THE MIRACLE OF

MIND POWER

by Dan Custer

WESTWOOD PUBLISHING CO.
312 RIVERDALE DR.
GLENDALE, CA 91204

D1075918

Seventh Printing 1983 Westwood Publishing
Glendale, CA 91204

Library of Congress Catalog Card Number: 60-14196

Printed in the United States of America
Inc.
ISBN 0-930298-22-5

ACKNOWLEDGMENT AND DEDICATION

My wife, Dr. Lucile Custer, who is a practitioner and teacher of mental science, has devoted so much time, thought and effort to the preparation and writing of this book that in all fairness her name should appear with mine as co-author.

We hope this book will provide an answer for all who wrestle with life's problems. We are grateful to our many students with whom we have worked and counseled; to the many whose "cases" have been reported, at least partially, in these pages. We are thankful to the large audiences who week after week have listened to our lectures, reported satisfying results and made valuable suggestions which we have tried to pass on in these pages.

Together, we dedicate this book to you, the Reader, and to whatever good you can take out of it. It was written for *you*.

Dan Custer

Table of

Contents

PART I

PART II

PART III

A Personal Message

from the Author

Man's Two Basic Desires

EVERY HUMAN BEING HAS TWO BASIC DESIRES: TO GET AWAY from pain and to arrive at pleasure. If these desires are to be satisfied, he must get along harmoniously with other people, adjust to his environment, and, most of all, get along satisfactorily with himself. If he lacks adjustment anywhere—inside or outside—he suffers pain—dis-ease—in his conscience, in his body, in his personal relations or in his pocketbook. Today few people are completely happy for few are without dis-ease—in mind, in body or in affairs.

If you are not as happy, as healthy, as prosperous as you wish to be; if you do not esteem yourself; if you do not have a feeling of complete satisfaction and fulfillment, this book is written for you.

There Is an Answer to Every Problem

Whatever your problem, there is an answer; and I believe you will find the answer in these pages. Certainly you would not take the time to read this book if you did not hope to get some ideas, some suggestions, some methods through which you might get away from pain and arrive at greater pleasure. *You want to do a better job of living.* You may want better health or more money. You may want love in your life or a feeling of peace and serenity.

Mind—The Greatest Power in the World

Whatever you desire *there is an agency which can fulfill that desire for you*—and that agency is *mind*. Mind is the greatest power in the world! And *you* possess and use Mind!

Ralph Waldo Emerson said:

"There is one mind common to all individual men. Every man is an inlet to the same and to all of the same. Who has access to this universal mind is a party to all that is or can be done, for this is the only and sovereign agent."

During the past century many books have been written about the miraculous power of mind and the good results to be obtained through positive thinking; but too few have been written about *how* to *use* mind; *how* to *think* positively; *how* to change from negative to positive thinking.

We agree, I am sure, that the mind man uses has within it unlimited possibilities; but we want to know *how* to use that mind to get the most satisfying results.

You, like thousands of others, want to know *how* to think and *what* to think; in short, *how* to direct *mind* so that you get the greatest satisfaction in your life.

The Most Important Thing in the World

You are the most important thing in all the world to *you*. Friends, money, family, even immortal Life would have no meaning for *you* if you did not exist. Your entire world of experience is centered in *you*. You may be a profound mystery to yourself, but you know *you* exist. You have desires and longings which demand fulfillment. You must express life in health and harmony if you are to be happy. You eat, sleep, play, love, study and pray so that you can do, be and have more of that which makes for greater pleasure—a greater sense of fulfillment.

Every act of yours in response to your desire to live better is preceded by some mental action—some decision. You desire certain results. You decide and act. Whatever experience you are having right now—good or bad—*mind* is the instrument you are using. Yet what a mystery is mind. Although no one knows all about mind, we certainly would not refuse to use what we do know to get the very best possible results.

Every day we use electricity. Although no one knows what electricity is, we use what we do know about it and get light, heat and motive power. As our knowledge increases, we get better results. It is said that someone wrote to Thomas Edison saying, "Mr. Edison, what is electricity?" Mr. Edison replied, "Electricity is. Use it."

No one knows how it is that when we plant a little brown seed in the ground, we get a radish. Fortunately we have learned how to plant the seed and get the result we want. So electricity, the seed, and *Mind* are all ours to use. Consequently it is just common sense to learn all we can about mind or electricity and then use it for a specific purpose to answer our needs. Your life can be a beautiful, glorious, successful adventure if you but wisely use the equipment nature has given you.

Life Can Be a Thrilling Adventure

If you will carefully read this book and do your best to put the suggestions into practice, I can promise you amazing results. However discouraged you may be, whatever may have been your experience in the past, you will find the help you need. You will not arrive at complete fulfillment just through a flip of the hand. No! It will take a bit of doing. But the results will be well worth all the effort.

Henry David Thoreau said, "Most men live lives of quiet desperation." They are at a loss to know why those unhappy and unfortunate situations arise in their lives. They try to retreat from the problems of living, seeking escape in alcohol, overwork, overeating or oversleeping. Some take to a sick bed, for escape is easier than courage. And then there are those who continuously resist and fight Life. For these people, living is just a succession of problems. You find frustrated people everywhere and many who are disillusioned. And yet I am glad to say there are also many who are happy.

Whether a person is a success or a failure, he uses *Mind*. One uses mind to become a success; the other, to become a failure. The difference is in the *use* of that magic power. No one needs to feel frustrated, weak, discouraged or unhappy. No one needs to live in poverty, sorrow or loneliness. No one needs to be a failure.

In a simple, understandable way this book shows how it is possible for you to secure through your own thinking that which you have the right to have—health, happiness, prosperity and peace of mind together with a feeling of self-esteem and satisfaction.

Something about the Author

Now, since you, the reader, and I, the author, are to spend several worthwhile hours together, you, naturally, want to know something about me. I am sure you want to be convinced that I write from experience and authority, for no one can write with any reasonable degree of authority about something which he has not experienced—something which he has not worked through in his own life. Unless one has examined, observed and experienced, he doesn't really know. Until one has come through the experience himself, all he writes is pure theory based only on speculation.

In my early life, I was forced to find the answers to some very serious problems. As a boy I had such a very well-developed inferiority complex that I would not walk along the best street in our town to go to my home. I sought the side streets because I felt out of place walking on the avenue.

At the age of twenty-one, I was refused life insurance because of a serious heart ailment. I felt inferior physically as well as socially. This sense of inferiority resulted in my being overly aggressive; consequently, I found myself in many unhappy situations.

At one time I became involved in a serious accident. Both legs, an arm and my jaw were broken. Physical illness dogged my footsteps. Finally, in my unhealthy drive for achievement, I suffered what was called a "nervous breakdown." Of course, I now know my nerves did not break down. I had a disordered mind and a broken body. The future looked dark and hopeless. At the age of thirty, I was a broken-down old man.

Now at the age of seventy, I am young, live, vital and happy. For the past thirty years Life has been very good to me. Many people may have more of this world's goods than I, but I have plenty and to spare. In fact, I have an abundance. For more than thirty years, my body has been a perfectly running machine which has served me well. I believe that today I have more physical and mental stamina than at any time in my life. I believe that I am better able today to serve others' needs. I do a much better job of living. I am happy and free. I would say, "I am almost content." For the past thirty years, my job has been serving others, which means that my own life has unfolded in a most healthy and satisfying way.

The pages in this book will reveal the story of many of my own personal experiences as well as those I have observed and what I have learned in dealing with thousands of sick, miserable, unhappy people. My psychological background has been of great value in the many years I have done ministerial work. In the past thirty years I have, I believe, synthesized a workable formula for happy, successful living.

Three Ways by Which Man Arrives at Knowledge

We have the Scientific method—which is the method of experience and experiment; we have the Philosophical method—which is the method of reason; and we have the Mystical Intuitional method—which is *the way of inner knowing*. All three methods are valid, but it is easy to see no one of these methods alone can be depended upon entirely to the exclusion of the other two. One may not understand a certain experience or one may reason from a false premise. Then again what seems to be a hunch or inner guidance may be only one's own inner desire speaking to him. I have discovered over a period of years that very satisfying results are obtained when a combination of all three methods is used.

As an ordained but not sectarian minister, for years I have spoken each Sunday morning to one of the largest audiences in California at the largest theatre in downtown San Francisco. In the aggregate many thousands of people come week after week to learn more about themselves and how to meet the problems of everyday living. Like you, they all want to enjoy health, happiness and prosperity. They would not continue to flock to that theatre Sunday after Sunday if they did not get results.

For some eighteen years I have had a daily radio program reaching thousands of people, and many thousands of letters have been received from people who say that my Science of Mind radio lessons have helped them to better understand themselves and have given them the key to a happier, richer life. Learning about themselves, and the more efficient use of their mind power, they live healthier, happier, more abundant lives!

What You Can Expect

At the suggestion of the publishers, I have brought together the philosophy, the science and the techniques pertaining to the use of mind which I have used over the past thirty years in helping thousands of people to experience health, happiness and successful living. They have asked me to tell you, the reader, what you may expect to get from reading this book and putting the suggestions herein into daily practice. I will present you with a key to the storehouse of happiness, peace of mind and security, and show you how to unlock the door.

Life Can Be an Exciting Adventure

You and I are about to set out on a journey into an exciting new land of adventure. We will study the science of Life, of mind, and of human personality. We will explore the depths of your mind, see how it works, and learn how to use it for your greatest good.

Now, you may ask, "But what is Life? What is mind? And what is a person?" I will reply, "To date no one knows the complete answers to these questions." I would say, *"Life is! Live it!* Man is a conscious point of Life, so accept yourself! Mind is the law of Life, the way life works, the instrument of life in creation. Use it!"

Mind—A Magic Power

As a conscious point of Life you use mind continuously. And as you learn more about mind and its powers, you will discover that mind is the Miracle Worker; and since you use mind, *you* may be called the magician. This being so, you should know all you possibly can know about this instrument which you use and as much as you possibly can know about how to use it.

The purpose of this book is to acquaint you with this great instrument, Mind, and show you how to use it to bring you *health, happiness, success*, yes, even your *heart's greatest desire*. If you will study and use the suggestions as they are pointed out to you step by step, *you*, like thousands of others who have used them, will get results beyond your greatest expectations.

Success—A Mathematical Certainty

There can be no question about the laws of successful living being available to everyone, and that they work exactly the same for everyone. I would say without fear of any successful contradiction that *success is a mathematical certainty* if you will scientifically use the laws of successful living which will be revealed to you in these pages.

The housewife who brings together the proper ingredients and works with them in the right way is successful in baking a good cake. There is no luck involved. This is purely a scientific matter. If you, I, or anyone else will bring together the ingredients for success, happiness and well-being; if we will but consistently use the known laws of Life scientifically in an efficient way, we will, without doubt, get the desired results.

This book is designed to open the door to a richer, fuller life; but, my friend, *you* must open that door. *You* must make the effort. I can only point the way and perhaps inspire you to make the effort. The instrument with which you must work is within *you*. You must not depend upon someone or something outside yourself. You do not have to get someone to behave or do something for you. Right here a great load should roll off your shoulders when you know that you have only to work with yourself and everything you need to work with is immediately at hand. You will be shown how to control your thoughts and develop a new pattern of thinking. You will be given the key to successful living.

To Learn How To Think Is To Learn How To Live

The most valuable thing you can learn is how to think so that you may live fully. Pains of unhappiness, failure and dissatisfaction are but nature's way of telling you that you are not thinking and doing as you should, that you are using the laws of life in an unhealthy way; while happiness, abundance, health and peace of mind is nature's way of compensating you for thinking in the right way and doing the right thing.

This book is not to be read through hurriedly as you would a mystery story; it is to be studied, pondered and considered. Some of the ideas presented may be new to you. Meditate on them until they become a part of you. Let these ideas inspire your thoughts and you soon will find that your desires are being fulfilled. You will see yourself being directed along the path of attainment in a practical way. You will change the old pattern of your life. You will joyfully climb the ladder of positive thinking, rung by rung, and what an exhilaration you will feel when you get to the top!

> Heaven is not gained by a single bound;
> We build the ladder by which we rise
> From the lowly earth to the vaulted skies,
> And we mount to its summit round by round.
> —Josiah Gilbert Holland

For ages we have been told that we must have faith, that we must change our beliefs, that we must love, and that we must use our imagination constructively. We agree that man "can be transformed through a renewing of his mind." We all know that "to learn how to think is to learn how to live" but too few of those who exhort us to change our states of faith have told us *how* to do it.

In my own counseling, I find that most modern-thinking, practical people want to know the philosophy back of mental action. They want to know why they have gotten into difficulties in the first place. They want to know about the power within themselves and how they may recognize that power, as well as how to use it.

In this book we start with ourselves. We come to an understanding of just what a human being is, what he has to work with, why he is as he is, why it is that he can change his experiences and how to go about making the change.

Problems Are the Result of Wrong Thinking

The problems which you and I have in our environment—these experiences of disease, failure and unhappiness—are but symptoms of something which is wrong on the inside. They are the results of mistakes in thinking followed by mistakes in acting.

The uninformed person simply wishes to get rid of painful symptoms but this does not get at the heart of the problem. The basic cause of the unhappy condition must be changed; and when one changes the basic cause, the effect automatically changes. When one establishes a valid cause for health, he no longer needs to get rid of disease. When he finds happiness, he no longer needs to get rid of unhappiness. When he brings together the elements for success, he is no longer a failure.

As you begin to understand the meaning of Life and how it operates within you and for you; as you begin to know something about what you are and why you are here; as you become aware of your inner faculties of mind, you will begin to see how you can live Life successfully and conditions will automatically change for you.

In every age, every country, every culture, men and women have been confronted by the same problems we have today—getting along with themselves, appreciating themselves, being happy and satisfied with themselves, getting along with their neighbors, adjusting to this world of environment, arriving at a feeling of success, freedom, security and peace of mind. No one wants the pain of sickness, trouble, unhappiness and inharmony in his relations with other people; nor does he want to live in poverty.

Everyone Can Have the Good Things of Life

Everyone wants the good things which Life has to offer and which bring pleasure and happiness. All these are available to each of us as human beings and everyone has the right to have the good things of Life if he does what is required—in other words, if he thinks right and does right.

If you make an electrical connection, plug in the light bulb, turn the switch and do not get a light, you are not angry with the electricity. You do not blame the laws of electrical engineering. No! You immediately set about to find the loose connection realizing that when you have done what you should do, you not only can expect a light, you will get it. This simply means if you do not experience what you want in any department of your life, you evidently are not doing the right thing; but, of course, you first must know what to do. You must be informed. That is the purpose of this book. It will give you the information you need and then show you how to use it.

Our Only Problem Is Ourselves

In this matter of successful living, our only real problem is with ourselves. While we may say our problem is with other people or with our environment, that is not true. Our problem actually is in how we handle the other person, how we adjust to him; it is in our attitude toward him and how we meet the situation. A dog growls at one man and is friendly toward another. Why? Because each has a different attitude toward the dog.

Part One

In Part One of this book we will study *you*. You will discover your own powers. You will come to an understanding of your environment. You will see how your body reacts to your attitudes and your thoughts. You will come to understand how you got into trouble and then you will see how to get out of it. You will learn to work in the field of causes rather than in the world of effects.

Part Two

Part Two deals with your use of the power of mind so that you may have and retain personal physical health, happy relations with other people, prosperity and right ideas. You will learn how to overcome a feeling of inferiority and sensitiveness; how to change bad habits to good ones; how to work with your mind so that you will always know what to do and how to do it. In short, you will discover the secret of turning failure to success.

Part Three

Part Three of the book deals with maintaining your new state of mind. These chapters are designed to inspire you to greater achievement. You will find there is no end to this road of happiness and accomplishment.

Again, I say, *"To learn how to think is to learn how to live."* Anyone who can change his mind and keep it changed can change his experiences. If you do not have complete control of your thoughts which inspire your acts, you can easily learn.

Yes, together we are starting on an interesting journey. This journey will be a fruitful, worthwhile, revealing experience. It will be an exciting adventure . . . and you, my friend, can look forward to the future with real enthusiasm.

PART ONE

chapter 1

What Are

You?

A SMART LOOKING, INTELLIGENT APPEARING WOMAN AP-
proached me at the conclusion of a lecture I gave one Sunday
morning, introduced herself and said, "I am a stranger here. I live
in a city a hundred miles distant. I am anxious to know what you
are teaching here because of the great change in my cousin, John
Roberts. He has been taking instruction from you and he is not
the same man he was six months ago. I would like to find what
he has found."

What the woman said was true: John Roberts was NOT the
same man he had been six months before. He had the same name;
he lived in the same house; he worked in the same office as six
months previously but he was now healthy in mind and body. His
disposition had changed. His affairs were certainly on the mend.
His bank account was much improved. His whole world had
changed; that is, his experience with the world had changed for
the better in what seemed to be a miraculous way. He had discovered something about himself which he had not known six
months before and he was putting this new knowledge into practice.

What Am I?

Have you ever asked yourself, "What am I?" And are you able
to give yourself a satisfactory answer to that question? If you are
to live a happy, successful life, you must arrive at some satisfactory
conclusion as to what you are, what you have to work with, what
your capacities are, and what you can and should do.

Let's agree right now that you, yourself, are the most important
thing in all the world to you. Self-preservation is nature's first law;
and if you did not exist, if there were no point in Life which
could be identified as you, then there would be no "you" to experience anything, would there? Everything in *your* world begins
with *you*. All of your beliefs are right where *you* think. Everything
you do, everything that you attract into your experience—love,
family, money, success or travel—all come about through some
mental action, either conscious or unconscious, on *your* part. Does
this startle you? Does this idea frighten you? I know that sometimes
people have been taught to turn away from themselves. They have
been taught they are unimportant, of no value; but that is an
entirely erroneous idea. It is not unhealthy to desire good for
oneself. It is unhealthy only if one desires good for himself alone.
Tennyson said, "Self-reverence, self-knowledge, self-control, these
three alone lead life to sovereign power."

Express Yourself Healthfully

Of course, selfishness is a great mistake; that is, trying to *get*
at the expense of someone else. However, self-expression is normal
and necessary. So we are advising self-expression—not selfishness.

It is evident if this self is to live in a healthy, successful way, it
must turn itself to healthful, creative, constructive expression—to
accomplishment. It must have a healthy interest not only in itself
but in other people, in the world, in the great surrounding Life. It
must give of itself and of its powers, of its love, and its devotion.
That is the expression of the self. But no one can give that which
he doesn't have. He cannot give a dollar to the needy if he has

no money in his pocket; nor can he lift the fallen if he has no strength.

The greatest teacher the world ever has known said that if you wish to be well and happy—arrive at heaven—you must love your neighbor as yourself. Now this does not mean you are not to love yourself. It means you are to have as great an interest in your neighbor's welfare as in your own. The inference is that it is normal and right for one to love himself *first;* then, however, one should go on to love his neighbor *as* himself; for it is a fact, no one can come to terms with Life unless he first comes to terms with himself. He will find it impossible to love other people until he loves himself. He must value himself, appreciate himself, if he is to find any real value in life or have any appreciation for others. He cannot have faith in other people, even in God, unless he has faith in himself.

You evidently are very important! What are you? What is this thing to which you refer when you say, "I"? When you say, "I," do you refer to your mind or your body; to your emotions; to your affairs; to your business; to your profession, or your family? Or do you refer to your experiences? Is it not true that your mind, body, feelings and affairs are just certain things the "I" uses and experiences? Instinctively you recognize that you are not your body for you say, "I have a body. I use a body." So you *know* you are not your body.

Some people, however, mistakenly believe that their physical bodies are themselves. Believing this, they make all their decisions from the point of view of the physical body and the material world. These people are asleep to their inner powers. They are unconscious of the real self. Believing they are their bodies, they are dominated by the demands of their bodies. Their time and efforts are largely devoted to answering the call of the body for food, shelter, and sense enjoyment. They do not control their bodies. For them the body is all important; so the body is in control.

Certainly the body is very near to us. It is the house in which we live. It is the means we largely use to express ourselves. It makes its demands upon us but we in turn make our demands upon *it.* We have control over our bodies if we but believe it.

Are You Your Emotions?

There are some people who believe they are their emotions—loves, hates, fears and faiths. They realize their bodies are under the direction of and subject to their emotions or their feelings. They know that their bodies respond to their feelings and so believing their emotions are themselves, they do not recognize their power to control and direct their emotions. Mistakenly believing their emotions to be themselves, they make their estimates and decisions from the standpoint of feeling; so they, too, are slaves—slaves to their emotions.

Are You a Mental Being?

Here and there, however, we find a person who believes himself to be a mental being. He knows that through reason he may direct his emotions and through his emotions direct and control his physical equipment. He may be a smooth running, highly efficient mental machine but he *still* is a *slave* to reason, to expediency. He may be a very efficient money-making machine. He may do very well in the creative arts, but he has failed to recognize that he is something else—something more: a point of Life using mind; and that he can choose how he will think or use mind. He still has not come to know that his mental operations are under the direction and control of a point of himself which is above and superior to the mechanical action of mind. This deep point of control we will call "spirit."

Are You a Spiritual Being?

A very few people have come to recognize themselves as spiritual beings. The definition of spirit is "that power which is aware of itself." The person who recognizes the deeper, more fundamental truth about himself knows he is a point of awareness, a volitional choosing point of Life. That person knows he is an entity aware of itself which can consciously direct mind to think what it should think. That person can, in fact, give his mental apparatus a problem to solve or a job to be done.

Very few people, however, consciously take control over their mental processes, which means few live full, satisfying lives. Those who do control their mental operations through intellect and reason, control their *emotions,* and consequently their bodies. They are the arbiters of their own fate, the captains of their souls. The person who recognizes his ability, his power, to do this has risen to a position of authority. He has taken dominion over himself. This person is truly master of his own house. He occupies the throne room. He lives in and from "the secret place of the most high." He has taken dominion over his world.

Until one comes to see that he, himself, actually is a conscious point of awareness, an entity which has free will, which can direct his mind, control his emotions and use his body, he is in effect asleep. He is unmindful of, oblivious to, his power to direct his own ship of life; consequently, he is unaware of his power to control his experiences. Dominion over one's experiences, one's world, is the result of his awakening to the truth about himself.

This point of yourself to which you refer when you say, "I," is an indefinable, immaterial point of conscious life. It is the center from which you may make all your choices and decisions. From that center "I" you may consciously, deliberately choose to use mind for whatever purpose you wish; and mind, being the creative law of Life, directs into action your emotions—your powerhouse, and your body—your physical equipment.

Long before the Christian era the ancient Greeks could think of no more appropriate inscription to have carved on their new temple at Delphi than those words of Socrates, "Man, know thyself." It certainly is the responsibility of each one of us to know as much as possible about ourselves; and we should know all we possibly can about this instrument, *mind,* which we use and about the *emotional power* which is ours to direct. Then we must know about the world in which we live so that we can fully and wholesomely express ourselves.

We, ourselves, surely are tremendously important because Life created us out of itself and designed each one of us to be a unique means for its expression. Each person is equally and tremendously important. No two people in the world are exactly alike; no two have exactly the same thoughts; no two have exactly the same motives or background; no two can express Life in exactly the same way. As a matter of fact, no two thumb prints are exactly alike and we are informed that actually no two snowflakes are exactly alike.

Since you are different from any other person in all history, you should have a feeling of importance and then justify that importance. To know that Life became you for a purpose and that you occupy a place no one else in all the world occupies; to know that Life with all of its powers, qualities and faculties became you, must cause you to have a deep sense of self-appreciation and self-esteem providing you justify your being alive and fulfill your purpose in living. No one can live healthfully or happily without self-appreciation and self-esteem.

Each one of us is Life personalized. We are each Life as a person; therefore, each one of us contains within himself all the intelligence, the power, the faculties and the instruments for the expression of Life. Each person has the ability within himself, the power and the intelligence at his command to express Life in peace and happiness, in abundance and satisfaction. All of the abundance of Life has been poured out for our good—for us to use. Good surrounds us. Each person has access to it and each person has an instrument which he can use to bring into his life whatever he wishes. That instrument is *mind*. When you *think*, you are using mind. Mind is the great creative principle—instrument or agent —of Life.

You Can Map Your Own Destiny

Each one of us can map his own destiny without limit as to what he will have or do or be. This idea may be shocking to some people because they feel weak and frustrated for they do not understand themselves—who they really are. They would rather have someone else take over the responsibilities of choosing and deciding for them—father, mother, sister, husband, minister, friend.

But, astounding as it may seem to some people, the truth is, each one of us is in fact an incarnation of Life, itself. If we are to be true to ourselves and true to the Life which we are, we will not deny the responsibility of choosing what we will do with our own lives.

Unfortunately, the average person does not understand himself and often does not even wish to know about himself. He does not know that at the point where he makes his choices, it is in fact Life—Infinite Life—making a choice. He does not know that the mind which he uses is in fact, the mind of Life, and that he has back of him each time he makes a decision, all the intelligence and the power of Life, Itself.

It should give each one of us a thrill to know that we can choose what we will experience out of all the universal possibilities of experience; that we do not need to let anyone else choose for us. Each of us being conscious choosing points of Life, we should be fully aware of ourselves and of our powers. We should know we can make our own decisions and then act accordingly without fear or hesitation. This power to choose is what makes each one of us an individual—a god in his own right—and our choices determine what happens to us—what our future will be—happy or unhappy —success or failure.

I think of a woman who is now radiantly happy, doing what she wants to do and doing it successfully. I distinctly recall the first time she came to see me. She told me she was referred to me because she was in mortal trouble. Bedraggled in body and soul and suffering untold mental tortures, I remember she said, "I would commit suicide if I had the nerve; I can't go on." Frankly, I hardly knew where to start with her for she seemed so devoid of courage or faith on which to build. To a degree I employed the "shock" method, telling her it took no courage to die; what she lacked was the courage to live. I told her there was no distinction in living when life was all easy; when there was no need for courage or gallantry. The word "gallantry" caught her attention. As we talked, although she had provided herself with an "out," blaming all her tragic circumstances on God, on other people and on conditions over which she had no control, it began slowly to dawn upon her that her own mistaken attitudes and misconceptions, expressed through her acts, had caused her present defeat. In that first interview, she got the idea there was some hope, some help for her. In the days that followed she came to realize how impossible it was for God to mistreat her; she saw that she had mistreated herself. As we brought her problems, one by one, out into the light and considered them objectively she was able to make a sensible analysis. Finally she reached the point where she could map a goal and she realized that her goal would be accomplished *as* she believed. Life began to have meaning.

Looking back over the history of this case I see that about all I was able to do for this woman was to help her discover herself. She came to realize that she was a perfect instrument through which Life could express and would, when given the opportunity. From that moment Life had her earnest and active cooperation. The results have been remarkably worthwhile and rewarding. She has found activities which delight her. Love has come into her life. She is successful and lovely. She is an inspiration to everyone around her—vibrant, happy and enthusiastically alive.

To come to an understanding of yourself will give *you* an awesome feeling of exhilaration. To know that it is up to you what you will do with the power of Life at your disposal will give you a feeling of enthusiasm or of fear according to what you believe about yourself. If you fear anything; if you feel weak and frustrated, it is because you don't know the real you, the wonderful, purposeful, important *you* which in reality you are. There is no limit to what you may do or have or be.

Most of us have been taught by parents or teachers to look outside of ourselves for the answer to our desires, so we have looked outside for power, for strength, for happiness—either unaware of, or refusing to look at that most important thing for us in all of Life —ourselves. It is high time for us to awaken to what the greatest teacher of all times, the one who has influenced present day Western civilization more than any other, had to say: "The Kingdom of God is within you."

chapter 2

The Magical Power

Within You

HAS IT EVER OCCURRED TO YOU THAT THE MIND POWER WHICH Edison, Einstein, Beethoven, Emerson or the Wright Brothers used is the same mind power you use? As a matter of fact the very same mind power used by the great throughout the ages is the power available to you. "There is one mind common to all individual men." There is one mind power and each one of us uses it.

You, Too, Can Perform Miracles

You may say, "But who am I to be compared with the great and the miracle workers?" The answer still is: "They used the same mind power you use." Of course, they may have used it more efficiently and effectively; but if *you* were to use mind more efficiently, with greater understanding, *you* would be able to do more, be more and have more.

Naturally, we have to start where we are with the understanding we have and expand that understanding, that knowledge, that information and use. We should learn all we can about ourselves and about this magnificent instrument of mind which we have to use and then we must use it.

Not long ago a young woman came to my office with a ballad she wanted published. She had tried many publishing houses and failed. She still felt the song was worthy. We helped her to come to a positive belief that there was someone who would publish that song. In her imagination she saw it being sold by the millions and sung on radio and television. She built the picture of success in her imagination. She let her intuition guide her as to what she should do. She acted in accordance with her deepest understanding and it didn't take long for the right publisher to come her way—a publisher who was most enthusiastic about the song—and the young woman's success has become an established fact. She changed her thought about the results; she resolutely maintained that new state of mind and she acted upon her very best understanding, which was all that was needed.

A man whom I knew well owned several large blocks of business property but all were heavily mortgaged. He had extended himself much too far for safety. His creditors seemed to be closing in on him. Fearful and anxious, he didn't know what to do. Bankruptcy was staring him in the face. He was frightened and ill. He told me that in his anxiety to save his fortune he ran here and there following every forlorn possibility, using every objective means he knew to meet the problem; but everything seemed to go wrong. I recall how he bit his fingernails as he nervously related one mistake after another and now there seemed no way out; he was at the end of his rope. He was convinced his creditors were about to take his properties away from him and there was nothing he could do.

I said, "Bill, why not change your attitude toward your creditors? Consider them as your friends—your partners. As a matter of fact, they actually are your partners since they loaned you the money to go into those business ventures. And they are your friends. They believed in you or they would not have extended you the credit." I pointed out to him that as partners they had rights in those properties just as he had; that he should try to look at every situation from their point of view as well as his own; in other words, he should begin to love his partners as himself, having the same interest in their welfare as in his own. I suggested that before he had meetings with his various creditors, he should condition his mind to think of their good as well as his own; to determine before each meeting that he would be just as devoted to their welfare as to his own. Naturally, with his changed attitude the entire atmosphere of those meetings changed. The attitude of his creditors toward him changed. We will make a long story short by saying a seeming miracle happened. The largest creditor, a bank, refinanced all of his property; and in a short time Bill became an executive in that bank in charge of the real estate department. His financial life was saved; his future assured. His faith in himself, his love for his neighbor, his devotion to and understanding of his creditors' position paid rich dividends. His changed attitude of mind brought about a complete change in his experience. He actually did as he wanted to be done by, with the result that his associates changed their attitude toward him.

Jim Drake, who owned a chain of stores, found himself in an awkward position. He, too, had extended his credit too far. For some time it looked as though he might lose everything he owned. Discouraged, despondent and fearful, he was drinking quite heavily before he decided to see me. I pointed out to him that where he had experienced failure because of his negative and distorted thinking, he could just as well experience success if he did some straight, positive thinking. Being an intelligent man he finally said, "Why, all I need is the right idea and that right idea will come through to me soon as I once again believe in myself and believe that I have the right to have the correct ideas." With that comment he relaxed, turned within himself for guidance; and soon he knew what to do. In all sincerity he made a plan for himself. It took courage, fortitude and determination to work out his plan; but he knew he had them for he knew the strength of Life was in him and he drew upon that inner power. Today, he is a richer, wiser, more worthwhile person than he ever had been; and he is a much happier man. During this transition he made many new friends. Today people have confidence in him and want to do business with him. This was not a miracle. This was not the work of something supernatural or superhuman. He had simply used the law of cause and effect, a law that never fails. He set up a new cause; consequently he had a different experience.

When You Think, You Are Using Mind

Through your thinking, which is using mind, you set a cause into motion and that cause moves into action producing an effect according to the cause. We see this all through Life. If you plant a poppy seed in the ground, you must get a poppy; you won't get a thistle. But remember—you must plant the seed if you are to have the poppy. First you desire a certain result. Let's say you desire to have a poppy. You imagine the poppy in bloom. You have faith that if you plant the seed, you will get the poppy and then, of course, you must plant the seed.

All of this is *mind* at work. Everything that happens is the final result of mind at work. Too long we have thought of ourselves as only a body with a brain, circulation and other bodily functions. We have failed to recognize that point of conscious Life which is back of the brain and back of the body. What causes the brain or the body to operate? What is responsible for their existence in the first place? We may have thought all this was the work of some great supreme god up in the sky or in outer space wielding a wand. We may have blamed an outside god or creator for our mistakes and failures—our inability to hold a job, our state of poverty, our misfortune, our sickness—the lack of good in our lives. Some people even blame an evil god which they call a devil. Many refuse to face the truth: the truth being that they themselves through their own negative thinking have brought about those very sickening, unhappy experiences.

The creative powers of Life are available to every one of us. Mind is the creative instrument. We each use it and we create that which we do not want or that which we do want. Most people are glad to take credit for their successes but would like to place the blame for their failures on someone or something outside of themselves. While they would not in so many words blame God for their troubles, they would say, "Well, God intended it this way. If He had wanted me to be well, He wouldn't have made me sick. If He had wanted me to be rich, He wouldn't have made me poor." These are childish alibis and the person who uses them is simply trying to escape his own personal responsibility.

I am sure at this point someone will say, "Now, why doesn't the author point the way to God and show how to come to a realization of God who can do all things?" Well, that is precisely what I hope to do but it may not be exactly in the way you expect; for as we continue our search together through these pages, I shall try to help you to discover God as the actual reality of yourself —the very power which you are using every day.

We are not looking for help from an outside God somewhere up in the sky. You and I are looking for an imminent, dependable God power—a supreme power immediately and always available to us—a power which we can use every day to bring greater good into our lives. I hope to help you to raise your own estimate of yourself to where you will realize that you have an unlimited ability to use the power of God. I hope to help you discover God as infinite power, infinite energy; the power that responds to your thought whether that thought is negative or positive. As you daily become more conscious of this power, you will discover for yourself that Life or God always responds to you according to your dominant habits of thinking, your attitudes, your faith, your beliefs —for *it is done unto you* by the Infinite Life, Itself, and always according to *your* faith.

Watch Your Thoughts

Watch your thoughts—your attitudes—your faith—and you will see for yourself how the power of Life responds to your mental states.

We are not discussing a mystical, mysterious, abstract God. We are discussing the warm, indwelling, usable, demonstrable, intelligent, loving power of Life which is not only the Life of this entire universe but the very Life of *you*. It is *your* life. It is *you* for you and your Father are one.

chapter 3

The Kingdom of God

Is Within You

HAVE YOU EVER BEEN DEEPLY IMPRESSED WITH THE WONDER of your own being? Are you sincerely thankful that you exist? You are a human being and humanity is the highest expression of Life on this planet. Do you have such a high sense of appreciation of yourself that you can do what the ancient teachers taught their students to do: strike yourself on the chest and say, "Wonderful, wonderful, wonderful me!"?

What do you see as you look deeply within yourself? Do you recognize that point of Life which says, "I am, I exist, I can look within myself?" That "I" is a point of Life which recognizes Itself and directs Itself. It is self-knowing and It is self-directing. What an interesting, complex organism you are!

At the point where you are aware of yourself, you recognize you have a desire to live, to exist and to express yourself. You desire to be happy and to be free. There is no limit to the desire to live and to live forever; to live richly, abundantly—gloriously. Your desire takes many forms; but as any desire is answered, you find that desire expanding. The more you get, the more you want. This

16

makes your desire *infinite* in nature, does it not?. It is without end. It is immortal.

Desire Is a Mental State

Desire operates through all of nature. Life continuously desires to express and to experience Itself. The plant desires to bloom. The tree desires to grow. The bird desires to sing. The desire within you, a human being, actually is the desire of Life to express; so desire is as endless as Life, Itself.

At the place within you where you desire, there is also a faith which says, "There is an answer to your desire." You believe that given time and opportunity, you can arrive at the answer to any desire. Everything you do is in response to a desire. Your faith directs you in whatever you do. There is no limit to where that faith can lead you. You may not be using it fully, but it is there. Faith is a condition of mind.

At the point where you think, desire and have faith, there is also a faculty called imagination. You have the ability to make plans—pictures—portraits—in your mind. Imagination is your plan-making department and it is under your direction. There is no limit to your ability to use imagination. It is an infinite faculty. Some people do not use it very efficiently but it is there to be used.

You can take an idea or the memory of an experience and join it with other ideas and memories and thereby come up with a new idea. You have the power to associate ideas and think through to a logical conclusion.

You Have an Inner Guide

As you look within yourself, you also find a faculty called *inner guidance.* Haven't you, many times, had a hunch or an inspiration which you knew without reason and without previous experience to be the truth; and when you moved out in that direction, you discovered it to be right? There is a something within you—a level ᶠaculty of your mind—which leads you to be at the right place at the right time, to say the right word and to do the right thing in the right way. If you were to recognize and fully trust it; if you were to be true to it and use it, there is no limit to where this faculty of guidance would lead you. So, it, too, is an infinite faculty.

The scientist sometimes describes conscience as an "inhibiting mechanism" or a mind faculty within you which would keep you from doing the wrong thing; it would keep you from hurting yourself or being untrue to the Life principle within you. This, too, is an infinite faculty.

Within yourself is the quality of intelligence, even wisdom; and while none of us experiences this quality as much as he should like, still none of us would assert there is any limit to the possibility of our experiencing wisdom. Infinite intelligence and wisdom is within each one of us.

Also there is love. Many people love the wrong person or the wrong thing. They may express their love impulses in the wrong direction and yet everyone must love something. The ability to love is limitless. We may experience that quality without limit and we may choose *how* we will express it.

Within each one of us is the quality of peace. It is always there ready to be experienced. Some people express that quality more than others do, but no one would deny there is no limit to the peace which may be expressed by anyone.

Within you is the quality of beauty. You may limit your expression of it or you may express it in a great and wonderful way; but, however much you may express beauty, there is still no limit to your further expression of it.

There is also the quality of joy and happiness. If you are not experiencing joy, it is not because there is no joy for you to express or experience. It is only that joy is not expressed through you and by you. Joy and happiness are always available without limit.

Isn't it amazing how a quick look within discloses infinite, never-ending qualities of intelligence, wisdom, peace, beauty, joy—in fact, everything you would like to experience? Also within you are all the faculties by which these qualities can be expressed—the faculties of desire, faith, imagination, reason and guidance.

Appreciate Yourself

Isn't it a fact those Life qualities which you would like to experience in *your* life and those faculties for expression make up the very being which you are? They *are* you! Would you not agree that these divine, immortal, never-ending faculties and qualities incarnated within you—in fact, natural to you—make up your real self? Would you not agree that as you grow in understanding of yourself and in your ability to use those faculties and express those qualities of Life, you expand into an experience of infinite, divine Life? Since your faith is without limit, your imagination is without limit; your reasoning powers are without limit; and since the love, peace, power, beauty and joy within you are without limit, would it not be practical to consider yourself actually to be a limitless being?

In addition to the faculties and qualities you have discovered within, you also have the ability to choose and decide. You can choose whether, how and to what extent you will use those faculties and you can choose what and how much of those infinite qualities you will express. This means through your power to choose and decide you can build the personality and the character you choose to build. Not only have you the inner power to choose, you also have the power to act in accordance with your choice. These are all mental faculties and spiritual qualities to be used, expressed and experienced by you as you grow in understanding of yourself. All of these qualities, together with the faculties through which they may be expressed are awaiting your use. The only limit placed upon the expression and the experience of this inner storehouse, power-house, is the limit which you, yourself, place upon it.

Naturally, you wouldn't be so foolish as to consciously refuse the blessings Life has given to you; but if you are unaware of those blessings, it is almost as though you didn't have them. One might have a million dollar bank account; and yet if he didn't know he had it or if he refused to draw on his account, the million would be of little value to him. He must know of his resources and use them, if they are to bless him.

Since you are Life, you incarnate the faculties and qualities of

Life. What Life is, you are! "Since the Father hath Life within Himself so hath He given to the Son to have Life within Himself." "All that the Father hath is mine."

The central point of yourself is that to which you refer when you say "I." There you choose how and to what extent you will express the qualities of Life and how you will use the faculties of mind. You may choose to express in a negative or a positive way. You may choose to express your faith as fear; you may choose to create pictures in your imagination of those things which you do not want rather than those you do want. You may express love as hate and you may refuse to express joy or happiness. There is no limit placed upon your ability to choose; therefore all the possibilities of heaven or hell exist at the point of your choice.

"There is nothing good or bad but thinking makes it so." Again let's remember that "spirit" is that power which is aware of itself. This deep center of yourself, "I," is aware of itself, so that is the spirit of you. That is the God within you. That is the thinking, choosing point from which you direct the creation of your world of experience just as the one Spirit of Life directs power throughout nature. You, then, are a person—a personalization—of the great Life. You are a point of God consciousness using God faculties and expressing the God qualities. When you come to this realization, you have discovered God, the innermost God, which is "closer than breathing, nearer than hands and feet."

Before we can successfully direct the powers of Life to produce for us those good things which we desire; before we take dominion over our world as we are designed to do, it is necessary that we become aware of this basic fundamental truth about ourselves. It is necessary to understand that at that point of awareness where we say "I," we are the God Life, Itself.

Get Acquainted with Yourself

We are now getting personally acquainted with the God-Life, the God-power, the God-intelligence, *which we ourselves are.* Recognizing our abilities and responsibilities, our duties and our privileges, we will proceed to use mind power for health, happiness and prosperity; for peace, joy and beauty. We will proceed to live gloriously. We now have a glimpse of what is meant by the Master's words, "The Kingdom of God is within you."

Some years ago, Jack Burnham, a man approaching middle age, frustrated in his work, dissatisfied with his advancement in life, came to see me. He was employed in an electrical power plant. As we discussed the divine being which in reality he was, he came to understand this central truth about himself. He accepted the fact that at the point where he was conscious, it was actually the God Life individualized as him, conscious of Itself as a human being —himself. That understanding of himself took the brakes off his thinking. His understanding of himself was lifted to such an extent that when he went to work each morning, he said to himself, "Now God is going to work." When he turned the switch in that big electrical plant, he said, "Now God is turning on the lights of the city." When he turned them off, he said, "Now God is turning off the lights of this great city." This consciousness of Infinite, Unlimited power took hold of Jack. He began to express greater wisdom, greater intelligence and power to such a remarkable degree that in two years he became Vice President of that large utility company.

Mind is the creative law of life; if we are to constructively, positively and creatively direct the universal power of mind to bring us our heart's desire, we must recognize that we have the right and the ability to do so. We must recognize that we actually individualize the Universal, God-Life.

You are not a little person with a little mind. No, the very life of you is the Life of God. The Mind you use is the Infinite Creative Divine mind which brought everything into being. Isn't that a wonderful idea to contemplate? Now, realize it's true about you. To the extent that you can accept this idea about yourself, about the mind which you use and then learn how to use mind, you have the key to the solution of all problems.

In the past most people have failed to understand this. I know there are still many who refuse to believe it. The average person, not understanding himself, feels weak, afraid, anxious. He doesn't understand that the limitless power of Life is his; that creative mind is his to use as he chooses. He doesn't know that Life stands ready to give him everything he needs provided he takes it lawfully. In his frustration, ignorance and self-pity, he begs and bargains with a God which he considers to be somewhere outside himself.

You Do Not Have To Struggle for Your Good

Not recognizing their own inner God power, people often feel weak, discouraged and unhappy. The asylums are filled to capacity and overflowing because of frustration and discouragement. Prisons are filled and we have wars because people do not understand themselves. They do not recognize or use their God power constructively. They look in the wrong place for their good, their happiness and their peace of mind. They neglect themselves. They do not understand the dignity of human life and the importance of human personality. They do not control their own thinking. They allow their thoughts to run wild in fear, hatred, jealousy and greed. Not realizing that Life responds according to their attitude toward It and their belief in It, they think they must struggle for their good. They mistakenly believe their good is opposed to the good of other people; consequently they desire their own good rather than that of their neighbor, their employer or their employees.

If this world is to be free of conflict; if the individual is to get out of his personal difficulties, there must be an acceptance of the tremendous values and power resident in every individual. There must come an understanding of the divinity and immortality of every person and his relationship to other persons and to his Source. There must come an understanding of the laws of Life, and people must be taught and inspired to use those laws for the greater good of themselves and other people.

There is no cosmic famine. Infinite good surrounds us. Everything we need for our success, our happiness and well-being is within us or surrounds us. Through ignorance and misunderstanding people often refuse to accept their blessings. They do not understand the automatic responsiveness of Life to themselves. Too few people understand or believe that it is done unto them according to their faith.

The average man refuses to recognize the basic laws of human relationships—the law of the Golden Rule, the law of love, the law of cause and effect. Therefore, the average person suffers conflict, frustration and unhappiness.

Moses, the great law-giver of antiquity, discovered the "I am" of himself was none other than the great universal "I am." He discovered that the point of awareness in him which said, "I. I exist." was none other than the Universal Life being conscious of Itself as a human being. He found God within. He found the Life of the universe was the very life of himself. What Moses discovered for himself you can discover for yourself. That was what Jesus taught. It was what Paul taught. It is what the great mystics have always taught.

You are the center of your experience. Your world of experience is formed and given direction by you at the point of your own individual thinking; inspired by your desires, planned by your imagination and brought into experience by your belief or your faith. The universal law of mind brings your experiences into shape and form according to the way you think in your heart.

It would be well for each one of us to quietly meditate each day upon this basic truth about the self; and as we come to a high realization of ourselves, fear will disappear from our lives. We will discover within the self all we need, to live as we ought to live.

chapter 4

The Magic of

Faith

Suppose a man has faith that he cannot get a job. Whether or not there is any justification for that faith, we certainly would agree it is a powerful force to contend with when he is trying to get a job. This man knows he is financially unable to take care of his family unless he has a job and yet he is afraid of the future. He believes he is a failure. He is convinced that he will not get what he wants and should have. He has profound faith in the negative. He has faith in his lack of power, in his inadequacy. He has faith in his *inability* to hold a job and face Life.

Positive Faith vs. Negative Faith

Suppose this man comes to understand that he need not be a failure. Suppose he sees that Life is only reacting to him according to what he believes about himself. Suppose he learns that since he has a real capacity and unique talents, he is needed somewhere in the business world; and that it is only his fear of Life or his belief about himself which stands in his way. If he will see this truth about himself and act accordingly, the Life forces will no longer act contrary to his need. As he comes to know more of the truth about himself, his faith changes from the negative to the positive. As his faith in himself and in his capacities changes, his experience certainly will change. Such a man does not need more faith. He simply needs to redirect the faith he already has. His negative faith pushes his good away from him while positive faith brings his good to him and him to it.

One day a man sat across the desk from me and told me that he could not find a job. He had been without employment for many months. He had a wife and three children. He was completely discouraged. I helped him to accept the fact that since he was alive, there was a place for him; there are no unwanted or un-needed items in Life. I helped him to see that since he had a family dependent upon him, there was an answer to his problem because of their need. Some employer needed him just as much as he needed a position. Moreover, if he would believe that the intelligent power of Life would direct him; if he would accept his inner guidance without question; if he could believe that Life had created him for a purpose and if he was willing to fulfill that purpose, Life would direct him and sustain him. In that one interview he became convinced of this. He left my office and within two hours had an excellent job. An inner intelligence directed him to the right place; and when he got there, he said the right words and made the correct impression. When he left my office, he had no more faith than he had when he entered; but he had a different *kind* of faith. He had changed his faith from a conviction that his problem could not be answered to a faith that it *could and would be answered.*

Faith is something very real in the life of each one of us. Faith actually is a state of mind. The religious exhorter often urges us to have faith. He commands us to have faith but what he doesn't recognize is that we already have faith. We would not be human beings without faith. We never have existed an hour without exer-cising it. Every experience we have, good or bad, comes to us by virtue of our capacity to have faith in something; and in the use of our faith we have made our heaven or hell.

Just as everyone loves something so does everyone have faith in something. No one needs to be urged to have faith but he must learn how to direct and use it. Probably the most important asset we have is our power to believe. We believe instinctively. The task before us is to change our faith from the negative to the positive, from faith in that which we don't want to faith in that which we do want. When we have done this, we have unlocked the "Holy of Holies."

I received a telephone call from a woman in Texas. Her daughter in San Jose was in a hospital. The doctors had told her the daughter not only had suffered a cerebral hemorrhage—a paralytic stroke —but a heart attack as well. Jane was reported to be in a desperate condition. We were asked to give a spiritual treatment for this daughter. In this treatment or scientific prayer we asserted and became convinced, along with the mother, that the natural forces of Life within the daughter knew how to heal the brain tissues; that intelligent Life had built her heart in the first place and still knew how to repair it. We became convinced that the intelligent power of Life was now working for her complete restoration. In our imagination we saw the healing now taking place. Through imagination and faith the forces of Life were directed to a complete repairing. Within a few days the daughter was reported well and ready to go back to work. Through a change in her faith about herself; through being surrounded by an atmosphere of positive faith; through our working together with the family so that she would be surrounded by a faith atmosphere, having faith in the laws of Life and the indestructibility of the soul of this woman; through actively harmonizing and cooperating with nature; removing the negative mental states and substituting positive ones; trusting the healing power of Life operating through her; by stimulating the Life forces to act through mental belief and imagination, this woman was healed. She is strong and well today. No one knows exactly how nature operated to bring this about. However, I do not know, nor does anyone know, how a radish grows from a radish seed.

We are learning to use mind in cooperating with nature so that we may experience more of the good that Life has for us. There is an intelligence in life which knows how to grow a vegetable from the seed. There is an intelligent power that knows how to heal and repair your body. Nature brings the harvest according to the farmer's faith. If a farmer did not have faith in the crop, he would not plant the seed in the first place; and he would continue to have a crop of weeds. Of course, through faith in the result he cultivates the crop. It should be pointed out that all appearances were against Jane ever becoming well. If she and the family surrounding her had been governed by the appearance of things, they would not have had faith in her recovery. If her faith and the faith of the family had not been redirected; if someone, somewhere had not transcended the belief and experience of people generally; if we had not looked beyond appearances, she probably would not be alive and well today. We are admonished by the great teacher, Jesus, not to be controlled by the appearance of things.

What Is Faith?

Faith is a conviction, a mental perception. Faith must rise above what our five senses tell us, for they only report the appearance of the physical world. Certainly faith can be negative or positive; but the faith that heals, that "removes mountains," must be a *certainty* about something which cannot be seen and cannot now be proved. Emerson said that all he had seen and experienced caused him to have faith in that which he could not see. Whoever reasons only according to what the five bodily senses reveal or believes that the only means of knowing is through seeing, hearing, tasting, smelling and feeling is controlled by appearances.

Man, himself, is something which cannot be seen. Life cannot be seen. The life of man is immaterial. We can only see what Life does. Every person must turn back to his true spiritual self and *discover himself* and know the *reality of himself*. He must get acquainted with himself. He must know that he, as a conscious point of Life, has the power to choose what he will do under any circumstances; therefore he is not under the dominion or control of anything outside as it appears through the five senses.

There are people who doubt this invisible nature of themselves. They say they do not believe in anything they cannot see, hear, touch, taste or smell; still, we know that love exists even though no one has ever touched it. We know mind exists although no one has ever seen it. We know Life exists although no one ever has put Life in a test tube or measured It with a yard stick. These are all realities even if they are invisible. Each one of us is an invisible reality acting through a body. You speak to me through the use of your vocal cords. Your body and your acts are simply your means of expressing yourself but it is your soul which speaks to my soul.

The person who lives only from the outside and makes all of his estimates from what his five senses tell him is concerned only with material things. He feels himself to be under the influence of, in fact, he is under the control of the appearance of things.

It is only through a living faith that you and I can escape from the bondage of sickness and poverty which are appearances; experiences to be sure, but not realities. We see the terrible power of negative thought all round about us. To be successful in this business of living, to be at peace, we should know we are anchored in a power and intelligence which is greater than we have heretofore considered our finite strength to be.

Into every one of our individual lives there comes a time when everything material seems to fail and there is nothing of a material nature which can answer our problem. To meet the problem and survive we must feel that we are anchored in something substantial and eternal, something which gives us a feeling of permanency. We must know that we actually are immaterial and imponderable and yet we are real. Since Life is, we are. Since Life is indestructible, we are indestructible. Our very nature is divine, infinite and immortal. The more we accept this fundamental basic truth about ourselves, the more free and boundless will be our thinking.

Emerson said, "It is the universal which gives value to the individual." He explained that the universal Life has individualized Itself in each one of us so each one of us is the *universal life as an individual*. We have universal powers at our disposal so it is the universal which gives value and permanence to us as individuals. If we can identify ourselves with a Life—a power, an intelligence —which has no limits, then it must follow that we believe our possibilities of experiencing health, success and prosperity must be limitless.

One of our greatest modern scientists, Dr. Jung, said that in thirty years of experience, he never had seen the cure of a neurosis without a return to faith. This is easily understood since fear or negative faith is the basis of neurosis. Certainly, this eminent doctor did not mean that we should return to a particular kind of faith in a circumscribed particular god; nor a particular brand of religion since his patients represented all kinds of religious groups from all over the world. He meant that we must discover something valid in which we can place our complete trust. We must have confidence. We must have faith in the honesty and integrity of Life and nature's laws and know that we have within ourselves the ability and the faculties through which we can be well, happy and successful.

This is something very intimate, very close and very challenging to each one of us. You may have had some unusually bad experience, some disaster, some loss, and everything turned black. The world may have seemed vile and you became negative. You may have decided that you would just put up with it and try to get along as cheerfully as possible. Perhaps it seemed to you that the world must have been created by a demon. This being so, of course, only a new thought, a new idea, a new state of faith, can rescue you. Something new must come into your mind, something which transcends this experience. You must think more positive thoughts, get bigger ideas and clearer concepts. You must come to believe that there is something within you which can lift you above these unhappy experiences.

Every one of us must believe there is more to us and to Life than that which is seen, felt, tasted, heard and smelled. We must know we are more than our bodies. Often we neglect to recognize the cause world within, the world of ideas, ideals and motives. Yes, we get so completely concerned with the body, so engrossed with our immediate environment, the appearance of the situation, that we discount the value of mind and spirit which are invisible.

Haven't you known two people in the same family—one sick and the other well; one a success and the other a failure? Their bodies are fed by about the same kind of food but one is sick and the other healthy. One has an experience of loss, becomes a failure and continues to be a failure. He thinks of himself as a failure so he lives a life of failure. The other allows that same experience to stimulate him, inspire him to new heights of thinking and fires him to consequent success. The man who has lifted himself out of the experience of the average has believed in something invisible about himself which can lift him out of and over the experience of failure. We readily recognize that the difference in the experiences of these two people was the result of their individual states of faith.

You should come to a personal decision and belief about the invisible powers of Life, mind and soul. The invisible is as real as the visible. Your faith is as real as your hands or your feet. Your love is as real as your heart. Your happiness is as real as your digestive organs.

When you live entirely on the biological level, believing only in the visible, you are just one of the race. You live on the level of the average—sick part of the time and well part of the time; poor part of the time and reasonably well-to-do part of the time. The average experience of human beings is your experience.

The person who lives only on the level of the body or even on the level of emotions, does not recognize that he has within himself the power to lift himself out of the race experiences. He can do this only by recognizing a higher level which transcends the information given him by his five senses.

When you live by appearances only, it is necessary to push things around in your environment. Things seem to be so big and you so small by comparison and you naturally feel frustration. To overcome the frustration you must come to think differently about yourself.

You Can Change Your Faith

I recall the owner of an apartment house. She was afraid she would lose her property because two of her apartments had been vacant for over a month. She had advertised them and many prospective renters had been to see them but for some reason they did not rent. Speaking of her problem she said, "There are many vacant apartments in San Francisco and there are many much nicer and more attractive than mine. As a matter of fact, I don't see why anyone should want to rent what I have to offer." I asked her, "You own the property, do you not?" "Yes," she replied. "Of course, but it is mortgaged and I am depending upon a full house to make the monthly payments and leave me something for my living expenses." "How many tenants do you need, Mrs. Green?" I asked. "Two," she answered. "Well," I said, "San Francisco is quite a large city and two tenants aren't many. Didn't you buy the property because you liked the location, the size of the apartments, and the type of building? When you bought it, did you not have enough faith in the good qualities of those apartments to make the investment knowing that it was good for you? Didn't you know it would be good for the number of tenants you need to keep it fully rented?" She thought that over, then said, "Why, yes, I had faith when I bought it; but now my faith seems to have wavered." I pointed out to her that conditions had not changed and she needed only two tenants. "Certainly there must be two people in this large city who want that location and the type of apartment you have to rent. Let's sit here together, now, and visualize those happy tenants already moved in, satisfied with their new homes, satisfied with the price, happy that they have found just the apartment they wanted." She got the picture. She changed her faith. In fact, she became so enthusiastic that she could scarcely get home fast enough to greet her new tenants. As a parting word I cautioned, "Don't rush. You are always in your right place. Remember you are directed by an inner intelligence. If someone calls and you are not there, they will call again." She relaxed but she wasted no time in getting home. In less than an hour after she got there, someone called and was delighted with the apartment on the second floor. It was just what he wanted. He took it then and there, and paid the rent. In the next three days she had three prospective tenants for the other apartment on the top floor. After she had rented it, the third man was so anxious to have it that he offered her $25.00 more a month than she had asked for it in the first place. He told her that he had looked all over that area for just what she had—a quiet place with a homey atmosphere and a view of the Bay, but until he discovered this apartment, he had not found exactly what he wanted. Naturally she was sorry that she could not accept his offer but she had already rented it.

This is not the story of a miracle. There is nothing supernatural about it. This woman changed her mind—her state of faith. She discovered it was not necessary to push people into renting the apartments. It did not take force. Worry didn't help. It simply took a change in faith. She came to see that her apartments were desirable, more desirable for two certain people than any others in San Francisco, and Life, being responsive, reacted to that belief as it had previously reacted to her belief that her apartments were not desirable or that others were more desirable.

Change Your Faith and Your Experiences Change

It is done unto you according to your belief. Change your belief and you change your experience. Life is real! But you cannot see It. You do not see Life nor do you see faith; but you do see what Life through faith does. You can see the evidence; faith is not less real than your mind for it is a state of mind. Your motives are invisible and immaterial. The real man is invisible; and when you remember that is true about yourself, you know that you really are indestructible and immortal. You are no longer a slave to your body, your environment or to your affairs. You are no longer under the control of competition from the outside. All your strength and force come from your faith in things unseen. Believe you are strong and you are strong! Doubt and you are weak!

Unless we depend upon, have faith in, that which is above and beyond the material level of substance, we will have little upon which we can depend. Most of us have put brakes on our clear thinking and we have put blocks before our imagination. When we learn to take the brakes off our thinking and unblock our imagination, we are free.

A new state of faith is not established through the use of will power nor by clenching our fists and furrowing our brows. It is not done by forcing ourselves to believe. We cannot blow up our faith like an automobile tire. We simply put a rational, logical foundation under it and then we act as though it were true. Many times people have said to me, "I understand this, intellectually. My reason tells me it is the truth but I have difficulty when it comes to feeling it and acting it."

A very intelligent man once said, "Faith without works is dead." And a perfectly good interpretation of that statement would be that your faith dies unless you work at it. Faith is activated through works. "Act as though I am and I will be." If you believe this surrounding universe of Life is one of love and responsiveness, that It sustains you, that It is interested in you, then act that way and you will be at peace.

If reason tells you that Life cannot be annihilated, that you, as an incarnation of Life, cannot become nothing—that *you* cannot be annihilated—then you have put a foundation under a faith in immortality. Then by all means *act as though you are immortal.* Certainly you will pass on to another experience some time but you still will exist. If you are immortal, you never actually die; so you may just as well meet your problem now. It is infinitely better to meet it now than to put it off until some time in the future. If you actually believe in your own immortality, you will not prepare to die; you will prepare to live. You will know that every act and every thought of yours changes you somewhat so every thought and every act will be carefully chosen in relation to your immortal future.

Fear or negative faith is but a condition of your mind. It can be changed or redirected through understanding, through reason, and you maintain that faith through action. Life does not react to you according to your hopes but according to your faith. Your faith is something which you become. It is something with which you have identified yourself so you *act* as though what you believe is true; and acting as though it were true, it becomes an actual fact in your experience. The great teacher, Jesus, suggested that "Whatsoever you desire, when you pray, believe that you have received it and you will have it." He was stating a law. He was saying that Life reacts to you according to your faith, according to the picture which you have in your imagination. It is done unto you according to your conviction—what you actually believe. To the extent you believe it becomes vital in your life.

The Biblical character, Job, after many losses, hurts, worries and frustrations, discovered, "That which I greatly feared has come upon me." He saw that those evils in which he had faith, those situations and conditions which he was convinced would come to him, actually became his experience.

The Four Fundamentals of Life

There are four basic fundamentals on which you should establish a positive faith. First, you should come to a positive faith in the goodness, the integrity, the honesty, the reliability and the responsiveness of Life or God. You should come to believe that the intelligent good Life of love brought you here; and since It did, It brought you here for a purpose. Having brought you here for a purpose, It is interested in you and It proves that interest by surrounding you with everything you need. Give real thought and meditation to this and you will without question come to believe it. You will come to believe that Life is actually good rather than evil; what you have heretofore called evil is merely the result of your wrong choices and your wrong use of that which is good. Life is *for* you rather than *against* you and it is up to you to harmonize with the laws of Life or the way Life acts. The modern counsellor is very much interested in what you believe about God for he wants to know whether you are afraid of Life or whether you have positive faith in a power available to you through which you can surmount your difficulty.

Second, you should come to a positive faith in Man; so recognize that Man is an individualization of or a personalization of the Good Life. If you can know that you are an incarnation of Life, that you have within yourself and at your disposal all the qualities and all the faculties of Life together with the power to choose how you will use those faculties and how you will appropriate those qualities, you will have faith in yourself. Having this faith in yourself you will know that other people also are fundamentally good. If you come to have faith in yourself, you will have faith in other people. You will know that you are not a machine operated upon by something outside of you over which you have no control. You will see that you are a free being with the power to choose where you will go and what you will do. If you believe that you are just a machine, you will not have a high opinion of yourself nor will you have a high opinion of other people. You are not just a piece of meat. You are an immortal soul. But depending upon what you believe about yourself, you will act; and you will treat others according to that belief. Naturally, this also means you will be treated by others according to your belief about yourself. If you believe that you are unworthy, others will consider you to be unworthy. If you believe yourself to be inferior, you will act inferior and others will consider you to be inferior. If you believe that you are adequate, that Life is devoted to your good and that you are important, you will automatically act that way and you will make the place you occupy important.

Third, you must arrive at a positive belief about the laws of Life; in other words, discard all belief in luck. The modern scientist has shown us there is no point in this universe where law is not operative. The person who believes in luck believes he is at the mercy of the winds of adversity. The one who believes that the laws of Life are available to him and that he can use them sees at once that he can direct and control his destiny. Do you believe that it is necessary for you to take everything as it comes, that you can do nothing about it? Or do you believe that you can inject new causes into the stream of Life, that you can accept new ideas for yourself and so have new experiences?

Then, fourth, you must believe in personal immortality; believe that when you pass on, you will continue to live. This is practical for if you believe you will always live—that death is not the end —then you know that you will have to meet your problem some time and common sense says it may as well be now as some time in the future—in fact, the sooner the better.

It is not necessary for you to get more faith. You just need to change the direction of your present faith. If you establish a positive faith in these four fundamentals—God, Man, Law and

Immortality—you cannot have negative faith in anything because all things and all situations in your life are represented in some way by these four fundamentals.

Some years ago I was teaching an adult class of men in the science of living. This class was made up of active business and professional men. Our discussions often revolved around this subject of faith. One evening a business man, a contractor, arose in the class and said, "All my life I have felt there was something wrong with me because I thought I did not have faith. I have tried. I have agonized and prayed for faith. Now it has finally dawned upon me that I do not need any more faith than I always have had; all I need to do is to redirect the faith I have."

Basically what you must have is a positive faith in Life, Itself. Since you are Life, common sense tells you that other people are Life, the same Life as you and that all people are sustained by the same Life. You must decide whether that Life is good or bad, whether it is a friend or an enemy. As you see it, you will experience it.

Since you are Life and God is Life, then you are a personality of the God-Life. If you cannot have confidence in that Life, in Its honesty and Its dependability, you certainly are of all people most miserable. Life is, however, dependable and does respond to you. It is all you have to depend upon and you do depend upon It every moment.

Life becomes everything; and since we have the power of choice and since we use mind or the laws of Life, then we can choose to bring into our experience whatever Life can become. Every person can pin his faith to an unlimited Life for the Kingdom of God is within him. He can know that he is anchored in an infinite reality; and when he knows that truth, he is set free of all limitation.

To know that you are important, to know that you have purpose, heals you of that unfortunate illness called aimlessness. You are aimless so long as your life is disintegrated. You must be pulled together into one piece, going in one direction. You cannot go forward if at the same time you are looking backward. You cannot fly off in several directions at once if you are to be effective.

To come to a positive faith in Life heals you of any sense of feebleness or lack. How can you feel weak if you know you are identified with Infinite Life and Infinite Power? To know that an infinitely responsive Life has brought you here and also sustains you will certainly heal you of all sense of fear or negative faith which is the greatest curse of mankind. Redirecting your faith is very important to your wellbeing.

You live by faith every minute of every day. Come to a *satisfying positive* faith and then act as though you believe it, for action is required if you would have a dynamic faith.

chapter 5

Your Limitless Power

To Choose

Isn't it wonderful to know that you have the power to choose what you will think, say and do?

This ability to make a conscious choice sets *man* apart from the lower animals. Through the exercise of his power of choice, *man* succeeds or fails in the business of living.

Good vs. *Evil*

That which man calls evil is the result of his using or directing the energies of Life in an unproductive and destructive way. The so-called evil man uses his God-given strength of mind and body in a destructive way while the good man, or the righteous man, uses his powers in a constructive, helpful and productive way. The strength, the energy, the power in itself is neither evil nor good. The good or bad is in its use and that is determined by man's choice. Man, himself, is not fundamentally evil; but because of ignorance, fear and frustration, he often chooses to use his powers in the wrong way. Ignorance is the only sin. I can use electricity to light my home or to electrocute myself. Man's power to believe can be used against himself or for his good. He can choose.

When we fear, we use our power to believe in the wrong way. *Fear, a negative state of mind, is, without doubt, man's greatest enemy. Faith, or a positive state of mind, is man's greatest ally. It* delivers him from the enemy.

A woman telephoned to me one Sunday afternoon and asked if she might see me for a few minutes before the lecture which I was to give on Sunday evening. This was more than a dozen years ago. She met me for a few minutes in a side room off the hall where I was to speak and said, "The doctors tell me I have cancer." I asked her why she wanted to talk to me about it and she said, "I want you to pray for me." I asked, "Do you believe that if I pray for you, you will get well?" She replied, "I know I will. There is no doubt in my mind. I have absolute faith that if you will pray for me, I will get well." Her conviction was evident. I told her I would do so and I did. That was the only conference I ever had with the woman on that subject. For some time I prayed or mentally treated daily for her health and the malignant growth disappeared. About a year ago I saw her. She told me she had been entirely well all these years. I am sure that with her faith she would have gotten well whatever kind of prayers I might have given for her, for she had absolute faith that my prayers would heal her. Whatever method is used to arrive at positive faith matters very little just so one arrives.

Probably the most profound statement ever made having to do with our success or failure in life, our sickness or health, our peace or confusion, was that of Jesus, "According to your faith it is done unto you."

You Create Your Own Experiences

Faith is simply your state of mind and mind is the creative law of Life. If you have faith in success, you will succeed. If you have faith in failure, you will fail. You are always creating, for you always have some kind of faith. You are always thinking and thoughts produce after their kind.

Every person creates his experience through his use of mind. Actually, what you call your mind is simply your use of the one universal creative *Mind* which has made and continues to make and remake everything.

"You may not be what you think you are; but what you *think*, you are." Much of the average person's thinking is uncontrolled; in fact, it is often misdirected. The average person is largely unconscious of the power of his thoughts. Misdirected thoughts bring into experience that which is not wanted. If you are at all conscious of what you are; if you have even a vague idea of the truth about yourself, you will recognize that you can control your thinking. Since what you think, what you believe, what you are convinced is the truth, becomes your experience; through choice of thoughts, belief and feeling, you can control your experiences. Thinking is using mind.

All form, action and experience is the result of mind operation on some level, in some way. Your experience with me and with this book you are reading is actually what you think about me, what you think about this book; and that is within your mind, within your awareness. Your experience isn't here where I am nor is your experience in the book. Your experience is within yourself, at the point where you think. When you think differently about me, you will have a different experience with me. When you think differently about yourself, you will have a different experience with yourself. When you think differently about other people and about Life generally, all your experiences will change.

When you listen to a lecture, it means to you just what you think about it. The same lecture will mean something different to another person because he chooses to think differently about it. When you think in a different way about your husband, your wife, or your business, you will have different experiences with them. All that you ever experience is the result of your thinking.

To learn how to think is to learn how to live. This is a tremendous idea. Don't refuse it! Your experiences extend out from you. Your experiences are the result of thought. Your choosing and deciding are within you. Your reasoning is within you. Your satisfaction is within you; so are your peace and your happiness—all within that infinite *you* which you are. You may say as you stroll in the quiet of the woods or enjoy a beautiful garden, "This is a peaceful situation;" but even so, the peace you experience is within your mind —in your own feeling. One man looks at a sunset and says, "It is beautiful!" He is enraptured, thrilled and inspired while another looking at the same sunset says, "The light gets in my eyes." Each man experiences according to his dominant thought pattern—according to his interest and his choice.

All the love you ever can know is within your mind; and the more love you express to others, the more you will experience yourself. Life within you and surrounding you responds to your thinking. What a complex, interesting being you are! You are a point of Life experiencing and expressing *Itself;* so of course, you are most important to *Life—*to *God.*

Mental States Express in Body and Affairs

You may have been ill after a great outburst of anger or an intense feeling of fear. That anger or fear was a state of mind. It was a state of faith which you chose and it was done unto you according to your faith. You may have had a feeling of weakness after a shock of fear or anxiety. You may have noticed that everything seemed to go wrong when you were mentally confused. You may have suffered insomnia as a result of an emotional upset. Yes, it is done unto you according to your faith.

One day I left my office to go to the radio station to make a broadcast. I had allowed myself to become upset and confused in my thinking that morning; and as I drove out from the curb, another car just missed my front fender. I continued down the street and had several near misses with other cars until someone did nick the corner of my fender. So, I said to myself, "My friend, it is about time you moved over to the side of the street and straightened out your thinking." After reasoning with myself for a few minutes, coming to an understanding of my own ability to control my thinking and my actions, I felt calm and quiet. I chose to change my state of mind. The inner mental conflict was dissolved and I went on about my business. Everything went smoothly the rest of the day.

Things seem to go wrong when we are mentally upset. We are late to work and late to appointments. People step on our toes and we seem to have to wait to be served. We don't get along well with people either at home or in business if we have a sour disposition. A sour disposition drives people away from us. But we should remember that a sour disposition is a mental state—a state of faith. If we want people to like us, believe in us and cooperate with us, we must sweeten up our dispositions—our mental states. We must remember to smile. Someone has said, "You are not fully dressed until you are wearing a smile." That smile is the result of a choice.

Our success or our failure is the result of our mental condition —our thoughts about people and about ourselves—our attitudes toward people and toward ourselves. The person who is kind and considerate, interested in others, interested in his customers, in his clients and loves them, is sympathetic toward them and has faith in them, has a good business.

A young woman friend of ours comes to my mind. I will call her Mary. She married young and had never worked outside of her home; but with the death of her husband she felt the need of some creative activity. In November she secured a position in one of the big department stores in Los Angeles where she lives. She never had been a sales person but she loved people. She was interested in them and in pleasing them. She was assigned as clerk in the scarf department of that big store for the holiday season. Even though she was the only inexperienced sales person in the department, she soon was selling more scarfs than anyone else. I was curious to know why this was so and I stopped to watch her from a distance to try to determine her secret. Another sales woman in the department with a rather sour, bored look on her face was waiting on a customer who seemed rather distracted and confused. The customer fingered scarf after scarf, uncertain what she wanted. Finally, after half an hour, the sales woman called to Mary, "Will you take my customer? I'm due for a coffee break." Mary took over the customer, smiling graciously as she looked into the frustrated woman's eyes. "Do you wish to buy a scarf for a young person or someone older?" she asked. The lady said, "I would like several if I can find what I want." "Well, tell me the color they like and the type of clothes they wear and I am sure I can help you. We have scarfs to suit every taste." Soon they were friendly and the customer relaxed. Mary said, "How about starting with this one?" and she held up a beautiful scarf, draped it about her neck and stood smiling. The woman smiled back and bought the scarf. In a matter of minutes she had purchased a dozen scarfs and went happily on her way. The outcome was that Mary was top sales lady during the month of December; and on the first of February was made head of the department, something without precedent in that store.

It is a fact our attitudes move out through our bodies into our affairs. Other people react favorably toward us if we sincerely give out good. Our desires, motives, attitudes and choices are mental states. We have believed that a sick body makes us irritable. We have believed that irritable people make us nervous. All too frequently this is putting the cart before the horse. When we are irritable, fearful, angry or when we are in mental conflict, we generate sickness in our bodies. Our bodies react to our mental states and so do other people. People react in a disagreeable way toward us if we are in an ugly mood; but what is that mood but a mental state? Yes, we are more successful in this business of living with ourselves and with others when we choose to have faith in ourselves and in others; when we honestly love and appreciate ourselves and express love and goodwill toward the people with whom we associate.

chapter 6

The Magical Power
of Decision

NOTHING BRINGS ORDER TO A DISORDERED MIND OR TO DIS-
ordered affairs quite so quickly or surely as coming to a decision
and deciding to let that decision stand.

The Importance of Making Decisions

When you consciously and deliberately come to a decision from
a logical premise and let that decision take hold of you, move
through you and through your affairs, you find that you are taking
dominion over your life. Until you do this, you are like a chip on
a stream without conscious course, goal or destiny; and so you
are unhappy. We all know this is true. Of course, we all want to
know how to make logical decisions—right decisions. This is a
decidedly personal matter—a personal responsibility and a personal
privilege.

Man is the universal Life personalized—individualized. Emerson
said, "Man is a piece of the universe made alive." Man is a piece
of the universe which has become conscious of itself. In fact, each
person is his own universe. Each one of us lives in his own world.

The point of Life called you or me is a conscious, choosing, volitional point of universal Life.

Life wants to express Itself. It wants to experience what It is and Its expression in health, happiness and harmony is heaven. As we express Life in harmony, happiness and health, we experience heaven.

In the Lord's Prayer, we pray that heaven be expressed in our world. Man wishes the universal qualities of Wisdom, Love, Peace, Power, Beauty and Happiness to be expressed in his individual life. Since man is an incarnation of Life, he incarnates the laws of Life. How he uses the laws of Life, how he makes the demand upon Life for those things which he wants is the result of his decisions. Nothing of real importance happens in our lives until we arrive at a decision. When we make a decision, we are really deciding how Life is to act for us.

One day several years ago I had been making outside calls until about four o'clock in the afternoon. I arrived at my office to find a man who had been waiting all day to see me. When I appeared, he was pacing the floor. He had eaten nothing nor had he slept for twenty-four hours, having driven from San Diego in his old car the previous night. He was wild-eyed and fearful. After I got him comfortably seated and had some food brought in, he told me his tragic story. He had lost his job. He had a lovely wife and two beautiful girls, but somewhere along the line he had taken to drinking heavily. He had become involved with another woman. He had forged his employer's name to some checks and now the police were looking for him. His wife had packed her clothes and was ready to leave for her mother's home in Seattle. He was desperate. He could see no way out. The day before he came to see me, he had bought some poison and had gone into a washroom in San Diego intent on taking it. Suicide seemed the only solution. He told me that he picked up a magazine from the floor of the washroom and happened to notice an article entitled "There is an answer to every problem." Under the title of the article was a statement: "There is a way out of every situation and a right way." That gave him hope. You may wonder where I came into the picture. Well, I was the author of that article which appeared in the magazine. Of course, he never had heard of me; but now he decided to have a talk with me before he carried out his plan of suicide. He said if there was a way out of his tragic difficulties, he certainly could not see it. I suggested to him that suicide would not help his wife and daughters. In fact, it would bring them only greater sorrow. I helped him to see that suicide was a selfish thing —a way out for himself, perhaps, but certainly not for those dependent upon him. That idea struck home! I asked him what he really thought he should do and it wasn't long before he relaxed; and with food under his belt he was able to look at his problem with some degree of objectivity.

We talked for several hours. During that time he came to see what was wrong. He came to a decision. He decided that he would do what he knew was the right thing to do. He became inspired with the idea that if he thought and did right, in the end only right action and happiness could come to him. He decided to depend upon the law of Life to deliver to him according to the choices he made.

You will remember Socrates' statement that no evil can come to a good man, that, "Whatever happens to a good man must in the end be a good thing"—and also the statement of David, "The righteous are never forsaken."

I assured this man that I could not look into the future and tell him what would be the exact result; but I did know that right thinking and right action could bring only right into his experience. He decided to return to San Diego and ask his wife to forgive him. He decided to tell her she had a perfectly valid reason for leaving him and he would not blame her if she did; but if she could forgive him, if she could decide to give him another chance, he would do his utmost to justify her faith in him. He decided to go to his old employer and tell him that he had a perfect right to send him to jail and he would hold no ill-feeling whatever if that was the decision. Should he be given another chance, however, he would get a job and pay back all that he owed, for he had learned his lesson.

Having come to a decision as to what he should do, deciding to do it and deciding to let his decision stand, the young man left my office with a degree of calm and peace. He had decided to do what he honestly felt was right. He had decided to take his medicine whatever it was—to go to jail if he must—but he would not run out on his responsibilities. He went home determined to be honest with his family.

One of his first acts was to completely dissolve his relations with the other woman. He decided to quit drinking and he let that decision stand. He honestly faced his employer whose name he had forged. His wife, his creditors and his employer felt his sincerity and reacting according to his change of mind, they took him at his word.

In less than a year's time he had paid off his debts. He had a much better position with his firm than formerly. He and his wife were buying a new home. Their daughters were taking music and dancing lessons. This whole change came about because of a decision, a mental act. Many times this man called me long distance even late at night, to express his appreciation of the wonderful good which had come into his life as a result of his making a common sense, logical decision.

A Decision Clears the Atmosphere

A distracted woman came to see me. She told me that she lived in a town two hundred miles distant. She owned a building in our city which she rented to a large supermarket. The building was designed for that purpose; but the owner of the market who had rented her building had written her that unless she made certain repairs to the building and reduced the rent to a certain point, he would move, for there was another building in the area which would suit his needs. She told me that she had very little time to negotiate with this man for she had received his letter but a few days earlier and now she had an appointment within thirty minutes to see him and tell him her decision. She told me that his demands were exorbitant, that she felt in all justice she should make certain repairs and should reduce the rent to a certain point; however it would be impossible to do everything the lessee demanded.

I suggested that she sit quietly and think of the problem not only from her own point of view but from that of the renter; that she then write down on a sheet of paper just exactly what *she* felt was right, what she could in all honesty do in relation to repairs and rental reduction; that she then take that paper and lay it down in front of the renter and tell him that was what she had decided and she believed it was right. I explained if she was absolutely honest and was as concerned about his good as about hers, that if he refused, she could then expect to find another tenant for her building. The building was created to serve Life and Life is honest. Intelligent Life can be trusted.

Within an hour she telephoned me that she had called on her tenant, had laid her decision before him, told him that was what she was able to do and she felt it was right. He read the memorandum, looked up at her and said, "I think so, too. Let's sign a new lease." This came about as the result of making a decision.

If we always act from the highest level of honesty and integrity that we know, considering the good of others as well as ourselves; and if we know, out of right decision, positive faith, sympathy and love, that the laws of Life will deliver only good to us, then right results are bound to follow.

A responsible woman executive with the telephone company called on me. She said her daughter, sixteen, was becoming quite a problem. This business woman was a widow. She and her daughter had lived with her mother—three generations together. The grandmother, who had to a large degree been responsible for the training of the daughter, had recently passed away. The daughter now refused to help with the housework. She would not even take care of her own room. She stayed out late at night and the mother was almost distracted. On the evening before she came to see me, the daughter had cried out, "Quit striking me!" thinking the neighbors might hear it and believe the mother was really abusive.

I suggested the mother write down on a sheet of paper exactly what she believed the daughter should do, looking at the situation from the daughter's needs as well as her own. She was to write down clearly just what the daughter should do in helping about the house, taking care of her room, what evenings she might go out, how late she might stay, and so forth. The mother hesitated. She was afraid if she showed that to her daughter, the girl would leave home. I pointed out to her that out of a right decision only right action could come. She made a complete schedule for the daughter as well as for herself. I told her to take it home, lay the paper before the daughter knowing with absolute conviction that since that was right, the daughter would agree.

She left my office having made a decision and within a couple of hours she telephoned me. Her voice had lost its tenseness. She told me that when she arrived home, her daughter had met her at the door, had thrown her arms about her mother's neck and kissed her. This was the first time the daughter had shown any affection for weeks. Naturally, she did not show the paper to the daughter. I suggested that she show it to the daughter only when she felt it was the right time to do so. That time never came. The daughter's attitude toward her mother changed completely as well as her attitude toward her school work and her home. With wonderful grace she helped about the house, took care of her room; and every Sunday morning following our discussion I saw the two of them sitting in the front row at the theatre where I lectured. This change for the good undoubtedly came about as the result of that mother's decision. The positive conviction on the part of the mother was unconsciously felt by the daughter.

When we are convinced of the truth and the honesty of any situation, we can expect the laws of Life to deliver; but we must *believe* they will. That is the secret.

One Sunday morning I gave a lecture at the Curran Theatre in San Francisco on the importance of making decisions. On the following day a business man who owned a large and valuable property for which he had been offered a considerable amount of money came to see me. He said that for weeks he had been torn with indecision as to whether or not to sell the property but having heard that lecture he had decided to decide. Sitting at my desk, he came to a decision to sell at a price which he felt would be right for him and for the buyer. This was considerably more than he had been offered. On leaving my office he went immediately to the people who had made the offer, told them exactly what he felt was right and within two days his decision was accepted. His property was sold to the great advantage of both himself and the purchaser. This transaction of over a million dollars was directly due to a definite conviction and decision on the part of my friend.

We Make Our Success or Defeat

Decision, imagination, faith, motives—all are mental states—states of mind—which move out into our experience. Through the exercise of these faculties we release and direct the dynamic God power within ourselves and which surrounds us. The Kingdom of God really is within us. The universal power of Life is the power we use. That power is omnipresent; it, therefore, must include the power we use.

There is but one Life. That Life is individualized as each one of us. The only place you and I can know and experience that One Life is in what we call "my life," "your life." The only place we can use that infinite principle of mind is where we think; so our work naturally begins with ourselves. Within ourselves is the God mind and we use and direct the God power. It is true, many people direct this power toward failure rather than success, toward sickness rather than health, toward confusion rather than peace.

Wherever you are, whatever you do, you are always confronted with yourself; but if you will look deeply within that self of you, you will find a bottomless pool of infinite qualities and faculties which in all probability you never have used fully. These qualities and faculties await your discovery—your direction and your use. Why not decide now to use them? To know that infinite intelligence is yours to use and infinite power is at your disposal means little to you unless you use them. You use them through decision, through imagination and faith. Within you is the power to reason. Within you are the miraculous faculties of decision and of imagination. Within you is the ability to choose. Within you are all the tools, so to speak, that you need in order to express Life as richly and as abundantly as you desire. It is only necessary to know those tools are available and then learn how to use them.

Do Not Underestimate Your Abilities

Do not discount yourself. Do not sell yourself short. You are a marvelous being. Life operates through the law of mind and that law of mind is yours to use. You only need, as I need, to learn about this law of mind, about the way Life acts, and use the law of mind for more wholesome, happy, abundant experiences. When you have learned this, you have learned the secret of healthy, happy, rich, abundant living. It doesn't in the least matter how long you have been using mind against yourself and against your best interests. Today you can begin to direct it into good and healthy experiences. The old weeds, briars and thistles in your garden of life resulting from wrong planting will, of course, continue to flourish if they are not uprooted and new seeds planted, but you can uproot and replant today and immediately you will begin to have a new and different result in your garden.

chapter **7**

Everyone Gravitates toward
That Person or Place
Which Is Most Pleasant

DON'T YOU ENJOY BEING IN THE COMPANY OF A HAPPY person? Since this is true, if you make the place pleasant where you are, other people will gravitate toward you. They will come to you—surround you; and if they like you, they will do nice things for you.

The Importance of Self-Esteem

Attracting people to you is a mental operation. Liking and loving people is something which goes on in your mind; so when others like you and respond to you, it is the result of a certain state of mind within you. If you like yourself, appreciate yourself and have a high opinion of yourself, you get along much better with yourself; and naturally you get along much better with other people. A good thing always to remember is that if you are to like other people, you must first like and respect yourself.

One who does not respect himself, esteem himself, will inevitably alibi. Being a problem to himself, he projects his shortcomings onto other people. The person who feels that he is a failure will excuse himself, rationalize his failure and say it is somebody else's fault. He does this in order that he may live in some degree of peace with himself or have some sense of mental harmony.

Every day we come in contact with people who dislike themselves; and consequently they project their resentment and criticism upon others. Naturally, this causes other people to react automatically in resentment and resistance toward them.

Your personality expresses your emotions and attitudes. Do you direct your emotions into healthy, pleasant channels or do you let them run wild until eventually they control you? How much better you feel physically when you are happy! Fear, anxiety, hatred, jealousy all register in your looks, your facial expression, in your speech, in your manner. Often a feeling of anxiety shows itself in stooped shoulders and dragging feet. You get along much better with yourself, and consequently better with other people, when you are happy; when you have faith in yourself and faith in other people. You will have faith in other people when you have faith in yourself; when you have faith in Life.

Isn't it easy to understand that happiness is not something to be found outside yourself, not something others can bring to you? It is not dependent upon some outside person or experience. Happiness is a state of mind, a state of consciousness, which you can recognize, develop, feel and appreciate. Like faith, it is an inner thing which can be cutivated. You may think you cannot be happy until you have arrived at some particular good or until you are completely well, or until you are married to the right person; or perhaps you are reserving your happiness until you have arrived at some particular accomplishment. This is putting the cart before the horse because happiness is an inner thing. Instead of being the result of certain accomplishments, the result of certain conditions, it in itself is one of the chief causes of accomplishment. A happy state of mind moves you into successful experiences. Automatically you are inspired to accomplish when you are happy.

Happiness draws the right persons into your environment. It attracts friends to you.

Mind Operates Like a Radio

Speak into the microphone and you are heard hundreds of miles away. Your voice is transmitted as clearly as though you were in the room with the person listening. This was difficult for me to feel many years ago when I first began radio work. The little gadget through which I was speaking seemed very cold and frightening. I could see no one responding to what I had to say. I could see no one listening to and smiling at me. Those who had tuned me in might even now be tuning me out; but gradually I was able to imagine all those listeners as my friends. I learned to like them. In my imagination I could see them smiling at me and I began to have a feeling of close personal friendship with my listening audience. As a result I have had thousands of letters from people who have told me they felt that I was speaking directly to them; that I was giving them a personal message.

We are now told by scientists that each one of us is actually a radio transmitter as well as receiver; that certain cells of our bodies and certain cells of the brain are transmitting sets and others are receiving stations. We certainly do set up definite mental vibrations at the place where we think and the result is that a corresponding something happens in the body, the affairs and even in the thinking and acting of other people. As we become more acquainted with the amazing powers of Life today, this doesn't seem at all strange. Without a doubt it happens because there is but one mind, one medium, common to all people—a Universal Creative Mind which everyone uses—and a thought or movement at one point in that Mind is actually active at all points. Emerson told us, "There is one mind common to all individual men."

Thoughts are real. We, ourselves, can generate thoughts and transmit them to others. We can easily observe how our bodies, our affairs and other people respond to our thoughts. Our thinking is reflected back to us in our environment. It is done unto us as we believe or as we use mind. Not only is this true with our bodies, our affairs and other people, it is true with all of Life. Your dog responds to your thought and to your feeling. If you hate a dog, he responds very differently than when you love him. Even plants respond to our thoughts about them.

Quite recently some scientists have been engaged in very interesting experiments with plants. It is reported that one plot of plants was loved and blessed while another was cursed. The plants which were loved and blessed grew abnormally fast while those which were cursed, shriveled and died. This may sound fantastic but the person who loves his garden and loves his plants has a much different experience with those living, growing things than does the person who hates, resents or is indifferent to them. Some of these experiments, I am told, were actually carried out by operators as much as one hundred miles distant from the plants which they blessed or cursed.

You have heard someone say, "That person has a green thumb." You may even know someone with that reputation. But this is simply saying that plants respond to love. I know an orange grower in Southern California whose grove is in an area where other growers use smudge pots but this man never has needed to use smudge pots. Each day he goes about through his orchard blessing his trees and telling them how he appreciates their heavy growth of fruit. In fact, he told me that each of his trees has a name and he feels a close personal love and appreciation for the accomplishment of each individual tree. This may sound foolish to you but I was with this man when he went to the bank to get a check for his crop and the banker told him he had the second finest crop in the whole area.

Our Bodies Respond to Love

We know our bodies respond to love and appreciation. Browne Landone, who lived to be nearly one hundred years old, said that while he was in his seventies, he went down with a heart attack. The doctors told him that his heart was worn out; that he probably would not last ten hours and certainly not more than ten days. Knowing the power of love, he began to talk to his heart, telling it how he appreciated what it had done for him, how it had taken abuse from him but how efficiently it had operated even though at times he had made it especially difficult. He promised his heart that if it would repair itself, he would be very careful and considerate of it in the future. He claimed that as a result of assuming a different attitude toward his heart—one of love and appreciation —it was completely rebuilt and operated efficiently for him for another twenty-five years.

Everything reacts to your thought about it for everything is alive. Your business responds to you for it, too, is alive the same as your body, people, animals and plants. Everything is governed by mind.

You know you can choose your thoughts but the fact that you can create and recreate your experiences through your thinking may never have occurred to you. A woman, working as a ticket agent for a bus company, told me people were so unreasonable all day long, asking foolish questions, expecting her to do the impossible, until she was so tired she hardly had sufficient strength to get home at night. I asked her if it were possible to change her attitude toward those people. Could she think of them as friends coming to visit her and then think of her work as an interesting game? The idea appealed to her. She decided to change her attitude, to give a friendly smile to everyone who came to her window and to answer their questions pleasantly no matter how ridiculous those questions seemed to be. She decided to make an effort to like everyone who came into the depot. And it worked! The very first day she went home without feeling tired and she was ready for a friendly evening with her family. She found the people whom she served to be much more agreeable than usual. Why was this? She had changed her attitude. She had formed a new habit of thinking. She liked people and they liked her. She had learned her lesson.

Henry Van Dyke wrote:

> Four things a man must learn to do
> If he would make his record true:
> To think without confusion clearly;
> To love his fellowmen sincerely;

To act from honest motives purely;
To trust in God and heaven securely.

Our thinking and loving, our motives and our trusting, are all mental states.

Mind is the great creative principle of Life. It is yours to use consciously. Through your state of mind or your state of faith, you may create for yourself whatever you choose to create. You may not like what you now are experiencing in your body, with other people, or in your affairs. Then change your mind, your state of faith, your attitudes and you will have different experiences.

What Is Scientific Prayer?

If a wrong state of faith has brought unhappy results, then common sense says that a right state of faith will bring happy results. Mental treatment or scientific prayer is the conscious changing of your mind, changing your faith from negative to positive. A different thought here causes something different to happen out there because the same mind is operating there which is operating here. The change may be noted in your body, in your human relations, or in your affairs. Change your mind where you are and you get a different result.

As an adult human being, you have the power of conscious choice. You can consciously choose your states of mind—your states of faith. As a matter of fact, you actually can make and direct your destiny. Through using mind consciously you can remake and re-create your world. Animals or vegetables cannot do this, for they do not think consciously. They live entirely by instinct even though they do use mind; but you, the highest personalization of Life, have the power of conscious thought, of consciously choosing what you will think. As David wrote in the eighth Psalm, you have dominion over the fowls of the air, the fish of the sea and over the beasts of the field. In fact, all things are under your feet.

To the extent that you use mind consciously, you take dominion over your world. Mind is the great creative instrument of all life. You may or may not use it for your greatest good. That is entirely up to you!

chapter 8

The Magical Power of

Creative Imagination

You HAVE THE FACULTY OF CREATING PICTURES, PATTERNS AND plans in your mind; and Life, being responsive, flows into experience for you over those plans and patterns. This faculty of image making is called imagination. Everyone has imagination and everyone uses it, either to make plans for what he wants or for what he doesn't want.

The mental pictures which you contemplate and *accept for yourself* are the plans you give to Life. Those plans are directed and controlled by your faith. Faith is a mental conviction. It is that which you are convinced is true for you or that which you are convinced will happen to you. That which you consciously or unconsciously believe to be true—that which you actually believe will happen—will determine the type of picture or plan you create in mind. Life moves into action over that plan. Your imagination is the engineering part of your mind, your plan making department.

Make a Plan for Yourself

If Life is to flow into the experience you desire, you must first make a plan and then hold steadfastly to that plan. The plan or picture should be vivid, clear and distinct. As you hold to that pattern persistently with unwavering faith, it must eventually manifest in form. If, however, after making a picture of what you desire, you then superimpose the picture or pattern of *not* having what you would like or of *not* being the kind of person you would like to be, you will fail to demonstrate what you want.

When Jesus said, "Believe that you have and you will receive," I believe He meant that we should make a vivid mental image of what we desire and then maintain the feeling of having it. When we maintain an inner feeling—a conviction of having—Mind, being the law of Life, begins to do whatever is necessary to bring the desire into fulfillment. Through our imagination our desires are fulfilled.

When you imagine yourself a success; when you feel that you are a success, you will undoubtedly succeed, for Life automatically moves you in that direction. If you live in the faith and the feeling of health, no power on earth will keep you from being well. The mind of Life is always opening channels to demonstrate for you whatever you believe you *have* and whatever you believe you *are*.

Conscious image building is *creative imagination*. When you persistently hold to a vivid mental picture, all the powers of your being are automatically turned to your becoming and accomplishing that which you see yourself as being, having and doing. The faculty of imagination, like any other natural faculty, can be directed. It cannot be repressed or refused expression but it can and should be directed toward the experiences we desire. Remember, imagination is a creative faculty. It is powerful. We automatically move in the direction of that which we imagine, so we should be careful what we imagine for ourselves and for others.

Let's suppose you are to make a speech to a large gathering of people. If you imagine yourself as not being prepared, as stuttering, stammering and making a spectacle of yourself, it isn't likely you will be successful. You may say to yourself, "I can't speak with all those people looking at me! I wonder if my clothes look all right?" Of course, you have built up a horrible, nervous fear. In your imagination you have created the wrong kind of picture. You have made a totally wrong plan. It will make little difference how much you may drive yourself or how you may assert to yourself,

"I *will* make that speech, anyway!" You will fail. You may even be ill because of the mental conflict.

Suppose, however, you say to yourself, "Anyone who can stand up and talk to one person, can stand up and talk to a hundred or a thousand persons. These people are all my friends or they wouldn't be here. They are interested in what I have to say. They are not interested in me, personally; but they believe I know my subject. I am well prepared. I have given it much thought and, of course, I know more about it than anyone here. What I have to say will be helpful. I am here to serve. I believe I will be able to explain my subject so clearly these people will see it as I see it." Now, if you use your imagination in this fashion, you will not be devastated by fear; you will be confident and you will give a good lecture. You have built a vivid, positive picture in your imagination.

This point may also be illustrated in the woman who tries to stop blushing or who bursts into tears at the slightest provocation. A sense of shame, loss or embarrassment is vivid in her imagination; and try as hard as she will, she cannot help the blush or the tears.

Coué taught people to say to themselves, "Every day in every way I am getting better and better." When you say that over and over to yourself, the imagination takes hold; and you automatically become better and better.

Coué gave another striking illustration of the power of imagination when he said that if a plank a foot wide was laid on the ground, no normal person would hesitate to walk it confidently for any distance; but suppose that same plank should be suspended ten stories high across the street from one building to another; it would be quite a different matter. Few people would dare to walk it. In their imagination they would have the picture of falling. At such a height most people would get dizzy, lose their sense of balance, even in thinking about it. It is the same plank, the same width; but a hundred feet up in the air the powerful imagination takes over.

You use this picture making, plan making department of your mind in all your creative activities. For example, you may wish to break an old habit or learn a new one. You do it best through the use of imagination.

I knew a man who thought he should stop smoking. He often said he could either stop or continue to smoke as he saw fit. He didn't stop smoking. Then one day he pictured to himself the advantages to be gained by stopping the habit. He decided he wanted those benefits. He pictured himself as feeling better. He pictured all the good results that would come into his life as a result of not smoking. He pictured better health and the money he would save. When this new picture was firmly fixed in his imagination, every part of his being was directed toward a demonstration according to that new picture of himself, and automatically he stopped the habit. He told me that he very shortly lost all desire for smoking.

Don't Force—Just Calmly Imagine

In the past people have worshipped at the shrine of the will. They have tried to develop will power. They have believed that in some way will power was tied up with getting what they wanted from Life. Sometimes people even have believed they were lacking in will power and became discouraged. Today our modern mental science parts company with this belief about the power of will. In fact, it is now pretty generally agreed there is no such thing as a "will" faculty. What we formerly referred to as will power is simply the forcing of oneself to do that which he does not wish to do—something contrary to his emotional desires. Imagination is now regarded as the creative faculty.

We all know people who seem to get things done without any fuss. They do not seem to drive themselves. Everything seems to work smoothly for them. They seem to be busy most of the time but it does not seem to require any special effort. This is because they want to do what they are doing. They do not force themselves nor do they pity themselves. In their imagination they see the good results of their acts and they live in the anticipation of good results. Their imagination directs their efforts and there is no conflict between what they wish to do and what they know they should do.

We also know people who are always pushing, hurrying, wrangling—willing this and willing that. They push themselves out of bed in the morning and push themselves around all day, forcing their minds to think and their bodies to act. Then when evening comes, they say, "I have accomplished very little today. I have gone here and there, rushing and striving. I am all tired out driving and pushing myself, all to no avail." These people are using up an enormous amount of energy and at the same time tearing themselves apart, for through their imagination they have not directed themselves out on an easy, comfortable, pleasant path nor clearly imagined the value to be gotten out of their efforts.

In your imagination you should live in the fulfillment of your desires then you will move forward with enthusiasm and with little loss of energy. If you have finished your work for the day and decided to go to your home, it isn't necessary for you to force yourself to get your coat and hat, pick up one foot after another and force yourself to walk to the garage, get your car and drive home. If you will enthusiastically imagine yourself as being at home with all the comforts of home and then just let yourself go, automatically you will do everything necessary to arrive at that pleasurable experience. Subconscious Mind—the responsive, creative part of mind —takes over when you imagine the result and when you are fired with enthusiasm.

Don't Make Mental Images of What You Don't Want

Unfortunately, many people imagine themselves into sickness, failure and unhappiness. So many people are enthusiastic about their diseases, their worries and their problems, believing unhappiness and frustration to be their normal state. Being enthusiastic in describing their problems, they only bind the problems more tightly to themselves. If they would be just as enthusiastic about health, success and accomplishment as they are about their worries, losses, diseases and failures, they would have very different experiences.

I know a young man who became president of one of the country's largest banks. He had no special pull or influence and few people could understand how it was possible for him to be promoted from the position of ordinary clerk to the presidency of that bank in such a short time. He told me the secret of his success. The moment he entered the bank's employ, he imagined himself as its president. When he waited on customers at the window, he imagined himself doing his work as though he were the president of the bank. Whatever his daily tasks, he imagined himself as the president doing that work. He kept his eyes on the president's chair and eventually—very soon, in fact—he occupied that chair. He wasn't aggressive. He didn't push people about or throw his weight around. He simply used his creative imagination in a positive way fitting himself for the position. Imagining himself in the higher position caused the powers of Life to flow off through him toward this new and better experience. The president, an older man, retired and the young man was elected to fill his place.

Suppose this young man had said, "Here I am stuck in this big bank. Hundreds of employees around here have been with this institution much longer than I. Many are better equipped, better prepared, than I. Many have more training and more pull. It will be years before I have any opportunity for advancement. Others will get all the breaks. I am always unlucky!" If he had accepted that picture of defeat; if he had projected that picture through his creative imagination, he certainly would not have had the larger experience.

Henry Ford, one of the world's richest men, said, "You can have anything you can imagine yourself as having." Jesus said, "Believe that you have got it and you will have it."

You must activate your imagination and use it for a good purpose. Live in the consciousness of already possessing that which you desire. Imagine it as yours now. Build up the feeling of success, of health, of happiness, of whatever it is you desire and no power on earth can prevent that desire being fulfilled. It will be attracted to you and you to it.

You Can Use Your Imagination for Good or for Ill

You can use your imagination to drag yourself down or lift yourself to the heights. If your imagination is directed by fear, anxiety, resentment (a negative faith), you most certainly keep yourself from having those things which you want and which rightly belong to you. If you are experiencing less than the good you desire, you can establish new thought patterns and *redirect* imagination through an unwavering faith that all good things belong to you—which they do. If you hold to this belief steadily, nothing can keep your desired good away from you.

I know a woman who never leaves her home. She will not go out into the street or even into her yard. The moment she thinks of leaving the shelter of her home, she imagines all the dreadful things that might happen to her. If she steps out of her house, she immediately gets weak and dizzy. This is called agoraphobia or the fear of open spaces. She does not control her imagination. It controls her. I know other people who have claustrophobia or the fear of closed places. Fear has been allowed to direct their imagination.

Once I knew two men who in earlier life had been partners in business. The business failed. One of the men let the experience get him down. He imagined himself a failure. He believed other people thought him a failure. He never recovered from the experience. He was a failure as long as he lived. Dwelling upon his loss and failure and upon what he believed other people thought about him, he became ineffective and he shortened his own life. Through his negative thinking, he brought to himself the very thing he feared. His partner likewise lost all his money but he didn't lose heart. Neither did he lose his ambition nor his belief in himself. He said, "My business failed but I did not fail. I will make use of my past experience and build another business. I will take a lesson from this. I will rebuild my fortune." And he did! He saw himself as a success and he became a success. He built a substantial business and he did much good. He helped many people. He was worthwhile. He made the world a better place in which to live. These two men had the same original experience but they reacted in different ways. One used his imagination to become a complete failure. The other used his imagination to become a success and with his success he became a great benefactor to mankind.

We are always using the power of imagination whether we know it or not. We can't help using it; but through our power of choice and decision, we can determine *how* we will use it. Faith can be used positively for our greatest good or negatively as fear and bring disease and failure. Love, a basic emotion, can be turned to hate; or we can love the wrong thing and get ourselves into trouble; but used correctly, love is one of our greatest blessings.

As individual conscious points of Life, we have the power of choice. The two men of whom I spoke were both surrounded by the same Life. Their original experience was the same. One accepted his good, the other rejected it.

Creative Imagination Is Not Day-Dreaming

The day-dreamer does not make a plan which he really intends to carry out. He does not accept it for himself. He does not put himself into the picture. He sits on the sidelines. In effect he says, "I will take my satisfaction in reverie. I will find my pleasure in dreaming. No one can take my dreams away from me." The dreamer who doesn't couple his dreams with action does not believe that the good he desires is his so he doesn't get it.

If one has faith that the good he desires is available; if he imagines himself in the midst of that good—if in his imagination he believes he has it; if he feels the good Life inevitably will move him on in the direction of his desires, he is not a day-dreamer; he is a creator—a creator of his own destiny.

If in our imagination we create pictures of bondage for ourselves, we put ourselves in bondage. Through misdirected mental planning we forge chains of slavery about ourselves and go through life as slaves. How foolish it is to do this to ourselves when we can think whatever thoughts we choose to think and direct ourselves to the ideal goal by holding the ideal image persistently in our thoughts, in our imagination. It makes no difference how long we may have been using our mental powers in the wrong way; we can start immediately to use them in the right way. It doesn't matter how long we may have been sitting in the darkness; when light is brought in, the darkness disappears.

Our bonds of restriction and trouble will be broken when we

no longer hold plans of limitation in our imagination. We can redirect our faith and mentally create new patterns of freedom which will create new experiences for us. We are not bound by old limiting beliefs when we identify ourselves with freedom, with abundance, health, success, peace and happiness. Our prison walls will automatically crumble away, for our outer world always reflects our inner states of mind.

chapter 9

Love and Faith

Influence the Imagination

You ARE NOW BEGINNING TO GLIMPSE THE MAGIC OF YOUR mind. You are beginning to see how it is that you, yourself, are the magician—for you use mind. It is becoming clear to you that thoughts are things. You now understand your thinking is using mind, which is the creative law of life. Since you accept the premise that the one mind or creative law exists everywhere, it is now becoming clear that your thoughts, your beliefs and the mental images which you hold in mind manifest as experiences in your world. In fact, you now see how it is that you can actually think good or ill into your experience.

You Think in Pictures, Plans and Patterns

Those mental images you present to Life are influenced, even directed, by your love, that is by your emotional state, and by your faith; therefore the plans and pictures which you make in your imagination are usually made without your conscious knowledge or direction; but having the power to choose, you *can* consciously make them as you will—if you will. If you make a plan—a blueprint—for yourself, then adhere to it persistently and act as though it were so, you will finally experience it. Life cannot refuse to move out over the pattern made by a conscious thinker if that plan is held persistently in mind. Do not refuse to use your imagination and by all means do not fail to use it constructively.

Put your imagination to work. Mentally make your plan. Give it shape and form. Then hold that picture in mind lovingly, confidently, easily but persistently. Do not push or coerce but with all confidence hand the plan over to Life with complete faith in the demonstration. In this way you are directing the creative law of Life which cannot help responding to you any more than the seed can refuse to grow when you plant it in the soil and give it loving care.

Unfortunately it is true that many people unconsciously make pictures in their minds of what they do not want and they hold to those pictures most persistently. Those pictures of what they don't want are the result of their negative beliefs and their negative emotional states. If a person does not love himself healthfully; if he believes himself to be unworthy, weak, a creature of lack, rejected by Life, unconsciously he makes a picture of himself as a failure. If he has a critical, unloving attitude toward himself, he may picture himself as sick; or in his imagination see trouble dogging his footsteps with more and greater troubles just ahead. Since it is the nature of Life to respond, it can do nothing but deliver according to the pattern he has given it.

You have read the story of Job in the Bible. Job was a rich man, healthy, with a fine family; but he became morbid. He made some serious mistakes and became very critical of himself so he imagined himself as losing his family, his herds, his flocks and his money. In his imagination he saw himself alone, destitute, without friends, and that is exactly what happened to him. He lost his family, his friends and his fortune. In his adversity, seeking to justify himself and alibi his failures, he blamed his friends and he blamed God; but all his blaming, ranting and raving didn't help matters. Conditions got no better until one day he came to the realization that he, through his own misuse of the infinite creative power, had brought those unhappy experiences upon himself and he uttered those famous, unforgettable words, "That which I greatly feared has come upon me."

He suddenly saw that the same power which had brought him failure could, if used constructively, bring him success, and being an intelligent man, he began to create different pictures in his imagination. He changed his attitude toward himself, toward his friends and toward Life. He even prayed for the good of his false friends. When he changed his faith from the negative to the positive, his fortunes were soon rebuilt. The story ends with his having a fine family, twice as many cattle, sheep and camels as well as many more friends than he had at the beginning. He recognized the creative power of mind when he said, "Thou shalt also decree a thing and it shall be established unto thee." A revised translation is, "You will decide on a matter and it will be established for you."

Your Plans Are Influenced by Your Emotional States

The pictures or plans in your imagination will inevitably be influenced by your attitudes; therefore by what you really believe about God, yourself and others, law or luck, and immortality, as we discussed in Chapter IV. If you are dominated by hate or fear, your mental images will certainly be influenced by those emotional states. Knowing that your fear thoughts influence your mental images, in the face of your fear, you may strive to create a picture or plan of what you should like to be or do. Through forcing yourself, you actually may be able to hold on to that picture temporarily; but as soon as you stop forcing, your fear or your distrust will automatically distort that picture and it will be replaced with another, one that you do not want. The dominant state of your subconscious mind or the way you think in your heart will eventually control the plans made in your imagination.

Now, there is an easy, efficient way of changing negative to positive images. Suppose you decide to take a healthy, sympathetic interest in other people and in yourself. Suppose you decide to love yourself and others healthfully. Suppose you come to believe that divine faculties and qualities are actually incarnated in every person whether he knows it or not and as a result you come to a high appreciation of yourself and a high opinion of others. You see the goodness in yourself and in others. Suppose you recognize the love and responsiveness of all Life round about you and you see this love and goodness available to every human being. Suppose you see that the power to use creative mind is given to you and you desire good for others as well as for yourself. Isn't it clear that you automatically will create pictures and plans according to that new state of faith? Dominated by a healthy interest of love and appreciation, will you not give creative Life a plan of health, abundance and peace; and won't Life respond to that plan? Of course it will, for Life never refuses. It always responds to your belief—your state of mind.

If you have a feeling of inferiority and of guilt and therefore depreciate yourself, you will draw mental pictures of yourself which really are not worthy of you, that wonderful divine you which is an incarnation of the good Life. The author of Ecclesiastes wrote, "Lo! this only have I found, that God hath made man upright but they have sought out many inventions." When you consciously change your attitude toward yourself; when you change your belief so that you love and appreciate yourself, the picture in your mind will change and your experiences will change. Remember, though, you cannot long maintain those new pictures if you force them contrary to the way you think in your heart.

Most People Just Muddle Along

Love is an emotional interest. We automatically give our attention to whatever we love. We desire all that is good for those we love, so we first must learn to love the self healthfully and thereby have faith in the self; then we learn to love others and all of Life so that we have faith in others and in Life.

You and I must let go of our old negative states of mind, if we are to live in health and happiness with ourselves and with others. We must lift ourselves above the average. Most people muddle through life, troubled in their bodies, in their affairs, and in their human relations because they won't let go of their old negative beliefs. It is possible to substitute a positive faith for fear. It is possible to let go of the old hurts, the old frustrations and failures and become profoundly, healthfully interested in ourselves and in others. It is possible to substitute love for hate; and since love influences our faith and since our faith directs our imagination, it is easy to see what Paul meant when he said: "Love is the fulfilling of the law"—the law of faith which governs our imagination and our affairs. We can change our faith by changing our interests, our attitudes; by becoming genuinely interested in people; by desiring good for ourselves, for others and for Life; by becoming interested in the joy, the unfoldment and the expression of Life, Itself. When this idea becomes firmly fixed in our consciousness, we can take control over ourselves, and with control over ourselves we have control over our world of experiences.

In the next chapter, we will discuss forgiveness or the releasing of the old negative states of mind so that new patterns can be projected and easily maintained. "Mind is the power that molds and makes." To be efficient in your use of mind it is necessary to remove the old states of fear, hate, criticism, resentment or resistance; every negative thought, belief, idea or feeling which influences your use of mind in the wrong way. Love and faith continually direct the creative forces in the right way.

Truly, "as a man thinketh in his heart, so is he."

chapter 10

The Magic of Prayer

and Forgiveness

YOU HAVE THE RIGHT TO WHATEVER YOU WANT AND NEED IF you operate lawfully. To know that an infinite, intelligent power exists and that it will respond to your positive approach and answer your needs should give you the greatest satisfaction. The most valuable knowledge you can possess is to know how to use creative mind or the law of Life so that what you want and need will be delivered to you.

Some Prayers Are Answered—Others Are Not. Why?

Contacting, communicating with and working with infinite, intelligent, creative power is usually called prayer. You may call it spiritual or mental treatment. It doesn't matter what you call it. For the moment we will call it prayer. Intuitively man knows that he is made to have dominion over his world. He has an inner urge to exercise that dominion. Throughout history and in every race, some people have gained dominion over their world and experienced health, happiness and satisfaction; others have not. We cannot believe that Life singles out certain persons on whom to bestow

Its benefits. It must be that certain persons have discovered the laws of successful living and have used them. James, writing in the Bible, said, "Ye ask and receive not because ye ask amiss." Another translation is, "You ask and do not receive because you ask wrongly."

People of all ages, all countries and all religions have experienced peace, satisfaction and success. God is no respecter of persons. Those who have been successful beyond the average have consciously or unconsciously recognized the existence of an intelligent, responsive power and found how to use that power.

Jesus told us how to get those things from Life which we would like to have when He said, "So I tell you, whatever you pray for and ask, believe you have got it and you shall have it." This is very simple but it isn't exactly easy. It calls for faith in good, faith in Life and also for the exercise of the imagination. The reason most people lack the faith that their good is already available and that they have the right to have that good is answered in the paragraph following Jesus' suggestion to believe that you have and you shall have. He said, "Also, whenever you stand up to pray, if you have anything against anybody, forgive him so that your Father in heaven may forgive you your trespasses."

Two Steps in Effective Prayer

First, there is forgiveness, which means clearing your mind by releasing all past hurts and failures, all sense of guilt and loss. After you have forgiven, *believe that life already has provided what you need and that it is yours now.* These two mental operations will set creative law into motion to bring you whatever you desire; for when you forgive, you let go of all inner resistance to your believing that you have the right to have. You must believe that you have the right to have your good; otherwise you cannot believe that an honest Life will deliver it to you. If you can believe you have the right to have, then most certainly you will believe that the laws of Life will bring that good to you. If you have let go of all past hurts, all sense of guilt and shock, you do not deny your right to have. Forgiveness, then, removes whatever has blocked creative mind from operating positively for you and for your good.

No one can go forward if he is tied to the past. No one can think straight and efficiently if his mind is cluttered up with thoughts of hate or memories of hurts and mistakes; hence the necessity of forgiving so that we can love ourselves, our neighbor and God. Most of us carry in our feelings some sense of hurt, mistake or loss. So long as we continue these negative states of mind, we live over and over the old experiences.

Psychologists tell us that at least seven out of ten persons carry throughout life a sense of guilt, a feeling of having sinned or made a mistake from which they never have felt release or sensed forgiveness. A person who has a sense of guilt, who believes himself to be a sinner, cannot feel that he has the right to have good come to him. Since he does not feel that he has the right to have it, naturally he does not expect it; therefore he holds his good away from him however much he may pray, beg or supplicate.

Many people have a deep sense of loss or grief because some member of their family or friend upon whom they greatly depended, or perhaps money or position, has been taken from them. This feeling, even though but a memory, continues to dominate their thoughts. They feel rejected. They believe Life is opposed to them. They feel ill-treated by the world or by other people. This keeps them from believing they already *have* or that they will *get* what they desire, for it is done unto us as we believe. These memories of shocks and fears cause resentment and jealousy. This is an unsavory condition.

God does not punish us. We punish ourselves through carrying in our souls the feeling of past mistakes, shocks and losses. It is *highly important* that we understand how our feeling of having sinned or made mistakes stands in the way of our feeling that Life will give to us lovingly and generously.

So long as we feel that Life has dealt unjustly with us, we are not in harmony with Life. We feel out of tune with It. So long as we have a sense of sin or a belief that we have made mistakes and not made full amends, we will not enjoy the love, the goodwill and the appreciation we should feel for ourselves. When we have hurt someone else and have not forgiven ourselves, we feel a barrier between us and the person we have hurt. So long as we feel that someone has hurt us and we have not responded in love and goodwill to that person, have not understood the motive for his actions, have held him away from us and ourselves away from him, we are not mentally in harmony with him so we have a feeling of separation. It is very easy to see why forgiveness is necessary.

A feeling of harmony with and love for other people is very important and also we must know there is a corresponding feeling of love and goodwill for us. We must love God or Life and feel that God—Life—loves us and responds to us. There must be an uninterrupted flow of goodwill between ourselves and other people and between ourselves and God. This, of course, has nothing to do with orthodox religion. It has nothing to do with theology. It only has to do with effective living—with healthy accomplishment and happiness. Remember, love, or your emotional feeling toward yourself, others or God, influences your faith; and faith, directing your imagination, determines your experiences. So, forgive "seventy times seven" if necessary.

Forgiveness Is a Principle of Nature

Nature always forgives. Nature is the great giver and the great forgiver. Should you cut your hand with a sharp knife, the forces of nature set about immediately to repair the damage. It was a mistake to cut your hand but nature does not withhold the repairing of the wound. Nature immediately forgives and starts at once to make repairs. If you eat food which does not agree with you and you have indigestion, nature immediately starts to repair the damage. Although it was a mistake to eat the wrong food, you do not need to go through the rest of your life with indigestion. Nature even repairs the ravages of the battlefield by covering it with grass and flowers.

We find the principle of forgiveness in our social system. When there seems to be no alternative, bankruptcy laws provide a way through which a business man, if he has overextended himself financially, if he has made a mistake and finds that he cannot pay his debts, may go before a judge, confess his mistakes and be forgiven. His debts may be cancelled. He can start life again freely as a respectable citizen. The load of debt is lifted from his shoulders.

All through nature we find this principle of forgiveness. It makes for health. When through accident or wrong thinking we become ill, nature forgives. Nature brings us back into harmony, back to health, back to happiness and peace if we do our part, so to forgive is natural. If we are to be well and happy, we must be true to our nature. If we wish to be at peace, to be free, to be successful, to give our creative nature full expression, we simply cannot carry along negative, hurtful memories which clutter up the free flow of Life. Negative thinking must be replaced by love and faith. The suggestion of Jesus that we should forgive if we have anything against anyone or anything is very practical; and of course, "anyone" includes ourselves, all people and all past experiences. It even includes God.

We will devote the next four short chapters to a further examination of this extremely important matter of forgiveness.

chapter 11

Forgiving

Yourself

SEVERAL YEARS AGO, I GAVE A SERIES OF SUNDAY EVENING lectures at the Y.M.C.A. Auditorium in Pomona, California. A man wearing carpet slippers, his feet shuffling along the floor, attended regularly. One evening after the meeting, he approached me and said, "What can be done for me? For nine years I have suffered from what the doctors have told me is arthritis. I have tried many cures but I get no relief." I told him it might be necessary for him to change his thinking or his dominant state of faith. He asked, "Will it be necessary to change my opinion about God? I belong to an orthodox Christian sect." I assured him that it would be necessary to change only those opinions which were harmful to him. I reminded him it is done unto all of us according to our faith; and that if any wrong beliefs had been causing trouble in his body, then those beliefs should be changed if he wanted to get well.

Many people dislike changing their minds. They are like the rich, young man in Jesus' time who was bound by his possessions. He was unwilling to free himself even though Jesus told him that by doing so he might experience heaven. The young man went away sorrowing, if you will recall; but he still held on to his possessions. Likewise, many people insist on holding on to some old, outmoded belief which stands in the way of their experiencing health, success or happiness. They would rather keep their old beliefs than step forth into freedom. We might call this a kind of spiritual pride. Many people are really afraid to learn something new, afraid their old comfortable familiar world will be upset. We must realize we never are bound except as we bind ourselves and no one can set us free but ourselves.

A Deep Sense of Guilt Can Make You Ill

My arthritic friend came to see me. He told me his trouble started during the financial depression several years before. Medical men had advised him that his illness was due to fear and that he never would be rid of his difficulty until he quit being fearful. Then he said, "But I am over all that. I lost my fortune, to be sure, but that doesn't bother me now. I have a comfortable home, a small ranch, a fine wife and I get along all right; but I still have this physical trouble." I asked him why he felt he must continue to have the arthritis. At first he said there was no reason for it. Nevertheless, I felt pretty sure he hadn't told the entire story so I insisted he come clean, just make a clean breast of what was troubling him that caused him to believe he should continue to suffer.

After some hesitation he relaxed. "I am going to tell you something I never have told a living soul—not even my wife." Then came the story: in the midst of the depression he had made a serious mistake. He had taken some money which did not belong to him. He had made amends immediately afterward; no one was hurt; in fact, no one knew about it, but somehow he never had been able to get the "sin," as he called it, out of his mind. He said that undoubtedly his physical difficulty was coming to him, that he deserved it and that he was being punished. This man had prayed desperately for forgiveness but he never could feel that God had forgiven him, so he never got a release.

I then asked him why he didn't forgive himself, explaining that if he would only forgive himself, he would be forgiven. This he couldn't understand. Since he was a devout churchman, I read him the first eight verses of the ninth chapter of Matthew which tells of Jesus healing a man sick of palsy. As you recall, this man was healed through feeling that he was forgiven of his sins. Jesus simply said, "Son, be of good cheer; thy sins be forgiven thee." Some of the scribes hearing Jesus tell the man that he was forgiven said that He, Jesus, blasphemed God by forgiving sins. Apparently those old scribes also thought that an outside God had to do the forgiving, but I called my friend's attention to the eighth verse, which is often overlooked. It reads, "But when the multitude saw it, they marveled and glorified God which had given such power unto men."

Our arthritic friend immediately saw that forgiveness was within his own power; that he needed only to release the old memory and start at once thinking and doing the right thing. This man never had seen that verse in the Bible before, nor the sixth verse—"But that ye may know that the Son of Man hath power on earth to forgive sins." Certainly his feeling of relief must have been great because he was waiting for me at the door of the auditorium the following Sunday evening and he told me that his arthritis was gone.

The next Sunday evening, with great enthusiasm, he told me, "For nine years I hadn't done a full day's work any day; but last week I worked all day, every day, without pain." Apparently, all this man needed was to believe that he had the right to be well. Life had been delivering to him according to his expectancy— according to his belief. So long as he believed he should be punished, he held on to his trouble. When he believed that he had the right to health, Life responded to him in health.

We are told that a sense of guilt is the most common cause of mental and nervous disorders. It manifests in the malfunctioning of different organs in the body. A sense of guilt is sometimes called a "conscience distress." It certainly is a distressed conscience; and so long as we labor under a sense of having done wrong, or so long as we nurse the memory of a wrong done to us, we will experience tension and strain in the mind which inevitably causes trouble and distress in the body. Hence, the need for forgiveness.

When you forgive yourself, you are forgiven. It is important to understand that forgiveness takes place within your own consciousness. The tense situation is within your own mind; and letting go, releasing, is within your own power.

Many times, people have told me they can't go on with the memory of that past sin hanging over them. A few years ago I had a visit from a fine woman of our acquaintance and her first words to me were, "I can't stand it any longer. I am losing my mind." This lady had a beautiful home and money. She was married to a fine man and she had two fine sons. Her story indicated an overwhelming sense of guilt. Before her marriage she had not been as good a girl as she might have been. Her mother had died when she was quite young and she had been at loose ends for a while. Indiscreetly she had tried the "primrose" path.

Now, years later, married to a man who loved her and whom she loved, her sense of remorse was so overwhelming that she felt she had no right to be the wife of such a good man and the mother of such fine boys. She felt she wasn't entitled to the comforts and luxuries life had given her. She told me she had been to many doctors and practitioners, all to no avail. She was completely miserable, mentally and physically. I asked her, "Are you a good woman now?" She replied, "Why, yes, of course! I have been a good wife and mother since I have been married." Then I dropped a bomb shell! "If you are a good woman today, you are just as good as though you never had been bad, aren't you?" This startled her. "Please say that again." I repeated, "If you are good now, then *you are good* and that's all there is to it! If you are a good wife and mother, you are good now! That's the truth about you now, so you have the right to have good come to you *now!* The past is of no consequence. It has no power over you except as you hold fast to it in your thoughts, believing you have to suffer."

Well, this woman exhaled a deep breath. Her whole body relaxed. She said, "I feel as though a load of brick has been lifted from my shoulders. For years I have thought I must suffer for my past mistakes until life became unbearable. Now, I see if I am good, I am good; and the past has no power over me." This idea was all she seemed to need to free her. Today, a charming, happy, brilliant woman—a magnificent woman because she is free—she spends much of her time helping lonely young girls in addition to being a good wife and mother. Anyone can have this same freedom! Whatever the past, it is of no consequence now.

"Today Is the World Made New"

The only past we need consider is the past we are creating today, for today will be tomorrow's past. David told us to do good and trust in the law. If a person is good, he is good. God holds no grudge against us. God isn't jealous nor does God mete out punishment to anyone. We punish ourselves by breaking a universal law —the law of cause and effect. Life is good to us. It always forgives us as we forgive ourselves. When we stop making the mistake and do what is right, knowing that from good only good can come, the natural law of cause and effect delivers good into our lives. To gain forgiveness for past mistakes, we need only to turn away from the mistake, think right and do good. We can hold resentment against ourselves only within our own minds. Within is the only place we can find forgiveness and release. Forgiveness—release— comes when we realize that the past experience for which we have felt guilty was only a mistake due to ignorance; and with forgiveness, we move into richer, happier, healthier living.

If we deliberately turn from our past mistakes after making whatever amends we can; if we firmly determine not to compromise the principle of right, we will find that we have transcended the old mistakes. They will no longer have any power over us for we will no longer remember them consciously or subconsciously. We forgive the self when we appreciate its good intentions; when we love ourselves healthfully.

The truth is, we are all gods, even though, as Robert Browning said, "in the germ." *Forgive yourself. See the good in yourself. Express the good and expect good to return to you.*

chapter 12

Forgiving

Others

HAVE YOU EVER HEARD SOMEONE SAY, "I CAN FORGIVE BUT I cannot forget?" But it's a fact one cannot really forgive without forgetting.

What Is Forgiveness?

Forgiveness is clearing the mind. It is not just putting aside an old matter for future reference. Real forgiveness is blotting out, completely obliterating the incident and starting all over with a clean slate. It is making a new beginning. The old offense is as though it never had happened. It is not a personal favor when we receive forgiveness nor is there any personal glory attached to us when we forgive. Forgiveness is a practical everyday principle of health and progress. It is unblocking the stream of Life so that It may express healthfully; and until we learn the art of forgiveness, we will not get far in this matter of happy, healthy living. When we release others, we release ourselves.

The person who says he can forgive but not forget desires the credit of forgiving the other person but at the same time wants to nurse his wound. Even though we feel someone has harmed us, no point is gained by continuing a feeling of ill-will toward him. We may not want to associate with that person again and it may not be necessary to do so; but if we refuse to forgive him, we bind ourselves to that unhappy experience and to that person. We live the hurt over and over. Each time we think of him, we will be hurt again. We will die a thousand deaths. We will feel a thousand times cheated; but when we release him, we are free.

If we harm someone and he forgives us, he is released. He is free. That forgiveness is a mental act on his part; but if we continue to carry a sense of guilt, we are not released even though he may be. Unless we release ourselves, we continue to suffer. We are not free. Let me tell you of a personal experience. One time I thought I had harmed a friend of mine and I was very unhappy about it. I was ashamed. I thought he avoided me. With my sense of guilt, of course, I avoided him. Then, one day I went to him and apologized. I told him I was very sorry for the wrong I had done him. He said, "Is that so? I don't know of any wrong you have done me. For some time I have thought you avoided me but I didn't know why." You see, there was no sense of inharmony on his part. It was entirely in my own mind. Within me was the feeling of being cut off from a friendship because of a wrong act on my part, so I *was* cut off because I had cut myself off.

Are we justified in holding a grudge against a person who, although he made a mistake, honestly felt that he was doing the best he could do? Shouldn't we have sympathy for him and forgive him?

If you think someone has mistreated you and you condemn him, fail to forgive, fail to understand and release him, you never really feel at peace. You never feel just right. But when you let go of the experience, release the other person, giving him the same consideration you would like to have him give you under the same circumstances, you are practicing the Golden Rule. Would you want someone to hold a grudge or resentment against you if you honestly were doing the best you could? He harmed you. It was a mistake; but when he made the mistake, he undoubtedly believed he was doing his best just as you did when you made a mistake.

He may have been weak and the mistake was easy for him. Perhaps he was under some pressure you didn't know about. Whatever his reason he should be accorded the same treatment you would want for yourself under the same circumstances. See him as honestly mistaken. He may still have a desire to persecute you but how many times should you forgive your brother? Seven times? Jesus said seventy times seven.

Now we are considering only your own good, your peace of mind. Love your neighbor as yourself and accord him the same consideration you desire for yourself so that *you* may be free. You may say his sin must be punished, but why must it? What is the object of punishment? Is it to rub it in so the offender won't make the same mistake again for fear of the consequences? Suppose the other person already realizes he was in the wrong? Suppose he is already sorry for it? Is anything to be gained by continuing to punish him or by avoiding him? If he has changed his attitude and viewpoint, nothing is gained by either of you through continuing the punishment. Mahatma Gandhi taught, "Hatred injures the hater, never the hated." We need insight and understanding!

Resentment Is Healed by Forgiveness

A highly intelligent middle-aged woman, the principal of a high school, came to me for counsel. She told me she was completely fed up with living, life held no satisfaction—no joy—for her. Some years before, her husband had deserted her and married another woman. She never had remarried. She said she was lonely and that she worked very hard to make both ends meet on a rather meager salary. Other women were happy with good homes and loving husbands, but Life seemed to pass her by. As Mrs. Baker's story unfolded, it seemed that her husband had given her a raw deal. One thing she particularly resented was that during the time she was married to him she had endorsed a bank note for fifteen hundred dollars which he did not pay and which she had been compelled to pay bit by bit from her salary after they were separated. Now, even though her ex-husband was quite well-to-do and able to pay, he had not reimbursed her. In fact, he ignored her; and the note being long since outlawed, she had no standing in court. Her mind was full of bitterness. Resentment fairly dripped from every word. She said, "I just can't seem to be able to stop thinking of his unfair treatment of me and now that I am getting older, I seem to have no opportunity for a happy domestic life."

I told her she must divorce her ex-husband; to which she replied in astonishment, "I have been divorced for ten years!" "Yes, legally, perhaps, but you still are bound to him with ties of hatred and resentment. You are not ready for another marriage. You must release him, forgive him and free yourself from the old experience. Try blessing him, praying for his success, his health and his happiness." This was a bitter pill but she took it.

Several interesting things took place. One day she called me by telephone and told me she must see me at once; a miracle had happened. She fairly bounced into my office and spread fifteen one hundred dollar bills over my desk. "Where do you think these came from?" she asked. Then she continued. "I have been praying honestly for my ex-husband's good. As you know I have neither seen him nor heard from him for several years. Today he telephoned me and told me he wanted to see me. He came. He told me there was something on his mind that had been disturbing him for several days and with that he laid those fifteen one hundred dollar bills in my lap. Then he told me he realized that he had treated me unjustly; but that if at any time he could help me in any way, I should call upon him. It seems unbelievable, doesn't it? I feel as though I have been dreaming." "A miracle," you may say. No, she had let go of her resentment. She had forgiven him. She actually had loved and prayed for that person whom she previously considered to be her enemy. She had forgiven him and he had reacted to her forgiveness.

Now the scene shifts.

At the time I was trying to help Mrs. Baker, I also was counselling a business man whose wife had deserted him for her music teacher. He was living alone and very resentful. His resentment was being reflected in his business.

I gave him the same suggestion I gave the school teacher—he must divorce his wife. In colorful language he told me that he had been divorced for four years; but I pointed out to him that he had not let go of his ex-wife in his own mind, that he must forgive her and wish for *her*, every happiness he desired for himself.

One evening he said, "I have been visiting you regularly for a year. I certainly have changed during that time. My business and my personal affairs are in much better shape. I am relaxed. I feel free. I have forgiven my wife. I am sure that she is married to a man who suits her temperament much better than I. I have learned my lesson; now I only wish for her every happiness. I hope that she and her husband are prosperous. Today the old experience means no more to me than an item in the newspaper."

He was on the way out of my office as Mrs. Baker was coming in. I introduced them in the doorway. Of course, you know the result. A few weeks later I married them; and, as all stories go, they are living together happily.

A very wise man, two thousand years ago, in teaching people to be happy, well and successful said, "But I say unto you, love your enemies, bless them that curse you and pray for them that despitefully use you and persecute you." Why? So *you* may experience heaven.

I am sure the reason most people do not get the answer to their most fervent prayer is that instead of a prayer of positive faith they pray with hate, resentment, a feeling of rejection or inferiority. Their mental processes are all clogged up with rubbish which should be dissolved—forgiven. How can we expect to get good results through mental means if we do not remove those personality obstructions—if we insist on keeping the stream clogged up?

When someone hurts us and we carry the memory of that hurt throughout the years, we come to have the feeling of being rejected by all of Life. Mr. Allison, a man of sixty, told me he never had been a success because twenty-eight years earlier his business partner had absconded with the money of their partnership. He blamed his failure in life on the defection of this old partner. I suggested that he forgive the old partner and thereby remove every excuse for failure.

Some two or three years later this same man attended a class I was giving in human relations. One evening he asked to speak to the class. He told his story: for twenty-eight years he had blamed his failure in life on a partner who had absconded with his money. He explained that I had told him to forgive that old experience and to pray for the good of this partner whom he had not seen for many years. "I didn't know how to pray for him but I decided to wish him all the good that I wanted for myself so I did it in my own simple way. I have always wanted a good automobile and I like to smoke good cigars. So in my imagination I saw this old partner driving up the street in a fine Cadillac, smoking a big cigar. In my imagination I called to him. He stopped. He seemed a bit embarrassed; but I said, 'Bill, it is all right. I understand. I forgive you. I hold nothing against you. I am glad you are successful. I am glad that you have the very things I like myself. The old experience is forgiven and forgotten. You are free and I am glad you are, for I have freed myself.'"

Mr. Allison went on to say that immediately his affairs took a turn for the better and now he was financially quite successful and very happy.

To release the other person, take the incident into your consciousness and work it over, analyze it until you understand it. As a matter of fact understanding is forgiveness. When you completely understand, there is nothing to forgive; so with understanding it is not difficult to wish the person who harmed you all the good you want for yourself. That attitude takes the foundation completely out from under your resentment and you have made a friend of that person in your own mind. That's the way to make a friend. Wish him health, success and happiness the same as you wish for yourself. When you change your mental attitude toward him, you are in a position where he can be a channel through which good can come to you. Do the job completely! Wash your mind of it entirely and it is done! When the person who harmed you comes to your mind after you have released him, just say, "God bless him" and mean it. Then forget it. It is done. In a short time you never will think of the offense again because you are completely released.

People have said to me, "But all of this is very difficult to do. I try but I just give up." Well, do you want to go through life without trouble or would you rather hug your hatred and your resentment to you? You may have either. The choice is yours. One man said, "I really have tried to forgive the man who hurt me but I can't." I asked him, "Have you tried honestly?" He said, "Yes, I have." "Have you ever gone up to that man and said, 'I forgive you, George.'?" I asked him. Well, no, he hadn't done that. I insisted, "Have you ever said, 'God bless you, George. Suppose we let by-gones be bygones. I hold nothing against you.'?" He said, "No, I haven't." "Did you ever do anything? Write a cheerful letter or send a birthday card?" The answer was, "No." He hadn't tried to forgive. He had just sat back and allowed his hatred and bitterness to consume him; at the same time hating himself for not doing what he knew he should do.

Forgiveness Must Move into Action

Faith without works is dead. Suppose someone takes something from you that you feel belongs to you. Whatever it is, there is plenty more, isn't there? All of us have had things taken from us. Your experiences are no different than others. There is more good around you than you ever will be able to use. Things don't belong to us, anyway. They are just ours to use while we are here. There is plenty of money and there are plenty of opportunities for friendship. Set the other person free and you set yourself free; but so long as you hold resentment, a cosmic link—a mental chain—ties you to the person who hurt you and ties the hurt to you.

We may have a conscious or unconscious resentment against someone whom we feel harmed us in our childhood, a person who frustrated our ambitions and whom we feel is responsible for our present state of inferiority and our lack of success today. That feeling of hatred, that unconscious anxiety, to a very large extent, will keep us from living a happy, successful life today. As a child we may have felt that our parents did not love us enough, that they treated us unjustly. We never will get over it entirely until we understand why they acted as they did. When we understand, we will forgive. Our experiences will change from darkness to light, from hatred to love. For forty years we may have hated the one who punished or spoiled us, making life miserable for us; but in a moment of understanding we may see clearly that the parent who spanked us or spoiled us was, himself, spanked or spoiled by someone in his own childhood. He was only compensating his own feeling of hurt and frustration when he treated us the same way.

The wise, the sensible thing to do is to love, to understand, to forgive. Love is the greatest healing power in the world. When we love, we understand and sympathize. When we love, understand and forgive, the power which we have directed as hatred, revenge, resentment and bitterness, will flow through us as love, goodwill and sympathy, bringing us many rich and unexpected blessings.

chapter 13

Forgiving

the Past

MRS. HENSEL, THE ONLY DAUGHTER OF A WIDOWED MOTHER, was married to a successful business man, and her mother had an apartment in their home. Mr. Hensel took frequent business trips and he always liked to have his wife accompany him. This necessitated leaving the mother with friends or having some friend stay with the mother while Mrs. Hensel was away. On one occasion while the daughter was away with her husband, the mother died of a heart attack. As a result, Mrs. Hensel developed a deep sense of guilt. For years she condemned herself with the thought that she hadn't given her mother the care and attention due her.

Guilt Causes Mental and Physical Illness

Torn between what she thought was neglect of her mother and loyalty to her husband, she developed nervous indigestion, spells of remorse and a general discontent. At the time she came to my office, she was on the verge of a nervous collapse. Miserable herself, she certainly was making those around her miserable.

Mrs. Hensel had a beautiful daughter in her teens. I asked her to imagine herself in her mother's place and her daughter in hers.

What did she think her daughter should have done if she were placed in a similar situation? At once she replied, "Why, I would want her to go with her husband, of course. I certainly wouldn't want her to stay home looking after me." Then she suddenly realized that she had believed her own mother was less charitable, less loving and kind, than she; and, of course, with that understanding, the feeling of self-resentment was removed. Free from remorse she adjusted to life and is now a healthy, happy woman.

Looking at the consequences of what seems to have been a wrong act, we are inclined to say, "I should have known better. In fact, I did know better. Why did I do it?" We did it because at the time, even in spite of our better judgment to the contrary, we thought we were doing the best we could. When someone believes he is doing the best he can, even though later it proved to be a mistake, you cannot refuse to forgive him, can you? Give yourself the same consideration.

Understanding Is the Cure

When we know the truth; when we understand, there is really nothing to forgive. If in our imagination we can put ourselves in the other person's place, understand his background, why he did as he did, we usually can sympathize and automatically will forgive. Solomon said, "With all thy getting, get understanding." Refusing to forgive is very shortsighted. If we do not forgive, we are only hurting ourselves. When a thing is done, it cannot be undone. The only sensible thing to do is to understand it, forgive it and then release it from our consciousness. So long as we continue to condemn, so long as we fail to forgive—free the person who hurt us—we never will be at peace while the person who hurt us probably goes on his way completely oblivious to the way we feel. Somehow through a change in our own thinking, we must give that person the same treatment we would like given to ourselves. If we are unable to forgive in spite of our endeavor to think love and goodwill, very likely we are trying to release without understanding, without putting ourselves in the other person's place.

Jesus suggested that you pray for those who despitefully use you and persecute you. Mrs. George, the mother of three children, for some twenty years had been having regular seizures which were diagnosed as epilepsy. She told me that when she was a young girl, her father had violated her; but she was sure this very shocking experience was not the cause of her difficulty, for she had forgiven him. Some twelve years previous to her visit to me, her father got very sick, and on what he thought was his deathbed made a complete confession of his whole horrible mistake. Mrs. George and her mother both forgave him; but he did not pass on and for years she and her father had been friends. As a matter of fact, she said the families had dinner together at least once each week.

I felt sure her forgiveness was not complete; so I told her that I believed she would get well if she would carefully follow my instructions: go into a dark room twice a day, get down on her knees and pray aloud for her father; in all sincerity pray that her father have all the good she desired for herself—health, peace, happiness, and so forth. This she did and after that visit she never had another seizure. Apparently the *act* of getting down on her knees and listening to herself ask for his good was needed to complete the forgiving process.

Mrs. Arnold, a woman in her sixties, a mental science practitioner, told me that she was mentally unsettled and confused. She had a nice home in the valley but she wished to sell it and move into the city. Originally she had lived in the city but following the death of her husband, she had sold her city home and moved to the country. Unhappy in the country, she returned to the city. She had repeated this moving process several times, never getting the peace she sought. When speaking of her husband, she evidenced a great emotional state, and I suggested that it was possible she did not firmly believe in immortality. She was indignant. "That's a preposterous suggestion! Why, I am a mental science practitioner!" "Yes," I said, "but seriously, do you believe that your husband still lives? Is it not true there is some doubt which has been the cause of your unsettled condition of mind?" After some thought she agreed that might be the difficulty. A few conversations followed in which I brought to her evidences of immortality and assured her of my own personal conviction in immortality. Her confusion disappeared. She did not sell the country home and the last time I saw her she was busy, happy and at peace. It is a fact mental confusion causes confusion in our affairs.

A husband in his sixties brought his wife to see me. He told me that unless she could find peace of mind, it would be necessary to place her in a mental institution. At my invitation to tell me about her trouble, she said frankly, "I am afraid of the future. I am afraid my husband will die and I will be left alone." I assured her that I had seen her husband but a short time before and he seemed perfectly well. "Yes, I know, but I am afraid he will die and I have no other family." As she talked, she evidenced great emotional stress. I discovered that in her early life her husband had traveled in his business and she had accompanied him. Under the circumstances they felt they should not have children.

I helped her to see that her present mental conflict probably was the result of a sense of guilt for not permitting herself to have children. She had brooded over the situation, she told me, until she felt herself to be a murderess; and she now believed she should be punished for her sin. As soon as she was able to see that she had done what she then felt was the best she could under the circumstances, she forgave herself. She felt at peace and now she is calm and happy.

It would be well for each of us to sit quietly each day and say to ourselves and mean it:

"Today I release every unhappy experience of the past and everyone connected with those experiences. I bless them with my love and (in my imagination) I see them having all the good I desire for myself. I recognize that all people everywhere are made of the same substance of which I am made. Each of us is a part of the great, infinite Life which is all the Life there is. In that Life we *all* live and move and have our being. Since this is true, I forgive myself for every mistake I ever have made; and I forgive everyone who in any way has harmed me, knowing that out of every experience, as I understand it, good will come to me. Each mistake I have made is a stepping stone to greater understanding and to greater opportunities. I bless every experience of the past. No past experience can harm me today or in the future. I completely forgive as I would be forgiven."

chapter 14

Forgiving

God

WE HAVE DISCUSSED FORGIVING OURSELVES, OTHERS AND THE past. Now we must forgive God for those experiences which we have consciously or unconsciously blamed on the Creator.

God Is Not Responsible for Trouble, War and Sickness

This is difficult for some people to understand. They think God is responsible for a suffering world. They even may feel they could do a better job of running the universe themselves. Many people, as they look at the chaotic conditions of the world today, seem to feel that God has failed in the job. They do not understand that God has nothing whatever to do with the unhappy conditions in the world. Those weeds or conditions sprout in the negative thinking—in the negative faith of man himself; and yet some people always have blamed God for their troubles and afflictions.

God has been reproached by those who have felt the loss of a friend or a loved one. God has been reviled and blasphemed by those who would make Him responsible for all the sin and suffering of mankind. Some people even have believed that when God did not want to do some certain dirty work Himself, He made a deal with a fallen angel to bedevil man. One day a woman said to me, "I hate God for all the troubles and tribulations He has brought upon me." I am sure this did not affect the Creator but it surely did fasten troubles and difficulties upon this woman. There are many people who should forgive God if they are to be happy, if they are to lead lives of prosperity, health and satisfaction.

Many people feel that injustice and unkindness have been brought to them by some outside force over which they have no control. They feel that in their youth because of ignorance and inexperience they made mistakes which caused heartaches. They believe they suffered loss of fortune, loss of loved ones—shocks which have resulted in fears and anxieties—all of which they had nothing to do with creating. They believe God has put obstacles in their way. Not through their own choice were they born into families and environments which were not wholesome; they hold God accountable. Until they can find release, see the truth, let go of all condemnation and resentment against anyone, any thing, any power outside of themselves; until they cease to condemn themselves, they will be unable to go forward into positive, creative, harmonious and healthy activity.

Every Situation—A Stumbling Block or a Stepping Stone

Meeting, understanding and transcending problems gives us greater power and wisdom, greater ability to meet other and larger problems in the future. It is a fact, there is nothing good or bad but thinking makes it so. A problem will not result in our being weaker and less able to meet life if we see it as a challenge—an opportunity. Every situation may be "a stumbling block or a stepping stone." All progress has been the result of overcoming some problem, meeting some challenge. Life is continually challenging us. When we find our own inner power to advance, we grow. Life forces us to call upon our inner power. Our success depends upon our growing and developing to meet challenges. If there were no challenges, we would not grow. The seed germinates and the plant forces itself through the hard crust of soil against the power of gravitation. When we realize this is nature's plan to force growth and development, we will be thankful for the problems and challenges which Life has put before us.

Many people believe that a lack of education has caused them to miss many things in life which they otherwise might have had. Of course, we know that lack of formal education does not necessarily limit one's expression of Life or opportunities for happiness. Many of our greatest philanthropists were poor boys who had no formal education.

I have known people who have carried throughout life a feeling of hurt because of lack of love and appreciation in their early childhood. I have known others who reacted to their early hurts by a greater appreciation of cooperative effort, a greater appreciation of the value of love and close harmony in the family; and they have seen to it that there was no lack of love or appreciation in their own families. They learned a valuable lesson from that earlier experience; consequently they treated their own children in a much better way than they might have otherwise. They turned the early experience which might have been called an evil into good. We can if we will see good in every experience. "Every adversity has its seed of opportunity."

One of the best ways to forgive your past hurts, shocks and losses is to make a list of the good things that have happened in your life as a result of those experiences. If you will be perfectly honest with yourself, you will make a considerable list of blessings which you wouldn't have enjoyed if you hadn't experienced those misfortunes.

Mrs. Palmer, nearly blind from childhood, for years felt bitter and resentful. A number of other physical disabilities besides a sense of social inferiority was the result. While she was able to see partially, still it was quite difficult for her to recognize other people. If she came into a group seated about a room, she listened very carefully so that she might recognize voices. Few people knew that she did not see perfectly. Often she was embarrassed by friends who would say, "I met you on the street yesterday but you cut me cold. You looked at me and never said a word." Then instead of telling the truth she made some excuse and naturally her resentment against her condition was intensified. I suggested she make a list of all the good things which had happened in her life as a result of this physical disability. She did this. Among others she had met her fine husband whom she deeply loved; and as she continued to think about it, she found many other blessings that had come to her as a result of her defective eyesight. As she turned her thoughts to the good she had received, the basis—the foundation—for her resentment was removed. She began to bless her eyes. She relaxed. Her eyes relaxed. She experienced a great personality change and certainly a very important change was that her eyesight improved. In fact, she came to see almost normally. She transcended the problem. She transmuted that which she had heretofore called evil to a great good, and now she is living a most harmonious, happy, successful and healthy life.

Our happiness and success depend upon how we react to experiences. Remember the deer developed fleetness of foot because it drew upon its own inner power to escape its enemy. Man has developed reason and intelligence through making a demand upon his inner self to overcome the challenges of nature. It is our privilege to do one of two things—either accept, see the good, forgive, release and go forward; or resent, pity ourselves, think only of ourselves and be utterly miserable. There is no question as to which is the healthy thing to do.

Throughout history many men and women who have been the greatest benefactors of the race, might have felt themselves ill-equipped. Carver, the great scientist, might have resented his being born a Negro, but he didn't. He was intelligent, he realized the dignity of all men—that all men are created equal. Instead of being self-centered and nursing his hate, he turned his attention to serving the world of men, and he became a great and beloved person. He knew he was one of the family of God—the human family. He recognized his divine heritage. Lincoln might have resented his early environment and lack of advantages. If he had, he would not be known as our best loved American.

Many people have told me their lives were ruined because they were born rich and were not required to work or to make any effort to harmonize with other people. Others have told me their problem was early poverty. Every condition, every situation is a challenge to our understanding. We have the ability plus the responsibility and we have the know-how to bring ourselves into harmonious relationship with Life so that we may live gloriously.

Harmonious Adjustment Is Health

Perfect bodily health is the result of perfect adjustment on the physical level—adjustment to food, to the weather, getting along harmoniously with the physical world. Mental health results from harmonious thinking—right thoughts and mental harmony. Spiritual health means adjustment to the Over-Soul, which is our immediate environment, for in Him we live and move and have our being.

It is not necessary to suffer because of past mistakes, losses and shocks. We simply take the lesson out of each experience, release it and go on to healthier living. God does not punish us. We punish ourselves through the natural law of cause and effect. Punishment ceases when we cease doing wrong. We let go of the past and start doing right and Life takes on a new tone for us. Every challenge is an opportunity. We cannot remain static. We cannot hold on to the past or the present whatever it may be if we wish to move into the future without struggle. If we hold on to past mistakes and past hurts, we are living over and over those memories which cause us mental suffering. We hurt ourselves and close the channels through which our good may come to us. Our responsibility is to express Life richly, fully.

It is only common sense to forgive the past, ourselves, others, and God. Only then can we be free of fear, worry, anxiety, a feeling of rejection, inferiority, resentment, and self-pity. Only then can we believe we have the right to have good come to us. If we can believe that we have the right to have good come to us; if we believe that it is natural for us, then trusting the natural laws of the universe we must expect that we will have it. Only through forgiveness can we pray the prayer of faith. Only through forgiveness can we let go of the past which is absolutely necessary if we are to go forward to a satisfying goal. My good friend, Irene Stanley, wrote:

We have to let go of the rung below as we reach for the round above.

There's no other way to climb, you know.

You have to let go of the rung below.

Each upward step brings more of the glow and more of the sun of love,

But we have to let go of the rung below as we reach for the round above.

chapter 15

Self-Analysis

and Re-Education

IN THIS CHAPTER I SHOULD LIKE TO HELP YOU WITH SOME self-analysis. We will discuss you, your problems and some techniques of their cure from the viewpoint of applied psychology. We are including this chapter at this point in order that you may have a fuller, clearer view of yourself as an effective, worthwhile and important person. I want to throw all the light possible from every direction on *you*, so that you may understand yourself, see the way problems develop and prepare you for the second part of this book, in which we will discuss ways of using your great instrument *mind* to get rid of troubles, rather than acquire them, and to arrive at your fondest desires.

A Negative Mind Is the Cause of Much Illness

Dr. Freud, founder of psychoanalysis, discovered that when the dynamic urges of Life in man are repressed, sickness of body or some personality breakdown follows. When those dynamic urges are not consciously directed, they frequently flow off into wrong channels causing sickness of mind or body. They are given wrong direction usually because of negative states of mind or complexes which are harbored on the subconscious level of mind.

Now let's consider how dominant states of mind develop and what happens when we permit them to remain in the subconscious mind.

For example: I am sure you have seen an old fashioned well, six or eight feet in diameter, walled up with stone and full of water. Imagine you are that well. Now think of that well of water as bottomed in the great ocean of all water which we will call *infinite life*. Water from the subterranean depths of the great ocean of Life moves up through that well into experience at the top. The only place you can see the water, the only place you experience the water, is at the very surface of the well. Isn't that right?

Comparing yourself to the well, let's call the surface your conscious mind. That is where you are aware—where you are conscious of experience; therefore it is called the conscious mind. Just below the conscious level or surface of Mind is the area referred to as the subconscious—"sub" meaning "under." In the subconscious area of mind you carry along all the mental images which you use every day—the multiplication table, your name, names of friends, addresses and telephone numbers—which you do not consciously think about all the time. As you need them, however, you usually bring them easily to the surface of your consciousness.

Below these conscious and subconscious levels there extends the great column of water which is the larger part of yourself—the unconscious part of yourself—which is immediately related to and merges with *all* Life.

How Complexes Develop

You have conscious experiences at the surface of your awareness, or on the level of consciousness. As an illustration let's say you may have had an experience of deep hurt. You may have lost a member of your family upon whom you depended, a fortune or a much loved friend; and you feel rejected. You don't understand it; you are wounded and you don't get over it. You drop the memory down into the subconscious or unconscious part of yourself. Later you have another experience of hurt and you drop that memory down into your inner self where it attaches itself to the original hurt. One after another hurt follows until all those unhappy memories of hurt join together and become a *complex of rejection*. You have come to think Life is unkind to you and every thing and every one is against you.

You may make a mistake. You wish to be rid of the memory and not understanding the way Mind works, you say, "That's over. I can't do anything about it. I'll put it out of my mind and never think of it again." You tell yourself you have forgotten it but you have only dropped it into the unconscious part of yourself. Later you make another mistake and you drop that memory into your subconscious mind where it joins with the one already there which you really haven't forgotten. Other mistakes follow. All these memories join together and a *guilt complex* is formed. You believe you are a sinner. These memories repressed in the subconscious are not forgotten. They continue to be active.

You may seem to be unable to meet Life effectively, confidently and you conclude you are weak. You drop the memories of a number of unsuccessful experiences into the subconscious and you have an *inferiority complex*.

These complexes which have not been resolved block your success in Life—your happiness—your faith in yourself.

In each case the original hurt was charged with emotion. Other memories of similar experiences dropped in with the original hurt developed a dominant negative state of mind in the subconscious and a complex was created.

A complex is a deep-seated, subconscious feeling usually caused by a succession of disagreeable or misunderstood experiences which have been pushed down into the subconscious mind and buried there. We say, "I have forgotten that experience and will have nothing more to do with it"; but the resultant feelings are sent up to the surface of consciousness long after the original experience which caused them has been forgotten.

Returning to the idea of the old fashioned well, you can see how the pure water coming up from the bottom to the surface (conscious mind) is discolored in its expression by negative complexes of inferiority, fear, anxiety, or guilt. This discoloration manifests at the surface (conscious mind) as experiences of sickness, unhappiness, frustration and trouble. Since we don't like these experiences, we must do something to get rid of them. In some way we must replace these dominant negative states of thought with dominant positive states of faith, love, goodwill and happiness so that the pure stream of Life moving up from the bottom of the well (you) is clear and pure when it reaches the surface. Only as Life flows upward through a clear, pure subconscious state can it become a stream of health and beauty.

The subconscious part of mind may be purified or cleansed of those complexes of hurt, loss, fear and anger in many different ways, but regardless of the method used it must be some form of forgiveness. The negative complexes lying in the subconscious produce a scum at the surface of our lives contaminating every objective experience. The cause of this scum must be removed if we wish to live in peace, health and happiness. How can it be done? *By consciously changing our states of faith.* But until we have faith in the power of good constantly manifesting in us, for us and through us; until we remove from the deep levels of our subconscious nature those complexes of fear, inferiority and depression, our frustrations and failures, our unhappy experiences in body and in affairs will continue. They must be met, understood and forgiven.

We are surrounded by other wells—people—some of which contain negative complexes. Sometimes the water in those wells gets badly polluted and may seep over into ours unless we have our walls properly protected. In other words we may accept the race belief— the beliefs of other people—unless we carefully insulate ourselves; unless we live our lives as distinct individuals making our own decisions through our own inner guidance. It is necessary that we keep our consciousness—our own individuality—inviolate.

How to Get Rid of Negative Complexes

Harmful complexes can be brought out to the surface of conscious mind through psychological analysis which is reaching in from the top, getting hold of them, bringing them out to the light of day and understanding them. With understanding, the emotional content is dissipated. This is a good way of doing it if the analyst is a good fisherman.

Another way is to pour love, goodwill, faith and happiness continuously into the top of the well. That will completely eliminate all harmful complexes.

To illustrate: suppose you have a bottle of muddy water. There are two ways of replacing the muddy water with clear water. You can empty out all the muddy water and pour in clear water or you can pour clear water in at the top continuously until all the water becomes perfectly clear.

Two Ways to Get Rid of Fear and Hate

Pour in love, faith and goodwill for yourself and for all people. See every experience as good or analyze out the fear and hate by understanding their cause.

When you hold resentment against someone or against yourself—if someone has hurt you or you have hurt yourself—in reverie or in sleep you will let the bars down and the hurt will try to come out. When you sit quietly and relax your mind, you may begin to think about the person who hurt you. That is nature's way of telling you to get rid of the unworthy, unwholesome memory.

Complexes often express through your dreams. The trained analyst knows that everything that happens at the surface of your mind has some connection with something below. Whatever appears at the surface is colored or influenced by that which is below. If you will tell the analyst your dreams or what you think about habitually—what your troubles are—through the law of association of ideas he reaches down into your subconscious mind and finds your negative complex.

Normal Instincts Must Be Expressed Healthfully

The desire of Life to express is basic in *all* Life. The desire for the perpetuation of the race—the sex desire, the desire for self-preservation and the desire to accomplish—all are normal. To be healthy our normal instincts must be given healthy expression.

Nothing normal and instinctive is bad; that which we consider bad is the wrong or perverted use of that which is basically good. Any vice is a perverted virtue. When understood and properly directed, the sex desire leads to beautiful family life. When misdirected or expressed without proper direction, the result is trouble.

While normal instincts cannot be repressed without peril to our health and well-being, it must be clearly seen that all inner drives should be directed out on the highest possible level if we are to be healthy and happy. Our natural drives cannot be given healthy, wholesome direction if our subconscious mind is dominated by a feeling of guilt, a belief in evil, or by fear.

Four Fronts on Which Life Expresses

Life has four major ways in which *it* desires to express Itself through you. There is the way of creativeness—your work; the way of recreation—your play; the expression of love through you; and Life desires to grow spiritually and intellectually.

Think of a Greek Cross in which all four points are equal. Let this cross represent your personality. Label the first point *work;* the second *play;* the third *love;* the fourth *worship.* A balanced personality expresses equally and fully on the side of work, on the side of play, on the side of love and on the side of worship. You must not only express on these four fronts but you must express *healthfully* if you wish to have a well-balanced, healthy personality. One projection is just as important as another.

Work is creative activity. You are not satisfied with yourself unless you are creating; unless at the end of the day, at the end of the week, at the end of the year, you can say, "I have created something. I amount to something. I did something worthwhile." You must have work, employment or creative activity that is satisfying to you.

It is important that you play—have *recreation.* Play is the free flow of life. Play is the expression of the simple joy of living—the release of Life Itself. Play is the dance of the sunlight, the ripple of the water in the stream; it is the rustle of the leaves, the song of the bird, the laughter of a child. It is the pure joy of expression. It has no end in itself except the joyful expression of dynamic Life— the joy of living and expressing. Recreation is as important as creation.

Just as important as work and play in your life is the giving of yourself emotionally to Life—the pouring out of the self emotionally upon something or someone without restraint—the letting go of the self—the emotional giving of the self to something.

Worship Recharges You

You must have some ideal toward which you are moving if you are to be well. Real worship is recharging your spiritual batteries. It is giving expression to your deepest nature. It is an awe of Life— a reverence for Life. It is the communion of your soul with the great surrounding Life—the great Over-Soul. It is unifying with Life. It is the growth of your intelligence and reason—the unfolding of your mind. It is coming to the realization of yourself as a spiritual being, to a sense of unification with the greater Life. It is discovering the deeper levels of yourself. This is very important. You must in some way, somehow, express through worship or your true nature will be repressed.

Many people say they can't imagine what is the matter with them. They have plenty of money and still they don't feel just right. "I am not satisfied with myself. I am not satisfied with Life," you hear them say. That is because they are unbalanced somewhere in their expression on the four fronts of Life.

This is *most* important! You always work at something but you must express that activity on the highest possible level you know. You must give expression to your work in a way that gives you the highest satisfaction or there will be a conscience conflict within you. You won't esteem yourself and if you don't like yourself, you are almost sure to be sick. For example, if you have no interesting creative activity, you may start to gamble, which would be a perverted form of work. But no gambler is happy. Anyone who makes a business of gambling is not happy because deep down within him he feels and knows he is anti-social.

This same thing is true of play. We must play healthfully. Everyone knows there are many unhealthy kinds of play.

It is also natural that you love something. The Life force within you will attach Itself to something or someone even if it must turn back upon the self in self-love, for you are bound to love. You can love the wrong person or the wrong thing and have much trouble. Even though it may be a perverted form of love, still you will love. You *can*, however, give healthful expression to love and you will be happy.

Many kinds of perverted worship or superstitions exist. These cause fear, failure, weakness and often sickness.

Work, play, love and worship may be allowed to express in the wrong way; but when Life is *fully* and *healthfully* expressed on all four sides, you are happy and you have a feeling of confidence and worthwhileness.

Make a Diagram of Yourself

Each of the four points of the Greek Cross is important. Analyze yourself to discover where you are too short and where you are too long. Find out if you over-work, over-play, over-worship or over-love or if you are under-expressing. Discover where you are unbalanced in your expression of Life.

After you have completed the diagram and taken a critical look at yourself, make an ideal portrait of yourself and accept it as you. Make a picture of how you think you should live and express yourself. Analyze yourself alongside this ideal and see what you need to fill in, to balance your personality. I have a doctor friend who says he has now learned to diagnose his patients by looking *not* at their sickness but by discovering what is needed for a perfect well-balanced personality on the part of his patient. This is modern and no doubt a good way of going about the diagnosis.

When you have planned the perfect personality for yourself, decide what needs to be changed. If you will accept that ideal as *you,* you will find yourself automatically acting that way. You are giving new direction to the powers of Life when you accept a new plan for yourself.

Your Ego-Image

We all carry along with us a picture of what we *think* we are. It is a mental picture of how we think we move into Life, how we retreat from Life, how we look and how we act. This picture is called the "ego-image." We used to think our experiences of unhappiness and failure as well as our success, our sickness and our health caused us to have that picture of ourselves. Now we know we had the cart before the horse for the picture we have of ourselves is what provides Life a pattern over which It never fails to move. The picture we carry of ourselves in our minds is the cause of our experiences rather than our experiences being the cause of the picture.

Your mental picture of yourself is not the result—it is the *cause.* Your Ego-image is the mold out of which your experiences emerge.

The Ego-Ideal

Suppose you create for yourself an ego-ideal. You are a volitional, choosing, conscious *being.* Suppose you choose the ideal of what you would like to do and be. Suppose you accept that ideal picture as your new ego-image. In your mind project yourself into what you want to be—what you think you should be. The part of you which projects the ideal is called the *super-ego.* The super-ego may create a plan or a picture of the ideal. The *super-ego* projects itself into the field of *ideals.* Make this new picture—this new portrait of yourself—on the basis of the ideal self and replace your old ego-image with this new *ego-ideal.* This is the modern technique of personality building. *Replace the ego-image you carry with the ego-ideal.* Consider yourself from the viewpoint of the ideal rather than from the viewpoint of the image of what you have heretofore considered yourself to be. Believe you are that ideal! Believe you are healthy and happy, that you are healthfully expressing yourself in your work, your play, your love-life and your worship—your intellectual and spiritual life of growth. Now you are using your imagination constructively. Now ideas of what you should do will come to you. Then act! This will get desired results if you will be persistent and work at it with enthusiasm.

Get a little memorandum book. Make a list of everything you wish to demonstrate under the various headings: *work, play, love* and *worship*. Go over those lists carefully and determine whether you believe those things on your list exist; whether they exist for you; whether you can have them and whether you believe you have the right to have them. Read the lists over three or four times a day; and as you do, you will come to believe that you can have and be what you have listed. Accept the new picture of yourself. Meditate upon it. You will unconsciously move in that direction. *You* have created the ideal plan for your life.

Turn away from the image as it appears to be to the way it should be—from the ego-image to the ego-ideal. If you find you don't wish to do this, you are undoubtedly protecting some of those unhealthy complexes lying in the subconscious mind. You may unconsciously want to protect your fear. You may want to protect your inferiority complex or your sense of guilt. You actually may wish to consider yourself a sinner. All this may give you a morbid satisfaction. If you don't contemplate your ego-ideal now that you know what to do, you will be like the person who gets medicine from the doctor but doesn't take it; or the person who goes to the psychologist and says, "This is his fault. It is not my problem." You are protecting your weakness instead of finding your strength and using it.

Paul said you must put *off* the old man and put *on* the new. Deny yourself the pleasure of holding on to those negative states of mind. Watch that thought which tells you why you can't do this thing you want to do or know you should do. Ask yourself, "Why do I believe I can't express myself in the way I should in my work, play, love and worship or growth? Is there some real legitimate reason why I can't?" You can always find plenty of excuses but no legitimate reason. *Whatever* reason you give yourself for failure is a lie! It isn't so! You are alibiing, rationalizing, protecting your weakness, protecting your neurosis.

Move Toward Your Ideal

In the course of evolution the animal, as it grew into manhood, became self-conscious, which means it began to recognize itself—to recognize that it existed and that it had desires. Man has found that he can decide how he will go about getting the answer to his desires.

The desire to escape pain and arrive at pleasure has been incorporated into our nature as a means of forcing evolution or growth. The desire to get away from pain and arrive at the greatest amount of pleasure is a basic urge in all of us. We find that we can, if we wish, choose for ourselves the greatest good and the greatest pleasure. Choosing the greatest good will eventually bring us into Life's most glorious experiences.

Self-consciousness carries with it the ability to consciously choose. We have developed *reason* which is superior to our emotions so we can choose the greater good. We can choose to direct our emotions so that we won't do something today for which we will be sorry tomorrow. We have developed reason in order that we may direct our inner emotional powers outward in the best way—out to the greatest amount of good or pleasure. We have learned to choose the greatest good for ourselves and for others because we know we all are bound together in a cooperative enterprise.

Love Is the Answer

Our ideal is that which will bring us the greatest good. We can readily see why we should learn to love our neighbor as ourselves, for we are partners with our neighbor. Through cooperation we arrive at less pain and more pleasure. We learn to love God, for when we love God, we love everything—we hate and resist nothing.

That is moral which is good for you—that which contributes to your greatest good. There is no moral law aside from the law of healthy expression; but your greatest good cannot be separated from your neighbor's greatest good. If you do not live up to that which you believe to be the greatest good, there is an inner mechanism of mind which causes you to be unhappy—which causes you pain. This inner instinctive mechanism is called *conscience*. Your conscience hurts you.

Life is intelligent; and if you want to get away from pain and arrive at the greatest amount of pleasure, you must move toward your ideal. As an animal, guided only by instinct, you would have no hesitancy about killing someone who got in your way. You would have no ideal so you wouldn't have a conscience.

When you have developed simple self-consciousness, you may say, "I still want to kill him but my reason tells me if I do, his friends may kill me." You realize you will not arrive at the greatest pleasure by killing. You have advanced a step in your growth and you don't do something which will cause you pain. If, however, you permit the desire to persist in your mind even though you know better, you probably will kill him later. So long as you carry two images—what you want to do and what you should do—there will be a conflict within you. It is always wise to want to do what you should do. Learn to control your emotions in the light of reason and good sense.

When you make the next step in your growth, you don't even want to kill; you realize that a greater good will result through loving that person, through cooperating with him and by so doing winning his cooperation and that of his friends. You never will take these steps, however, until you consciously take hold of your emotions—those instinctive drives within you—and re-direct them through reason in the light of your ideals. "To thine own self be true, and it must follow, as the night the day, thou canst not then be false to any man."

You will not be true to yourself, to your neighbor or to God so long as you hold within yourself complexes of guilt, fear, hatred and resentment. These dominating states of mind will push you to do those things you shouldn't do. Until you release these negative states, there will be conflicts within you—conflicts which will express themselves in disease, unhappiness, confusion and failure.

If our instinctive drives get us into trouble, unhappy situations of one kind or another, they must be re-educated. When conflict exists between emotions and reason, the emotions eventually win. Since emotions—instincts—are older and more basic than reason, they must be re-educated—re-directed—if we are to live in a modern, civilized society without conscience conflict.

Fear and resentment often stand in the way of our expressing Life completely and healthfully. They must be replaced by faith and love. Our big job is to get rid of those inner complexes and conflicts, those feelings of inferiority, inadequacy, fear and resistance, if we wish to go ahead with enthusiasm for living. Otherwise, we just muddle through life.

We must come to a knowledge of the Truth about ourselves and take conscious control of ourselves. We must get to the place where we do what we were created to do. We must grow in our work-life, our play-life, our love-life and our worship-life. We must get rid of that which stands in the way of doing these things healthfully or we may resort to many methods of escape. We may alibi, rationalize and excuse ourselves, which only spreads salve over the wound; it does not heal it.

A man may be having trouble in his human relations. Everyone seems to be against him so he sues his friend, his business associate, perhaps even his wife. He may get a divorce or he may dissolve a business partnership but he still continues to have trouble because he takes himself along wherever he goes. The inner cause of the trouble must be found and eliminated. Until this is done, the man will excuse himself, saying, "It is the other fellow's fault—it isn't my fault." He gives himself many excuses so that he may have a better opinion of himself. He may excuse himself by saying, "God made me this way and so I suppose I must remain as I am, born to trouble. I can't do anything about it." Often he attempts to salve his conscience by self-pity but that, of course, doesn't cure.

Surface Symptoms

Running, fighting, wrong actions, unhappiness, conflicts in our environment and with other people, alcoholism, frustrations are all *symptoms* at the surface—all experiences which are the out-picturing of something wrong down below. Arrogance, sensitiveness, selfishness, a feeling of rejection, self-pity, timidity are just the results of what is held in the subconscious. It does little good to treat these symptoms. The underlying cause must be found and eliminated. Experiences of mental and physical illness appear at the surface of our lives. They are the results of inner maladjustment. We have to recognize and forgive our unhappy experiences. We must release them.

As we have discussed in the past several chapters, you will be healed of the hurt when you forgive and understand. Released from the past, you can visualize a satisfactory goal, go after it and attain it.

How does one unconsciously think from a false point of view about himself? Suppose after having had some hurt or made a mistake, you develop a feeling of inferiority. You conclude you are inferior to Life. You *say* you *are* inferior. As we have learned, you are not actually inferior, you are strong with all the strength there is. You are wise with Infinite wisdom but you *believe* yourself to be inferior. In reality you are a good person because you are Life and Life is good. Not knowing the truth about yourself, however, you may decide that you are a sinner, that you are bad. You feel rejected; you *believe* it. If you believe you are inferior or that you are a sinner, everything you do will be colored by that idea—by what you believe about yourself; and you will act that way. You cannot help acting according to what you believe about yourself, for "according to your faith it is done unto you."

The truth is, you are Life and Life is good. This is the truth about you and it is from this point of view you should see yourself. When you believe you are inferior, you are thinking from a false center— from a false point of view. In your thinking you have split yourself off from the real truth. The result is a split personality.

Split Personalities

All neurotic people are split personalities because they believe an untruth about themselves and they act that untruth. Right at that split is where their trouble develops and grows. That's clear, isn't it? The belief should be analyzed. The truth should be seen. The untruth must be discarded; truth must be accepted. Jesus said, "Know the truth and the truth will set you free." (John 8:32) As you know the truth about yourself, as you see yourself from the true point of view, you will act in the right way without inner conflict.

As you forgive yourself, everyone, everything; as you reintegrate yourself around the central idea of the perfect Life which you are, all the energies of your being will be released to move effectively in the right direction. Controlled by reason and intelligence instead of fear, you will be free to go straight ahead rather than in many directions at once as you may have been doing.

You can't move forward in the face of fear and be healthy. Fear will drive you in the opposite direction from that which you know you *should* go. You will be pulling yourself apart. In your desire to accomplish, your reason will pull one way and your fear acting instinctively will pull in the opposite direction.

Jesus said, when you are about to pray, if you have anything against your brother, go straightway and make peace with him. Forgive everyone and everything before you start to pray; otherwise you will be praying for that which you don't want. You will be praying a prayer of hate or fear. Get rid of the resentment. If you fear or hold resentment toward anyone or anything, pray first to purify your mind and heart.

Find the core of power within yourself. Recognize and activate it. Then your mental, emotional and physical powers will all be pulling in one direction. Establish your goal, your ideal, and you will move toward it. You can have whatever you want because both desire and fulfillment are in the mind within you. You wouldn't have the desire if the answer didn't exist for you. Your desire is the picture Life Itself is giving you of what you can be. However, you will not move toward the fulfillment of that desire if you harbor complexes of weakness, inferiority, resentment, hatred or fear. Confusion blocks your prayers.

Peace of mind comes when you have rid yourself of all inner conflicts—when you have established faith, love and forgiveness.

It comes with a conscious unification of the self with the Infinite Divine Immortal Principle, which is the principle of all Life. It comes when you have released all negative thoughts, beliefs, attitudes, retaining all that is positive and good.

At Night—Forgive

Before you retire at night, go back over your day and clear it. Forgive yourself. Forgive everything which hurt you. Then you will relax. Forgive each hurt before it has the chance to sink down into the depths of your mind and become a part of your subconscious states. Take care of it while it is still objective, still fresh in your mind. Unless you do, it will soon fasten itself upon you and become a chronic sore. Right now it is not chronic. If there is something you can do about it, decide what it is and then decide to do it.

Mentally you have gone back through your entire day's experiences since early morning. You have cleared the day. None of those hurts will remain with you during the night in your subconscious mind to upset your sleep or cause mental tension and disturb your slumber. A large part of your insomnia, if that is a problem with you, is the result of carrying the hurts of today and the anxieties of tomorrow to bed with you.

After forgiving the day, say and mean it, "I am through with today. Now I shall get ready for tomorrow." Visualize yourself getting up the next morning happy and well, refreshed, and full of enthusiasm for the day ahead. In your imagination make an ideal plan over which you wish to operate. See yourself doing everything you should do throughout the day—easily, confidently, successfully. Then use this thought, "I have finished with today. I have made plans for tomorrow. Now I am going to sleep. I shall rest in peace and awake in joy. I live always in the consciousness of abundance, health and freedom."

chapter 16

The Creative Principle

Within You

THE PERSON WHO DISCOVERS THE POINT OF AUTHORITY WITHIN himself and consciously directs his thinking, feeling, and acting from that high point of awareness becomes, so to speak, a god. He takes his place as the director of his own world, the arbiter of his own fate and the captain of his own ship of Life.

The Story of Creation

I am sure we all agree everything that any of us can possibly need exists in this world. It may exist as something intangible waiting to be brought into form. It may exist in parts waiting to be brought together into some new mechanism for the good of mankind. The story of creation is told in the first chapter of Genesis in the Bible. It was written, no doubt, by some inspired genius who saw deeply into the truth of man's creative power. He said the earth was without form and void but the spirit of God moved upon the face of the waters. This statement explains the creative power of mind.

You Are Creative

At that central point of awareness which you call "I," you are spirit; therefore you are creative since you are creative Life, Itself. As a conscious point of Life, you direct the law of Life—mind. At that point you are the God of your world. *You,* the Spirit of Life, move on the face of the waters and create. You can discover what Moses discovered, that the "*I am*" of yourself is the "*I am*" of Life or of God. The world is without form and void until something is done about it.

Within you and surrounding you are all the God qualities of intelligence, vitality, beauty, joy, love, peace and power; and all this is without form until through choice, decision and imagination you give form to those qualities. For example, beauty is an idea without form and void until you create a form. You may objectify beauty by painting a picture or singing a song. Through your choice, your mental picturing and your acts, you bring into objective experience that which heretofore has been without form. As a reality beauty exists for everyone. Give it your attention, give it form through your imagination, contemplate it with faith and love, and you will objectify beautiful experiences—a beautiful home, beautiful surroundings, a beautiful life.

Let me use this illustration. Pick up a pencil and draw a circle on a sheet of paper. Of course, the result of the first attempt is far from perfect. Try it again. The result is better. Practice again and again. Soon you will be drawing a nearly perfect circle. The more you think and practice *circle,* the more perfect will be your experience. Through faith and consistent practice you will approximate perfection. Does a perfect circle exist anywhere? Yes, certainly it exists in your mind. The image in your mind is a perfect circle but to experience it you must see it, have faith in it and go into action. As you give yourself mentally to the idea with persistent practice, you will approximate perfection, but it is necessary that you think perfect *circle* to experience anything like a perfect circle.

Suppose you contemplate or think about a triangle at the time you are trying to draw a circle. You will have no success in drawing a circle, will you? No, you must think circle. You cannot think oblongs, rectangles, or triangles if a circle is what you wish. You give your desire form by thinking perfect circle and by allowing that thought to move through your body. You must be interested in experiencing it. You love the idea. You give your attention to it with enthusiasm. You let that emotion move through your arm and your hands.

You contemplate the ideal. That ideal is the reality. What you draw on the paper is your experience with the reality or the ideal. Your thinking gives it form and through the automatic action of Life you have an experience with the reality. Through choice, decision, contemplation, meditation, faith, love, and persistence, you are drawn to the experience. There is and always has been the possibility of your experiencing circle. You may accept it for yourself at any time. It doesn't matter what thoughts or ideas you may have had in the past; those thoughts can be changed now and you may have a new experience. You may have always thought triangle or oblong therefore not experienced a perfect circle; but now, as you begin to think *circle,* you act in accordance with your thought, and you immediately begin to have some experience of the desired result.

Just as there is a perfect circle to be experienced, there is an ideal business. However, if you contemplate poor business, bad business, unjust competition, then creative mind directed by you, cannot and, of course, will not bring to you an experience of perfect business. You must meditate or think with faith about a perfect business. The possibility of perfect business already exists in mind. It only needs your mental action to bring it into your experience. You must accept that ideal for yourself. You must love it, contemplate it, make a decision and act as your inner guidance leads you. You can have perfect relations with other people but certainly those perfect relations will not be your experience if you contemplate inharmony, struggle, confusion, arguments and fighting. No, you must think harmony, perfect relationships, cooperation, successful experiences.

You direct Life according to your choice and your faith. It is the nature of Life to bring you into an experience of that which you contemplate with love and faith. The ideal perfect body exists and it may be experienced by you; but if you contemplate sickness, disease, maladjustment, then that ideal perfect body will not manifest in your experience. So think perfect body, perfect health. Think about someone who seems to express perfect health then know that is your health and contemplate it with enthusiasm.

Discard the old ideas and images of what you don't want and accept what you do want. You can begin to believe in perfect right action this moment—perfect right action in your business, in your affairs, in your relationships, in your body. You can believe in your good. You can give yourself to it. You can meditate upon the ideal and allow your thoughts to act out through your feelings and your body. If you do, the results you desire will come forth into your experience. The ideal of perfection already exists but it must be appropriated and brought into form. Life acting through mind brings forth according to your choices, your beliefs.

Infinite Life Gives You of Itself

Infinite Life which has become you has given you of Its creative powers. You can create your experience but you must recognize your ability to do so. You must recognize you have the tools, the instruments, and you must use them. You have tremendous powers, many of which you have been entirely unaware of. If unconsciously you have been using those tools in the wrong way to bring you what you do not want, at any time you can accept new ideas and use those God-given tools for what you do want. You can accept the ideal. You can quit thinking failure and think success any time you choose to do so and the moment you do, you will begin to have new and different experiences. As you continue in that state of mind, your experiences will get better and better. You will go on from "glory to glory."

What is the power you use? It is the power of Nature, the creative power of God. God is Omnipotent, or all power. God is Omniscient, or all intelligence. God is Omnipresent, everywhere present. You use the All Power, the All Intelligence at the point where you think. In fact, the divine mind and the presence of God are the very mind and presence of yourself. That power which creates a perfect circle for you, when you think it, is none other than the infinite power of Life. Meditate upon that power. Love it. Believe in it and trust it. It will never let you down. That is the power which can and will, when properly used, bring any desired experience into your life.

That intelligent power within you is the same power that grows a tree, grows the hair on your head and the grass of your lawn. It grows bodies, heals broken bones, and broken hearts. That power is Nature—Life—God!

chapter 17

Preparation for

Mental Treatment

Your belief about yourself, your fellowman, God, Law and the continuity of Life not only influences everything you do, but also what is done to you, whether you know it or not. The whole pattern of your life—everything you feel, say and do—in fact, every experience of bodily health, finance and human relations—is governed by what you believe about those major fundamentals. People respond to you according to the way you think and act toward them. Your body responds to your states of mind—your thoughts about it and your general attitude toward Life. In fact, all living things, animals, and even plants react according to your belief about them. Your family, your friends, your business associates, your customers, even the people you meet casually reflect back your attitudes, your thoughts, your deep, dominant beliefs. This is common knowledge.

A change of attitude brings a change of experience. Knowing this is true, if you do not like what you are experiencing, it is but common sense to change your state of faith, your attention, your attitudes. You should love what you ought to love and in the right way. You should use your imagination constructively. *Consciously* changing your mind for the purpose of getting a different result is *Mental*

Treatment. However, to give an effective treatment, either physical or mental, some preparation is necessary. In Mental Treatment we call this preparation *meditation.*

What Is Meditation?

Meditation is a conditioning of mind. It provides the foundation for a mental treatment. Through meditation you come to a belief— a conviction—that you can give an effective treatment. Through meditation you arrive at a positive state of faith about yourself, about others, about God, about the creative powers of mind and about the world. You work with your thoughts until you remove resentment, resistance, anxiety, worry and hatred; then you establish love, inner peace, confidence and a firm belief in the responsiveness of Life.

Meditation is the cleansing, clearing, and purifying of your feelings so completely that you see a good world and the people in it as all basically good. It is coming to the realization that good exists in every situation and that good may be taken out of every hour of your day. In meditation you come to realize or understand that you, yourself, are none other than the infinite Life of God which is all good. You come to understand that goodness and truth are not only the reality of yourself but of all Life that surrounds you. Meditation and Mental Treatment, contrary to what some people think, are not the *same thing.* Meditation creates the setting for a mental treatment; whereas the treatment itself directs the creative powers into specific action to produce a desired result.

The Importance of Meditation

You will have difficulty in arriving at a state of mind in which you believe you will have certain good experiences if at the same time you believe yourself to be a sinner—that you are actually bad. If you feel guilty, inevitably you will believe unhappy experiences are bound to come to you. You believe you deserve them and with this belief you will not receive your desired good. You must, therefore, come to a new belief about yourself. You come to this belief through quiet meditation in which you analyze your motives and yourself. You come to see what you truly are—a human God-being. You saturate your mind with this basic truth about yourself.

We have devoted many pages to forgiveness, to an understanding that our past experiences are not really bad or evil. Those experiences have been lessons out of which we can take much good. They have taught us about Life, its responsiveness and about our own powers.

If you believe you are inferior to other people; if you feel rejected, that other people are opposed to you; if you believe the world is fundamentally against you, then, of course, it is necessary to clear your mind of these negative beliefs before you can expect your good to manifest.

It is only after you have cleared your mind, sanitized it, so to speak, that you can give a mental treatment—scientific prayer—and have it effective. If you have not cleared your mind of negative thoughts, beliefs, attitudes and motives, you will very likely, although unconsciously, pray for what you do not want because your fear will automatically create that kind of a mental picture. You cannot believe that Life will deliver good experiences to you unless you believe you have the right to have those good experiences. It isn't likely that you can use your mind to get well if at the same time you believe you should be punished with sickness.

In their misunderstanding some people believe and say that God will not answer their prayers or that God doesn't want them to be happy; but this goes straight back to the dominant state of faith of the individual himself—his fears, his feeling of guilt, inferiority.

Meditation consists of relaxing, understanding and forgiving. Meditation itself is not creative. It provides the mental atmosphere in which creation takes place. To the extent that you control your mental states, you can give a mental treatment. *Anyone can give an effective mental treatment who can change his mind and leave it changed.* Let this statement sink deeply into your consciousness. It is very difficult, if not actually impossible, to change your mind and have it remain changed unless it is clear, at peace and free from tension and strain. Freedom, trust and peace of mind is the secret.

In meditation you eliminate hate, anxiety, worry and resentment and in their place substitute love. Fear is eliminated by positive faith. In meditation you exercise your right of conscious choice.

This power to choose, to decide, is probably your greatest God-given power. The power to choose what you believe about yourself and about others, to choose what you will love, to choose the plans which you accept in your imagination is your power to make your own heaven or hell.

chapter 18

The Power

That Heals

SINCE WE ARE ALL CONCERNED WITH THE HEALING OF BODILY conditions and human affairs, it is only natural to ask, "What is the power that does the healing? As we think with a purpose, as we change our states of faith and rechannel our imagination, we direct some power. What is it?"

Only One Healing Power

No doctor, psychologist, psychiatrist or mental science practitioner ever healed a patient. No honest, self-respecting doctor ever would say, "I healed a patient." The doctor cleanses the wound but God heals the patient. No honest psychologist or psychiatrist ever would claim he healed anyone. He helps to remove that which stands in the way of Life acting normally and he stimulates Life to move forward through the patient as health, but he would not lay claim to his doing the healing. There is only *one* healing power. That power is Nature, Life, God, Providence, Infinite Intelligence, Love —whatever you choose to call it.

All anyone can do, whatever method he uses, is to unblock the stream of Life, release It to go forward, direct It and stimulate It into action. Many different methods are used to remove the blocks which stand in the way of the perfect action of Life and there are many ways of stimulating Life into activity, but the power of Life is the *only* healing power. That power is within you as it is within everything. It can and it will, if properly directed, heal your body and your affairs of all disease. It will serve you whether you are black or white, Catholic, Protestant or Jew. It can heal you regardless of your church affiliation. Nature heals the cut on your finger even though you may be an atheist.

The inner creative power of Life which Paul called "Christ," and Jesus called "Father," and which the psychologist calls "subconscious mind," heals. Jesus seemed to be very much impressed with the idea that an infinite, intelligent, powerful and purposeful Life is the essence of everybody and everything and that It responds to our conscious use of It. He called that Life "Father," and He explained that the Father is within you. Since It is your Father, your source, It is interested in you. It brought you here for some purpose and It will sustain you. It will respond to your needs. There is nothing It cannot do for you.

To use It specifically for your needs it is necessary that you recognize Its existence as an infinite power and intelligence and that It will respond according to your faith, your belief and your love. Jesus suggested that you go into your closet or get quiet, close the door on all outside distractions, recognize and work with that inner subconscious intelligent power and direct it to answer your needs. He said when you pray, imagine you have received the result you want. Then He said this Infinite Father of Life will respond to your conscious choice and your conscious demand. *This is a most important thing to know.* It is exactly what the modern mental scientist does when he gives a mental treatment.

The one and same Life through Its instrument or agent, mind, operates through everything—the tree, the grass, the wind, the earth —for everything is alive. We see the action of this intelligent, powerful Life all round about us but in Man It has become conscious or aware of the fact that It exists as an individual—as a person. Intelligent Life operates through the animal, the mineral and the vegetable kingdoms as instinct, the law of tendency, the law of growth. In man, however, this Life of nature is aware of Itself; therefore man, as a conscious point of Life, may choose, decide and direct the infinite powerful principle of Life specifically for his own good and according to his own need. This mental act of decision and direction is called Mental Treatment or Scientific Prayer.

The Power to Choose Is Born in Every Person

Throughout the ages Life has developed and evolved to the place where the individual person with personal awareness has appeared on the scene. Self-awareness means the power of conscious self-choice, so the power to choose is incarnated within every person. The person who uses mind consciously may now make conscious choices and direct the law of Life for himself. He may use the only power there is, the power of God; and that power is infinite. The power of God is directed by the intelligence of God which is not only the intelligence of the universe but the intelligence within you. It is your intelligence. You direct the power of nature or the power of God through your states of mind, through your imagination. When you know and accept this about yourself, you have discovered the power of healing, the power of growth, the power of evolution; and you may consciously take hold of that power. As a human being you, a conscious point of Life, choose what It will do for *you*.

The power to believe is given to man and according to his belief Life operates for him. Isn't it wonderful that man has free will, that he can choose his belief? Unfortunately, most people do not understand this. They cannot see how it is possible for them to consciously choose their belief or their states of faith; consequently they live to a very large degree on the level of the animal or the vegetable without giving the powers of Life conscious direction. They believe in failure, weakness, unhappiness, disappointment; and because of their belief they have the average experience of Mankind.

It is a simple matter of *choosing* the image which you make in your imagination—the engineering department of mind—and then persistently holding to that new image. If you will do this, Life will bring it forth into objective experience for you. Unless you con-

sciously direct mind, it will bring forth according to your unconscious thinking. Most people unconsciously accept what other
people think, what other people believe; therefore most people
believe in limitation, trouble and disappointment. They accept those
states as normal but *you* can choose to have positive faith rather
than negative. You can take dominion over yourself and over your
affairs through becoming aware of that deep point of direction
within yourself, that point from which you choose what you will
think and how you will feel.

What Is Scientific Prayer or Mental Treatment?

Mental or spiritual treatment is specifically choosing ideas, concepts, pictures and plans of that which you desire to experience.
The idea or the concept is the mental form—the form in mind—and
you have unlimited ability to form concepts and mental pictures.
Mental treatment is simply a changing of ideas, eliminating those
which you do not want and substituting those you do want.

> *Prayer or mental treatment is consciously choosing a certain state*
> *of mind to obtain a certain result and then maintaining that state of*
> *mind. A mental or spiritual treatment is a definite mental act for a*
> *definite purpose. It is specifically directing mind to obtain a specific*
> *result.*

Mental treatment is enlarging your concepts. For example, you may
enlarge your idea of one hundred dollars to one hundred thousand
dollars. The verity is there. It exists. Not only does one thousand
dollars exist but one million dollars exist. How much can you believe?
What can you accept? What can you actually conceive *for yourself?*
The possibility of a perfect body or a perfect business exists, but
you experience according to your belief, according to the idea or
concept you hold *for yourself.* We should be very much interested
in this matter of mental and spiritual treatment because we want to
control our affairs and step out of the average experience of the race
of people. There is no real reason why we should be weak or why
we should fail or have trouble.

One time a man whom we will call Jack Wright was brought to

me by a former classmate who hoped something could be done for Jack. Mr. Wright was not only mentally and spiritually ill; he was physically in the gutter. He was said to be a confirmed alcoholic. Jack told me there was no use whatever in spending any time with him because alcohol had him. He was a slave to it.

I stood a book on the desk and told him to consider that book to be a bottle of whiskey and talk to it. I asked him to say to that bottle of liquor, "I am stronger than you for I can think and you cannot." Finally, after some persuasion, I got him to say it. Then I asked him to say, "I am not a slave to you. I can do with you whatever I wish. I can pour you down the drain or I can drink you if I choose to do so; but I will do with you whatever *I choose* to do. *I* am in control, *not* you." I worked with him for an hour or more and he saw he could think what he chose to think; he could feel as he chose to feel and act as he chose to act. This recognition of the power of choice lifted Jack to a new belief about himself. Through that appreciation of himself he was lifted above his belief that alcohol or anything else actually could control him if *he* chose to take control.

Only two interviews were necessary. He went out and got a job. From that moment alcohol had no more control over him. Within two weeks he had a better job and within six months he was superintendent of a fairly large factory. He reunited with his family and became a self-respecting person, respected by his associates.

That center of choice, of decision, that point within you which says, "I can choose, I can decide" is the point of Spirit within you. It is the deep center of yourself. Many people fail to recognize that deep spiritual center of themselves so do not choose to give their lives healthy direction.

Not long ago I met another man who for many years had been a slave to alcohol. Some four years previous I had helped him to discover and activate this center of choice and decision within him. I said, "John, you look very successful and very well. You seem to be getting along all right." He replied, "Yes, I have been getting along all right ever since I decided *who* was boss."

The key to your freedom lies right within you, in your power to choose and make decisions.

chapter 19

Steps to a

Positive Faith

FOR EMPHASIS WE REPEAT THE INSTRUCTION OF JESUS, WHICH is also the instruction given by the modern mental science practitioner as well as the modern psychologist, "Whatsoever you desire when you pray, believe that you have got it; and you will have it." Also we remember Jesus suggested that when you pray, if you expect to receive a positive answer to your prayer, you must forgive or release those negative states of mind which have caused you to believe or have faith in that which you do not want.

Through meditation you release the past. You let go of the old hurts. You quit believing you are inferior to and rejected by Life. You no longer believe yourself to be fundamentally a sinner and no good in you. You come to believe that infinite Life is your life and you contain within yourself all the faculties of Life. You come to believe there is available to you all the good that Life has to offer.

Someone may say, however, "I can understand if I use my imagination constructively, believe I have that which I should like to have and act as though I have it, Life will answer me; but how can I believe I have something which I really do not have? How can I *feel* it?"

You do not reach that level of positive faith easily or quickly if you have been a negative thinker. You can move up to that level of positive faith by taking certain mental steps. First, you desire something. Every normal person desires health, happiness and prosperity, but most people have not decided just what health, happiness and prosperity mean to them. These are abstract ideas. One may need food, but he doesn't go to the grocery store and say to the grocer, "I need food. I am hungry." He tells the grocer just what kind of food he needs and how much he wants. He gives a detailed order for the food he needs to satisfy his desire.

Desire is the foundation stone upon which demonstrations are made but our desire must be for something specific. As our desire evolves into a demand, the demand must be specific. Then our treatment or prayer can be answered. Many people are too timid to specify their desire. They are afraid they will not choose correctly. They are reluctant to take the responsibility; but if we are to be successful, we must be resolute and willing to take the responsibility. With sincerity, honesty of intention, high purpose and worthy motives, we will be led into making right choices. A desire for the greatest good will always prevent our making a mistake. Then whatever it is we desire, we must believe we have the answer.

Here are four mental steps to the belief that you already have:

1. Believe the answer to your desire exists
2. Believe it exists for you
3. Believe you can have it
4. Believe you have the right to have it

If you will write down clearly just what you specifically wish to demonstrate, why you believe it exists for you and why you believe you have the right to have it, then be willing to do whatever is in your power to bring it to pass, you will be using the creative law of mind positively and your demonstration will follow. Read over this statement of what you desire and your statement of faith in the answer two or three times a day and you will come to a deep conviction that you already have it. Through faith the demonstration is bound to be made.

A friend once said to me, "The moment I made a list of my desires and read it over, something happened to my faith. I looked at that list and said to myself with absolute confidence, 'Of course, I can have those things! I *can* have them and I *will* have them.'" The very act of *writing* the list clarified his thought and convinced him of the possibility of the demonstration. He had accompanied his faith with works.

Let's Clearly See These Steps

The first step in arriving at a conviction or a faith that we already have it is to ask ourselves, "Does the answer exist? Is this demonstration possible? Is it included in Life? Of course, I am not *experiencing* it now, but does it actually exist somewhere? Does that which I desire in my work, that particular job, or that particular income, that state of health, that friendship, or love exist anywhere?" Instinctively we know that Life could not desire anything unless at the same time the possibility of the answer existed. Life becomes everything and can become anything. The answer does exist. Someone has well said, "Desire is the thing itself awaiting transportation." The question, "Does it exist?" must be answered in the affirmative.

Next we ask ourselves, "Does this which I desire exist for me?" I might readily see that a beautiful home is a possibility in the universal scheme of things but do I believe that it actually exists as a possibility for *me?* "Do I believe that I can have friendship and companionship? Can they be included in *my* experience of life?" Until this question can be answered affirmatively, there is no point in moving on to the next step. Some people believe they are inferior to others because of race, family or early training. While they may believe that which they desire actually exists, they may be unable to see it existing as a possibility for them. Because of a sense of inferiority, because of a feeling of having been rejected by Life, they may think that while good is the normal experience of other people, it is not the normal experience for them.

A little logical argument with ourselves, however, will prove there really is no inferior or superior person. "Everyone is a god though in the germ." "Ye are all gods and sons of the Most High." We are not limited by family, race or early training. Previous experiences have nothing to do with our real selves. All people are free and equal—gods—human beings—divine beings. Many people who have risen head and shoulders above their fellow men were not born into this life with golden spoons in their mouths. Jesus was the son of a carpenter and the resident of a little country town. George Carver, the scientist, was a Negro, the son of slaves. Everything belongs to humanity. Universal good is poured out to everyone regardless of color, race or early experience. Lincoln was born in a log cabin and David was a shepherd boy. As they made specific demands, Life answered them. It will do the same for us. We work mentally with ourselves until we can answer the question, "Does this exist for me?" in the affirmative.

Now we come to the important question: "Do I believe I have the right to have this which I desire?" We may agree that which we desire exists, that it exists for us, and still not believe we have the right to have it. If we believe we do not have the right, knowing the law of Life is honest, we can't believe we will have it. We cannot expect an honest law to deliver that which we do not have the right to have. So let's examine this desire.

Certainly we have the right to make any demonstration of good for ourselves so long as it does not harm another. Surely we have a right to have that which is good for us and good for all concerned. "Is this which I desire wholly good? Will it bring harm to anyone?" We have the right to a certain kind of job, at a certain income, but we would not use mental means to take someone else's job. There is a right employment for each of us with right compensation. There is a right home. Some people believe because of past mistakes they do not have the right to have some particular good. They believe God punishes them by withholding their good. But common sense tells us that past sins or mistakes can have no power over us if we cease making those mistakes and do good. "Depart from evil and do good." If we desire to complete a certain business deal or sell a certain piece of property, we might ask ourselves, "Is it right that this transaction be completed?" We must know that we cannot expect universal mind to operate in our behalf unless we believe that which we desire is right for all concerned. We desire only right action.

To believe that we have the right to have would include a con-viction that we are doing everything we know to bring this good into our experience. If it is right that we should act, we know that the principle of guidance within us will tell us what we should do to make proper contact with the good we desire. We are willing to be led into right action. We cannot sit still and expect Life to pro-duce twenty-dollar bills and drop them into our laps. We do know that if our thinking is clear, mind will give us the right ideas as to *what* to do if there is something we *should* do. *If we believe we have the right* to some particular good and are *doing everything we know* to do to bring the desired good into our experience, it will manifest. We do not need the particular good which someone else is enjoying. We do not need to take anything away from any other person. This is a universe of abundance and there is plenty for everyone.

We arrive at the place in the analysis of our desire where we believe the particular good we desire exists; that it exists for us; that we can have it and that we have the right to have it. Since we believe we have the right to have it and since we have confidence in the integrity of Life and law, we must believe it is already ours. We cannot believe that an honest, intelligent universal power could not or would not deliver to us those things which we have the right to have. If we have the right to have it, it is ours now.

I have suggested the four steps through which you may arrive at a positive faith. If I may inject a personal note here, I would like to say that one of the greatest moments in my life was when I realized that if I knew I had the right to have a certain good, it would inevitably come to me or I would be led to it.

If we cannot believe in the integrity of Life, then we certainly have nothing upon which we can depend. In demonstrating those things which we desire, we are not attempting to perform miracles. There is no touch of magic. The laws of mind are as definite as physical laws. As a matter of fact, law is just the way Life acts. All law is super-physical and immaterial but absolutely dependable. It is something which you cannot see but you *can* see what it does. The law of creativeness is directed through faith. Life responds to us according to our belief about It and our use of It.

chapter 20

The Techniques of

Mental Treatment

SINCE LIFE RESPONDS ACCORDING TO YOUR BELIEF ABOUT IT and your attitude toward It, prayer or mental treatment should be as natural as calling on your doctor, your dentist, your attorney, your wife or your husband to do something for you. You are calling upon mind, the creative principle. You are dealing with the storehouse of all good. You are consciously making a demand for a specific purpose.

In any creative operation certain steps are involved. Mental science is meant to be scientific. If your treatment is to be successful, you must believe that you can change your mental state and get a certain result. Since you use creative mind, the "one and sovereign agent," you can use it to get specific results not only in your body, but in your affairs; and what is even more wonderful, you can use it to help someone else. You must have faith in the power you are using and have faith that you have the right and the ability to direct it. Mind, just like gravitation, is individualized where you use it; or like the principle of mathematics, which is universal, it can be used by anyone, anywhere, at any time.

Form is fluid, never the same from one moment to the next. Form, time and space are mental constructions within consciousness. Remember, also, all our experiences are within consciousness— within ourselves. We don't have an experience *out there*. We have the experience *in here*. It *seems* to be out there. We interpret it as out there but it is a mental experience. We objectify it mentally. Science demonstrates this; philosophy affirms it; the mystics have known it throughout the ages.

Since Mind Is the Creative Law, Your Mind Is Creative

Since you know you are personalized, individualized Life, and since you individually think or use mind—the creative mind—you are free to choose how you will use it. "I" is a point of Life which is aware of Itself and which is creative because *it* chooses how *it* will use the law of mind. That "I" is God individualized. Moses made that great discovery for himself and Jesus discovered it for Himself. When we discover this for ourselves, we feel a sense of power.

Jesus said, "If you will abide in me and my words abide in you;" in other words, if you abide in the state of awareness where you know you are one with the power and intelligence of the universe, where you know you have the ability to use mind, "then you may ask what you will and it will be done unto you." This is a tremendous idea, isn't it? Jesus demonstrated it, and I am sure you, like many others, have observed it in your own experiences. Jesus was not the *great exception*. Jesus was the *great example*. He showed us how to think and how to use the creative principle.

Mind the Engine, You the Engineer

This "I" uses Mind. We might say *mind* is the engine and the "I" is the engineer. The "I" or Spirit chooses—makes a demand—and creative mind responds.

When you treat mentally, you, yourself, do not *make* anything happen. It is "The Father within which doeth the work." The creative law of mind—subconscious mind—serves you and does the work. Its response to you is automatic. You discard the belief that you have to use will power or that there is some outside entity which manipulates things for you. You simply use the law of creativity. It cannot help responding. That is its nature.

All of Life below the objective level of consciousness is subconscious or subjective. It is *subject* to a conscious decision. For example, you give your garden a treatment when you dig up what you don't want and substitute what you do want. You will continue to have weeds until you change the cause. Those garden weeds might be compared to the result of the negative thinking of the race. But you can dig up what you don't want in your garden and plant what you do want *any* time you choose. It makes no difference to the principle of creation. You can plant potatoes even though potatoes never before have been planted in your garden. The garden doesn't choose. The law of growth doesn't choose. It can only respond. *You* choose!

How to Change Your Experiences

Do you want a different experience? You don't deny the objective world. You don't deny an experience of sickness, of inharmony or of lack any more than you deny the weeds. You simply say, "It is not necessary for this condition to continue." You choose to do something about it. You choose to use the creative principle in a different way. The innermost point of direction is Spirit or the "I." That is the starting point, the place where you are aware of yourself.

Spirit is that power which knows itself, the power which chooses. At the center of your being you are Spirit. At that point you may contemplate the thing as it *ought* to be. Contemplation is creative. It is giving a plan—a pattern—to Life. The "I am" contemplates. It changes the picture. You contemplate the condition *not* as it appears to be. You contemplate it as it *should* be. *You* are a Creator since you use the law of Creation.

As an individualization of God, you are as much God in experience as you *believe* you are and you are as much God actually as though no one else existed. You are not dependent upon anyone else for your individuality. You, too, are "The only begotten son of the Father."

When *you* desire, it is Life desiring to express Itself, for you are Life. Desire is a cosmic urge operating through you and reason has developed within you so that you may interpret Life's desires and lead them out upon a high level.

When you give a mental treatment, you are very clear and specific. If you aren't clear in your thinking, creative mind isn't clear as to what to do.

You do your work in your own consciousness. When you treat for your business, you treat it at the point where you think. If you treat for someone else, you certainly do it where *you* think. You don't do it "over there" or "out there" some place or where someone else is. You can't do it any place except where *you* think—at *your* point of consciousness.

Mental Treatment

A mental treatment is *not* hypnosis. It is *not* sending out thoughts. It is *not* believing that you do it. It is based in a belief that you direct the Law of Life into action through your thought, through the pattern of your conscious thinking.

It is possible that your thoughts operate something like radio waves. I do not *try* to make something happen one hundred miles away when I speak into a microphone. The law of creation acts automatically. The engineers at the radio station do not *make* something happen. They only provide the condition through which it happens.

When you give a mental treatment, you do not seek to coerce. You do not lay on hands. You do not say to God, "If you will give me a thousand dollars, I will give half of it to the Salvation Army." No, you do not attempt to make a deal—a bargain—with any entity. You do not supplicate and you do not beg. You simply clear your mind of confusion and perceive the presence of God—creative mind —to be right where you want something to happen, as well as right where you are thinking. The same mind is present in both places. At the point where *you* think, *you* direct it. At the point where you want something to happen, it is there and acts according to the direction given it. By conscious thought you direct action at the point where *you* want action to take place.

Nothing Is Incurable

Life becomes everything! Everything is Life. If we can realize that, we know nothing is incurable. Even though there are some things which we don't know how to handle, there certainly is nothing that Life can't handle.

We must refuse to accept the race belief that here is a situation which can't be remedied. We must refuse to join our belief with that of any doctor who says, "This is something that can't be healed." We must refuse to join with any lawyer who says, "You're in an unsolvable mess! No one ever got out of a mess like this." We must know there always is an answer to every dilemma, no matter how great it may seem to be. We must know that the creative, intelligent mind operating within us and operating everywhere knows how to solve every problem and it will when directed to do so. There is no great or small to infinite mind.

I recall a woman who phoned me after one of my broadcasts and asked if I would come to her home. She said it was very important. When I reached there, she was sitting up in bed, a quiet smile on her face as she told me her story. She had been in bed nearly a year. Only a few months before, the doctors had told her she had but a short time to live. She told me she was turning the dial on her radio in search of music when she happened to tune in on my broadcast. It intrigued her and she continued to listen day after day. She decided she could be well in spite of what her doctors had told her. She made her plans as to what she would do when she recovered. She assured me that before long she would be attending our Sunday meetings and in just one month she fulfilled her promise. That was many years ago and she is alive and well today.

Of course, we all know the story of Jane Addams, who was told by the doctors shortly after her graduation from college that she had but a few months to live—six, I believe. She told them that in that case she would make every moment count, that she would do all she could to make her life effective. She began her welfare work in

Chicago. The six months passed and she worked on, too busy to die. She lived for many years, founding the famous Hull House. Yes, there is an answer to every problem. There is a way out of every difficulty.

Five Steps in Mental Treatment

You should be relaxed if you are to give an effective mental treatment. Then, as Jesus suggested, quietly *recognize* the Healing Presence is Omnipotent, Omniscient and Omnipresent. Mentally, *unify* with It. The Father and you are one. You and the condition which you are treating and (if the treatment is for someone else) the person you are treating are all the same Life and within the same mind. Know that the Healing Power is right where you are thinking. It is also present where you want something to happen. You direct It through your thought—your imagination. Then realize that the thing is done as it should be. Release it, let go and give thanks! When you have done this, you have given a mental treatment. *Act* as though it were so and it will be so!

Here again are the steps:

1. Relax!
2. Recognize that you are dealing with the Creative Principle. Recognize Its Infinite Power.
3. Unify with It! "The Father and I are One."
4. Realize your desire is fulfilled! Imagine it fulfilled! Know it is fulfilled!
5. Release and give thanks. Enthusiastically expect results.

Some years ago I took instruction in golf. I was told to keep my left arm straight and my eye on the ball. I was taught the right stance. When I tried to think of all those things at the same time, I couldn't hit the ball. Still, I had to do all those things if I were to properly hit the ball directing it toward that little cup in the middle of the green at the end of the fairway.

In the beginning you will, of course, consciously recognize these steps; then work with them and with yourself until they become as automatic as driving a car.

Relax! The Chinese have a saying that "All things are possible to him who can successfully practice inaction." We should maintain a detached attitude. We must objectify the problem we are going to treat. Heretofore, you may have said, "I am sick." This is the equivalent of saying, "Sickness is a part of me." We must realize that sickness is but an *experience* of dis-ease which means *not* ease in the body. It is *not* a part of the *real* person. It is but an experience. To treat the condition mentally we should disassociate it from ourselves. So long as I think I am sick, I probably will continue to have that experience. To believe and say, "I *am strong and well*" is like planting a vegetable seed where weeds have been growing.

"I am poor." "I am troubled." Such statements are not true. You may be having certain unpleasant or unsuccessful experiences; but since they are no part of *you*, they do not need to continue.

You can objectify the problem only when you relax. Put it outside of yourself so that you can get a good look at it. See it for what it is—an experience. It is *not* a part of you.

Be Specific

Be very specific in your treatment. You are going to treat for perfect action in your arm, your stomach, your legs, some other person's health or in your business. You may want a new dress, a new car or a new home. When Jesus treated the man with the paralyzed arm, he was specific. He said, "Stretch forth thine arm!"

After relaxing, the next step is recognition. You recognize there is *one* Power in this universe, which is the power of all, the One Life, your Life and the Life of the person for whom you are treating. The same mind is operative everywhere. The same Life is in your body as is in your business. There is no evil in that Life. Evil would be your non-recognition of the God-Life or your use of It in the wrong way. Since Life is *not* evil, nothing resists your treatment. Life agrees with you. It always says, "Yea" and "Amen."

You are a point of Life which has the right to choose and you have the right to experience the results of your choices. Nothing denies you the right to choose. Your word gives direction to the power of Life. *Remember that!* Mind is your servant. That is nature's law.

You have relaxed. You have recognized yourself as identified with Infinite Intelligence and Power. The person or the condition you want to treat is also identified with It. This power is yours to use. Now use It.

The person who is in difficulty or who is sick has the belief that he is separated from the good of Life. Like the prodigal son he has gone to a far land and got into trouble. This is only a wrong belief— a belief in separation—standing between him and his good.

It is natural to be well and successful. We not only have the right but the responsibility of getting back into harmony with God's goodness. Life gives the sparrow all that it needs to eat and It clothes the lilies.

No reality of time, space or form stands in the way of our good because time, space and form are mental constructions. Since mind has created a certain form or experience, *that form or experience will continue until the old thought or idea which caused it is removed and a new thought is substituted.*

Remember, your difficulty, your sickness, your problem is the result of your own state of mind. So long as you don't dig up the weeds and plant vegetables, you will continue to have weeds. Never say, "I will leave it up to God." Rather, "I am going to take action here and now. I will do something about it. I will use the power given to me."

Bring Your Good into Experience

The condition is changed by changing your mind. The mind which you are using is also the mind of the person or the condition which you are treating. The same mind, the same law, is operative everywhere. It creates and continuously re-creates. You don't have to reach "over there" to have something done. You simply impress or direct the law of mind at the point where you think. You say *what* you want done. You don't specify *how* it will be done. There are not two Minds, two Laws, or two Powers. There is but *one,* and neither you nor the condition you are treating can be separated from that *one.*

Then you realize or imagine the work completed. You have made the picture—the plan—and have come to the realization that it is done. Accept the plan which you have visualized. Imagine it! Feel it! When it is done in *your* mind, it is done in creative mind. Believe you have received it and you will have it. In your imagination see it *done,* now. See your heart beating, the organs of your body operating efficiently and harmoniously. Believe! See the condition as it should be! See yourself well and happy!

Contemplate What You Want—Not What You Don't Want

Don't try to get rid of something. Simply substitute in mind what you *do* want for what you *don't* want. Don't deny! When you deny anything, you actually admit that it still exists. You keep it with you as your thoughts dwell upon it in denial.

Look at the ideal! Accept it as real. When you get to the place where you accept and know that the demonstration is made, you have a sense of peace. The demonstration is made in mind *now,* not sometime in the future. It is most important that you recognize *it is done, now.* So long as you see it in the future, it will always be in the future. Haven't you heard people say, "I am going to be rich some day. I am going to be well some day."? So long as you continue to believe that "some day" you will be rich and well, you never will catch up with the answer to your desire. It always will be in the future, for you are mentally holding the answer in the future.

Give your plan to Life and realize that it is done *now.* That is the pattern over which Life must move. Provide the mental equivalent. Set the Law of Mind in motion. You plant the seed and you trust the law of growth. You do not fear. You do not doubt. You do not dig up the seed to see if it is growing. That would be doubting the law of growth. That would be another kind of faith—a negative faith. You would be planting another seed on top of the one you just planted. You don't doubt. You trust. Mind knows how to make the seed grow into a plant once the seed is planted. Mind knows how to make and remake and *it* knows how to get your good to you.

You have planted the seed. You have provided a plan and you have turned it over to Subjective Mind, or the Father. Now in your imagination you see the harvest you desire. Be enthusiastic about it.

By all means, do not discount the element of *enthusiasm* which is most important! Nothing activates and stimulates Life quite so much as enthusiasm.

The Power of Gratitude

Being thankful helps you to believe. You can't be thankful for something you don't believe you have. So give thanks! When you have expressed your thanks, you have completed the job.

Now that you have completed your treatment turn away and go about your business. Should you turn back in doubt, I would suggest you do your treatment over again. If necessary treat again and again until your faith and expectation are positive, until you are convinced.

Easy Does It

To fear and doubt is to plant weed seeds on top of vegetable seeds. If you wrinkle your forehead and clench your fist, you probably are doubting it will happen. Easy does it! Plant your seed and have faith in the law of Life to deliver. It never fails if you believe.

The Infinite Power is always available and ready. It is waiting for you to use It. You don't press or agonize, beg or beseech. Your faith is not positive if you are pressing. If you find you are straining, check on your desire. You may be trying to treat against your feelings. For example, you may be treating to get well when you actually want to remain sick. I have known people who did just that. They wanted to be well but more than to be well they wanted to be the center of attention. One of our practitioners was treating a woman who, when she began to get well, said, "Please quit treating for me. I don't want to get *too* well. If I get too well, my husband won't let me keep a maid." She wanted to be well enough to go to parties but sick enough to keep a maid.

In mental treatment, remember, we are dealing with the creative principle of Life. We should choose the highest and greatest values we can imagine. In mental treatment we don't use will power. We use imagination and faith. We don't have to make things happen any more than we have to push our automobile when we are sitting in the seat, driving. You have seen people pushing on the steering wheel, haven't you? But that doesn't make the car go faster. The power is in the car and all you have to do is sit quietly, relax and steer the car where you want it to go. It will go wherever you tell it to go, even into a telephone post. "It is done unto you."

Maintain an Attitude of Expectancy

Maintain an attitude of positive faith—an attitude of expectancy. When the conscious and subconscious levels of mind agree, it will be done. When there is no denial, conscious or unconscious, you have no need to argue or push to get results any more than you need to force gravitation to hold you to the ground or force water to run down hill or force planted seeds to grow. All you need do is give the direction. You are dealing with a natural law. You can't *make* anything grow. Will power has no place except in persisting in your positive faith.

After you have given a treatment, it is very good practice to turn back and ask yourself, "What do I think will happen as the result of this treatment?" If you can't answer that in a completely satisfactory way, then you should treat yourself to know that you can give an effective treatment. Meditate upon your right and your ability to change your thoughts. Meditate upon the fact that as you consciously use mind, you consciously direct the power of Life. Then ask yourself, "When do I think this will happen?" If in your imagination you can't honestly see it as *already* happened, then treat again.

The Law knows no tomorrow. It only knows today. Emerson said, "This moment is as good as any moment in all eternity." That idea has always thrilled me. When I am "down" emotionally—when there is something in my experience not to my liking and I do not seem to be able to meet it successfully—if I can recall that *"This* moment is as good as any moment in all eternity," I know it is up to me to take the good out of *this* moment right now.

If you are confused as to whether you have the right to give a treatment, or if you doubt your right of choice, or if you doubt that you have given a good mental treatment; if *any* doubt arises, then treat again. Start from the beginning. Soon you will get to the place where there are no doubts and treatment becomes spontaneous, easy, and free.

Treat yourself to know that your faith is the faith of God. Please do not be shocked! *Your faith is the faith of God!* The faith of God is all the faith there is. There is one Mind, the Divine Mind, the Mind you use, and faith is the condition of Mind. So, your faith must be the faith of God. Know this, and you will have faith in *your* faith.

Keep Yourself "Prayed Up"

Having arrived at a conviction that your treatment is effective, maintain that state of mind. Maintain faith in your right and ability to treat or pray effectively, then you won't have to consciously go through all these steps every time you give a treatment. Jesus said if you will abide in the state of consciousness in which He lived, then you may ask what you will, and it will be done unto you.

David said, "He that dwells in the Secret Place of the Most High abides in the shadow of the Almighty." That person can make a demand upon Life and expect an answer. I like that word "dwells." Not the one who runs in when the weather is bad outside but he who abides there *all* the time. You can live in that dwelling place or you can go away and return again, as did the prodigal son, but that is a waste of time. Maintain a positive state of mind and you will move forward steadily, consistently. You will not go up three steps and slip back two. You will continuously go forward.

Trust Life

Trust the Life that brought you here. Trust the Life that sustains you. Know that the creative, healing power is within you and that it moves out through you healing and vitalizing everyone with whom you come in contact.

Trust the power which operates through you, for you, as you. Trust your digestion, your heart, your lungs. Trust your associates.

Trust Life. Trust the healing power as you would trust gravitation or the principle of mathematics. You don't know *how* it happens—*how* the Law brings it about. No one can say *how* it is done nor *why* it is done. No one knows how 5 times 5 makes 25. But it *is* done! We don't have to do it. Life operates through *law*. Life always speaks in the affirmative, which means if you say it won't happen, then it *won't*.

You can mentally treat for health, right action, abundance, expression and intuition. You can treat for *anything* because Life becomes anything and everything you or anyone else needs. There is no great or small to Life—to Mind.

Write Out Your Treatment

If you have difficulty in clearly visualizing the desired result, take a pencil and paper and write out your treatment. I often do that. Sometimes when I am unable to come to a realization that the results are even now accomplished, I write it out and through my eye impress it upon my subconscious mind. I often read aloud what I have written so that I may hear the words. I impress mind through the nerves of my body and above all, I *act* as though I believe it. "Faith without works is dead."

The Healing Power within you is a state of consciousness, a state of mind in which you accept the unity of all Life. All Life is unified —One. You are that Life. Everything belongs to Spirit. Take your good lawfully—and gratefully accept it.

Relax! Recognize the creative principle of life! Unify with it! Realize what you desire to have or have done! Release it with enthusiasm and give thanks! Make these five steps and you have given an effective mental treatment.

God is all intelligence, love and power. God is all goodness, truth, peace and beauty. "I and my Father are One."

PART TWO

Saadi, the medieval philosopher, said, "He who learns the rules of wisdom without conforming to them in his life is like a man who labored in his fields and did not sow." To prepare the soil and not plant the seed and enjoy the harvest would be very foolish. Jesus said, "If you know these things, blessed are you if you do them." Paul suggested we "prove all things."

Through twenty chapters we have labored in the field and learned the rules of wisdom. We have looked at ourselves from a high point of view. We have become acquainted with our amazing powers. We have found "All that the Father hath is mine." We have discovered the laws by which we may experience the good which Life already has for us.

The second part of this book will be concerned with making application of the principles we have learned. We will apply the laws of mind to health, happiness, prosperity and inner peace. We will go about specifically demonstrating what we want and should have.

chapter 21

How To Use Your Mind

for Physical Health

ONE OF THE FIRST PLACES WE SHOULD USE OUR NEW KNOWL-edge of mental science is in staying physically well, in overcoming disease and re-establishing health if we get sick. Vibrant health is certainly one of Life's greatest gifts to human beings. To keep well is our privilege and our responsibility. We should be enjoying abundant, physical health. It is ours, for we are Life; and Life is health, vitality and energy. If we are to fully express the Life which we are, we must experience perfect health.

To get well you would not try to get rid of disease. No! You turn away from the idea of disease completely and enthusiastically contemplate perfect health. Since Life is *you*, you must realize health is already within you. As you believe health is yours awaiting your expression, always ready to express through your body, you begin to experience it, for everything grows through attention. Drawing upon health and giving expression to it brings out greater and greater expression.

If you feel ill, immediately give your attention to the health which you have, instead of giving your attention to your lack of health. "Dis" means "the lack of or the absence of something" so "disease" means "the lack of or the absence of ease or health." When you think about and begin to express health, vitality, and energy, the experience of disease disappears. You've heard the rhyme, I'm sure:

> Think of sickness and sickness grows,
> Think of health and sickness goes.
>
> Think of poverty and poverty grows,
> Think of riches and poverty goes.
>
> Think of trouble and trouble grows,
> Think of harmony and trouble goes.

Darkness automatically disappears when light is brought into the room.

You have the right to health. It is yours now. Start building in your imagination a mental picture of perfect health. Firmly impress that picture of health on your creative subconscious mind—the mind within you. Visualize it clearly. Life is health and vitality. That is what you are, for you are Life. Through a positive faith in health you eliminate faith in disease. Remember your state of mind is your faith. It is done unto you according to your faith. Mind acts for you, building and rebuilding, creating and re-creating according to your faith. Let your faith be in health, in energy, in power, rather than in a lack of health, the absence of energy and power.

Never permit yourself to say you are anything you do not wish to be. Rather say and believe, "I am already that which I wish to be." Health of body and mind are already yours since the power of Life Itself is within you. Your contemplation of health and healthy activity stimulates the power and energy of the infinite Life to be released through you and energy will surge through you as radiant health and dynamic power. Contemplate, picture yourself as a powerful, energetic individual. Create that ideal picture clearly in mind then accept it for yourself.

Think of someone who expresses perfect health; one who performs every task easily and with enthusiasm; one who is able to digest his food perfectly and sleep peacefully. Then quietly, calmly place yourself in the midst of that picture. Imagine yourself to be the same Life as that person, expressing those qualities of Life. Imagine your body tingling with vitality. Know that a perfect intelligence within you knows how to repair and make whole every part of your body. The intelligence which knew how to create a perfect body in the first place still knows how to do so. It knows how to repair and the law of Life is always there to make the repairs. That intelligent power is the God-Mind in you.

Create a new concept—a new mental picture—of yourself! See yourself as vital, healthy, alive, active and say,

"That is I! It doesn't matter in the least what I have experienced in the past. Health is mine right now. I feel it pulsing through me with every indrawn breath. Every organ, every tissue, every function of my body is charged with radiant health, vitality, and power. I know that Life is now operating through the creative mind within me, rebuilding every tissue that needs rebuilding, removing every obstruction, mental or physical, to my experiencing perfect health. Every thought of mine that denies perfect health is eliminated right now.

"The infinite mind within me knows how to take food from outside my body and through a mysterious process of digestion and assimilation builds that food into living tissues within my body. The infinite mind within me is continuously performing miracles in me. Intelligent Life within me combines food, air, sunlight and water and builds a perfect body for me. The supreme intelligence, which is the intelligent power in every atom and every cell of my body, keeps my lungs breathing, my heart beating, my blood circulating and my digestive organs operating in perfect harmony. I know it. I trust it. I believe in it. I bless it. And I thank it for serving me so intelligently and efficiently.

"Life right now is cleansing, purifying, vitalizing every part of me. I am strong. I am well. I know there is nothing impossible to Life and I am Life. I depend upon Life. I trust It. The healing power of Life heals, strengthens and perfects my body right now. This I accept.

"I let go of every sense of fear and anxiety. I relax completely and let Life operate through my body unhampered, fully and freely. I am completely relaxed. Life circulates normally and naturally through every tissue of my body. Every cell is alive, tingling with perfect health. I am grateful for my health.

"Perfect Life now operates through my eyes. I see the beauty of Life everywhere without effort. My vision is perfect. I see clearly and perfectly. My ears hear only that which is good. I hear easily and perfectly without any sense of strain. My hearing is keen and clear.

"Every organ of my body functions perfectly. I love my body. I have faith in it. I trust it—every part of it. I *think* only good thoughts about my body, about other people and about every situation. I *hear* only that which is good. I *see* only that which is good and I endeavor to *do* only that which is good. I *speak* with wisdom, love and understanding.

"In a completely relaxed way, without tension or strain, I do whatever I need to do, whatever I should do, easily and confidently. I am always conscious of infinite Life expressing through me. I rest in quiet confidence. I sleep quietly and peacefully knowing that infinite Life with Its abundant goodness continuously operates through my thoughts, through my body and out into my affairs.

"I am strong. I am well. I am confident, relaxed and at peace. I am healthy, abundant Life."

chapter **22**

How To Use Your Mind

for Financial Security

FINANCIAL SECURITY IS ESSENTIAL TO HUMAN HAPPINESS.
Security guarantees personal freedom. We might honestly say money
is one of the greatest blessings Life bestows on human beings.

Money can be the means of bringing great good into your life,
and through your proper use of it, you can be the means of bringing
great good into other lives. Money symbolizes rich, abundant living.
It represents freedom and power. Like any of Life's blessings money
should be gratefully received, enjoyed and used for a good purpose.

Like air and sunlight, money is available to you. It surrounds you
and becomes yours when you use the simple natural law of giving
and receiving. Impress your mind with the idea that money is good,
that it is good for you, then quietly imagine the good you can and
will do with your money. Ask yourself, "Why do I want money?
What is my purpose in wanting money?" If your motive is right and
above reproach—if it is honest and good—then you know in your
heart you have the right to have money; and if you have the right
to it, you certainly can expect to get it.

Obtaining money or any good thing in the wrong way or using
it for some destructive purpose brings unhappy results but the fault

is not in the money; the fault is in the motive and in the improper use of the money.

Some people believe that to live in poverty and lack is virtuous, but we should know that as human beings we have the right to any good which Life affords, providing we use that good in a constructive way. We ought to rise above any experience of lack and limitation. According to your faith it is done unto you. Let your faith be in the goodness of Life, in yourself as a healthy expression of Life, in the immediate and loving response of Life to you and in rich ideas which bless you and serve others.

The story was recently published of a man who, discouraged and troubled over mounting bills he couldn't pay, read the well-known statement of Jesus, "For truly, I say to you, if you have faith as a grain of mustard seed, you will say to this mountain, 'Move hence to yonder place' and it will move; and nothing will be impossible to you." He read that statement again and again. The idea took root in this man's thinking. Out of that one idea he created and developed a substantial business manufacturing little plastic balls with a mustard seed in the center. First he made pocket pieces, but the idea grew and mustard seeds were put into rings, bracelets, earrings and tie clasps, reminding millions of people that it is their faith which makes them what they are. Here was a good idea put to use for the good of the world. Watch for those ideas. They come to all of us. When a good idea comes to you, do not brush it aside—use it! Put it to work for you and the good of others.

Ask yourself this question, "How can I best serve the needs of the world? What ideas, what unused talents do I have?" Let these questions linger in your thoughts. Expect an answer and an idea will come to you. Then do not belittle the idea when it comes, whatever it may be, for intelligent Life is leading you—directing you.

In the Bible in the fourth chapter of Second Kings is an Oriental story which illustrates the importance of getting ideas and using them. A modern translation puts it this way, "The wife of a member of the Prophets Guild once made an appeal to Elisha. 'Your servant, my husband, is dead,' she cried, 'and you know that your servant reverenced the Eternal. Now a creditor has come to seize my two children and make them his slaves.' 'What can I do for you?' said

Elisha. 'Tell me what you have in the house.' She replied, 'Your humble servant has nothing in the house at all, except a flask of olive oil.' 'Then borrow vessels here and there,' he said, 'from all of your neighbors—empty vessels—plenty of them; shut yourself into the house, you and your sons; pour the oil into all those vessels; and, whenever one is full, set it aside.'

"She went away and did so, shutting herself and her sons inside the house. They brought the vessels while she poured the oil. When the vessels had been filled, she said to her boy, 'Bring another.' He said to her, 'There is not one more.' Whereupon the oil stopped flowing. When she went and told the man of God, he bade her sell some of the oil to pay her debts and then live, herself and her sons, off the rest."

This is not a story of magic or of some miracle. It is a lesson teaching us how to overcome our difficulties and become prosperous. Widow, or the feminine, symbolically represents the subconscious mind which is the creative part of mind as distinguished from the objective or conscious, thinking, choosing part. The husband or the male represents the conscious thinking or objective mind. The widow—the feeling, creative, subjective mind—is full of fear; and when we fear, we lose our power to reason effectively. When we are in great trouble, we are unable to think straight and so lose our power to accomplish. Since the subconscious mind is the body builder, it gives form to whatever ideas are handed it. When we temporarily lose our power to reason clearly or control our emotions, we create a fear image in our imagination and that which we greatly fear comes upon us. When we are consumed with fear—fear of poverty, trouble and failure—we not only do not reason clearly, but we sink deeper and deeper into debt and trouble and finally lose all sense of values. We are controlled by our emotions.

In this story the widow in distress went to the prophet, Elisha. The masculine represents the reasoning power of mind. The prophet represents not only reason but also the higher level of intuition and inspiration.

This parable teaches us that when we are disturbed by fears, upset mentally—not knowing what to do—we should get quiet, calmly seek the level of inspiration within us and let that inner intelligence tell us what to do. This is what every one of us should do when beset by fears, worries and anxieties. Each one of us, as did the widow, should go to the higher inspirational levels of mind for the answer.

The answer to the widow was, "You are the one who will have to produce for yourself. You will have to use what you already have to get yourself out of your difficulty. The answer is right within your own house if you will but use it."

We all have this same responsibility. Someone else may help us, inspire us, or guide us but the place to get right ideas as to what to do, as well as the power to accomplish, is right within ourselves. Like the widow we are thrown back upon our own powers and resources. What do we have in our house? What do we have that we are not using? Ideas of service and accomplishment are the most valuable things we can have and they can be turned into wealth if we will but pour them out. *Ideas* are what we want.

The uninformed person tries to grasp from the outside as did the widow when she appealed for help. Many people believe in "pull." They think someone else should furnish ideas for them, but every person has wealth within himself, within his own house, if he will but recognize it, organize it and bring it into action. The widow had one small idea but it was enough. Inspiration said it could be of value to the world. She was inspired to borrow many vessels, indicating she was not to limit her outpouring.

It is reported that Henry Ford, one of the world's richest men, when asked what he would do if he suddenly lost all of his money and his business, said, "I would think of some other fundamental basic need of all the people and I would supply that need cheaper and more efficiently than anyone else. In five years I would be a multimillionaire again."

The opportunities for service are all around us. Opportunities exist on every hand. If we recognize and grasp these opportunities and use them efficiently, Life will deliver to us so that we can pay our debts and live well.

While the widow continued to pour out her oil, there were casks to fill, which means that so long as you and I continue to use our ideas, our energies, our opportunities, more ideas and more energy flow through to be used. When we quit pouring out, the flow ceases.

In the beginning the widow did not think very highly of her assets. She had but one little idea which she could use to serve humanity; but she found that when she began to use that idea, it was all she needed.

Everyone has a flask of oil within which may be valuable to the world. To recognize the value of his idea he must conquer his confusion, his worries and his anxieties.

When we quietly turn to our deep inner self for inspiration as to how we may best use that which we have, and when we allow ourselves to be led out into activity, we will find a way to pour out of that which we have, to serve the needs of others with profit to ourselves. We fill a need of humanity which in turn enriches us and takes care of us. Ideas for service are right within us, ideas for health, for happiness, and success.

Why not stop right here and list those abilities you have through which you may serve your fellow man and for which he will gladly pay you?

Simply scheming to get money is not creative nor is it wise. When we serve Life honestly and wisely, money will come to us normally and naturally and without great effort. It will bring us happiness and contentment. Fresh, clean air surrounds us. We accept it. We inhale it for a good purpose. If we had the same attitude toward money, without doubt we would be as abundantly supplied. There is no cosmic lack, but man through his lack of understanding often fails to see and accept his good. He does not recognize his assets nor his ability to serve Life and therefore be served by It. Security and happiness are the results of the proper, lawful use of the power and energies of Life. We should live and serve in such a way that we are convinced we have the right to have. Life will serve us when we believe success belongs to us; when we can believe we can have it and that we have the right to have it. Then, we will *have* it.

Do each thing you do in such a way that you are satisfied with yourself. In your imagination see yourself serving other people's needs in an ever greater and greater way. See this service bringing you greater and greater abundance. In your imagination see Life responding to you as a result of your unselfish service. Believe that money flows to you as readily as to anyone in all the world. Accept it when it comes, whatever the amount, with a deep sense of appreciation and use it wisely with gratitude.

Money is universal substance. It belongs to all people. It exists for all to use. Completely discard any false belief that you cannot or should not have an abundance of money. Money is necessary to the full, free, happy expression of Life through you.

Say to yourself,

"I use my money in a healthy, constructive, generous and good way. I do not turn away from nor do I refuse money any more than I turn away from and refuse to accept air or sunlight. I accept the generous gifts Life has for me with enthusiasm. I am not a slave to money but rather do I look upon money as my servant. It is good for me and I use it to bring good into the lives of others. Others are benefited through my right use of money. Creative, expansive ideas for financial success are continually coming to me. As I unselfishly seek to do more and more good for others, all the channels of Life—people, situations and conditions in my environment—pour out to me a greater abundance of money. I seek and find the value in every situation.

"Through the infinite power of Life within me, I do what I should do enthusiastically and successfully. Success exists for me. I have the right to it, for to the best of my knowledge and ability I am fulfilling my destiny here on earth. I express Life—the good Life—in a full and wholesome way. I meet each day with courage and with understanding.

"I have all the money I need with plenty to spare and to share. I know there is no shortage of money. I realize that money is spiritual substance. The capacity of Life to respond to me is limitless. It can produce a million dollars as easily as It can produce one dollar. I know that my state of faith determines the amount I receive, so I open all the avenues of my being, both mental and physical, to give out as well as to receive abundant wealth.

"I attract money. Money flows to me easily, freely and generously. It comes to me from the infinite source of all supply. I have a clear, definite, mental picture of wealth. I see myself with all the money I desire that I may live richly, abundantly, luxuriously. I have a feeling of great joy as I see myself giving from my store of wealth so that others may share my good. My heart is open to give out. My hands are open to receive generously.

"I make wise and safe investments. Each investment brings me generous dividends. Opportunities to make money come to me every day. They come continually and unexpectedly. It is as normal and natural for me to acquire wealth as it is for me to breathe. I am grateful for my wealth and I use it where it will do the most good. A continuous flow of ideas to increase my bank account comes to me, and I put each idea to work for the good of myself, not selfishly but so that I may give out even more in helpfulness and service. My success is steady and constant. Everything I do prospers.

"I have a lavish, dependable income as a result of my personal integrity. As I continue to use what I have in service to my fellow man, more flows in to replace the outflow. My thankfulness for and my good use of that which I have automatically brings me more and greater opportunities to make money.

"Money-making ideas take shape and form easily and freely in my imagination and they come forth into my experience as wealth and more wealth. Wealth is mine now. I accept it. I am grateful for it. I am grateful for my achievements. I am grateful for the abundance that is mine, now."

chapter 23

How To Use Your Mind

for Personal Guidance

In the Twenty-third Psalm, which is one of the best known and highly respected documents in the English language, David said the Lord guided him and cared for him as a shepherd guides and protects his sheep. He said an inner, guiding Principle guided him into peaceful, happy and profitable situations. It was with him even in the most trying circumstances. He believed in It and It responded to his belief about It.

What is the Lord? The Lord is the intelligent power of God in you. It is the wise, purposeful, creative principle in you which sustains you. It is the very nature of yourself, since intelligent life is the Life of you.

To have confidence and trust in God, or the inner, guiding Principle, is to have confidence in ourselves, in our intelligence and wisdom. It is to have self-assurance, which is the exact opposite of fear, timidity, discouragement and a feeling of inferiority. "Man, know thyself."

What are you? You are Life. Life became you, no doubt, as an instrument for Its expression which makes you important to Life. As you justify that importance, Life is interested in you and sustains you. That is a wonderful thought to contemplate. Since Life became you as a means of Its expression, you have a special job to do for Life. You are special because you are different from any other person in all the world. You look different. Your thoughts are different. You have special gifts, unique capabilities. You are able to express Life in a special way, able to do something in a way that no one else in all the world can do. Since you are especially equipped, if you do what you can and should do, you will have fulfilled your destiny, your reason for existing. Do that and you will, without a doubt, be happy. To the extent that you refuse to do that, Life will be unexpressed to just that degree. You are important. When you recognize that importance, when you perform the tasks Life has given you, when you meet your obligations to Life, when you live Life the very best you can, when you fill your niche, you will feel your importance. Inevitably you will have a feeling of inner guidance and high personal esteem.

You must be important in the universal scheme of things, or Life would not have created you out of Itself in the first place and endowed you with Its own qualities and faculties—faith, imagination, reason, the power to choose and to act. It would not have incarnated within you Its own qualities of vitality, energy, peace, love, poise, and happiness if you were not important to It.

Life has set before you a task. It has placed opportunities before you. It also has given you all the tools you need to perform that task. Life desires to live through you in a special way, gloriously expressing Itself, or It would not have created you. When you express Life fully in your own unique way, you are happy and successful, for Life is more fully expressed. Life, Itself, is happier, more successful, and as a result you have a sense of well-being. This is your compensation for doing what you should do.

Inner guidance comes when your motives are right, when you desire only to do the right thing in the right way, when your desire is for right action. "The righteous are never forsaken." When your desire is right, you have a very rich feeling, a feeling of self-respect and self-esteem. This feeling cannot and will not come to you if your motive is only to impress others or only to inflate your own ego or even if it is for money only or for some other objective compen-

sation. When you have done your best, given your best in service
to that which is right, you have a compensation much beyond
material gain. Naturally, you expect material compensation. You
deserve a reward and you will have it, but you will labor for that
which does not perish—a deep inner satisfaction.

Undoubtedly you have made mistakes. You may have been mistaken in your judgment but who has not made mistakes? When the
motive is right, mistakes can be transformed into stepping stones to
success. Simply forgive the past. Press forward confidently without
fear. When you do what lies before you to be done, giving it the
best you know, you will feel lifted, guided, directed, sustained, and
protected. Your strength will be intensified. You will have no fear
of results. When you do the right thing, in the right way, you have
all the power of Life working with you and for you. You rise to the
high hill of courage, when your hands are clean, when your cause
is just, when in your heart you know you have given your best.

Always do what you should do in the best way you know and by
all means turn back to yourself in appreciation and praise for doing
it. Of course, no one can do better than the best he knows; however,
if you do the best you know today, each day you will know more,
for your understanding will grow from day to day.

When you fear; when you are anxious about what will happen to
you; when your attention is entirely on yourself rather than on your
accomplishments, you will be confused, frustrated and uncertain.
You will not have a high opinion of yourself. You will be discouraged. When you do what Life has created you to do, when you are
true to yourself, you will not be fearful about what may happen to
you for you know that you are fulfilling your purpose in living. You
know you are protected and sustained by an intelligent, all-powerful
Life.

A man of my acquaintance developed a large business through
driving, scheming, and overworking himself. He went down with a
heart attack. His business became seriously involved. He owed
much money and he seemed to be facing complete failure.

When he finally saw that his business was an opportunity for him
to serve other people, when he came to see that Life had furnished
a business for him as a means of expression, a channel through

which Life could move in service to employees and the public, his tensions were released and his health returned. He began to see himself as the manager of the business operating it for the good of Life, Itself. His confidence returned and his business today is successful and profitable. It is all in one's state of mind.

Within you is a superior point of authority, a point of awareness which you call "I." That point of awareness is not controlled by any outer turmoil or confusion. It does not recognize failure. At that point you may choose. You make decisions. You choose what you will think, how you will direct your emotions, how your body will act, and what you will do. Contemplate that wonderful secret place of power and wisdom within you, that place never touched by outer experiences, and live out from that center. Never try to live from the outside in. That central point of awareness is the center of your own individuality where infinite Life Itself is personalized as you. Contemplate that inner point of supreme wisdom and power within you and you will know that you have complete dominion over your affairs and your activities; you will know that nothing outside you can or does control you. Determine that, beginning now, you will do everything that lies before you in such a way that you can turn back to yourself in approval. Do everything you do in a way that satisfies you.

Each evening sit down and quietly relax. Go back over your day with a feeling of satisfaction, a feeling of joy in your accomplishments. Make this a daily habit and soon you will go through every day with a feeling of peace and dynamic, inner power. You will appreciate yourself. You will have complete self-confidence. You will know yourself as the master of your destiny, for you will be making your decisions from that inner, secret place of infinite wisdom.

> You are not higher than your lowest thought,
> Nor lower than the peak of your desire;
> And all existence has no wonders wrought
> To which ambition may not yet aspire.
> Oh, Man! There is no planet, sun or star
> Could hold you if you but knew what you are.
> Author Unknown

With positive assurance say to yourself:

"I am poised, serene and confident. I can and I do meet each situation as it comes with calm, quiet assurance. The infinite wisdom of Life within me can and does solve every problem. I trust It. I rely upon It. The wisdom of God—of infinite Life—within me comes to the surface of my consciousness as I need it. It enables me to keep every problem outside of myself where I can observe it impersonally and calmly—where I can see it clearly for what it is —something for me to handle; and I do handle it easily and perfectly.

"As I analyze the problem, I see the truth about it. I look over it, around it and through it. As I do, I discover it is no longer a problem, it is a challenge, an opportunity; and I draw upon my ingenuity to handle it. I see it as no part of me. It is simply a passing experience which cannot and does not control me and the solution becomes simple and easy.

"I handle every task before me with poise and confidence, with serenity and complete self-assurance. I am always aware of that center of wisdom and power within me which knows what to do and how to do it.

"I have faith in my ability to achieve whatever I decide to achieve because I have faith in myself. I believe in myself. I appreciate myself for I know that the Life of nature, the Life of God, is my life. I meet each day with calm assurance. I have faith in my decisions for they are always made from that high God-level of infinite wisdom and awareness. I am always in complete control of all my faculties.

"My faith in Life keeps me courageous, confident, resourceful and strong. Whatever I say, whatever I do, is said and done with complete confidence and self-assurance. I walk with spring in my step. My eyes are observant. My head is held high. My voice is strong yet perfectly controlled. My appearance commands respect. My thoughts are calm and steady. I look people directly in the eye when I speak with them. I speak easily and fluently always giving a clear word picture of the thought I wish to convey.

"I am also a good listener. My friends and associates cooperate with me, for I take an active interest in their welfare. I have many friends because I am friendly. Other people respect me because I respect them and because I respect myself. I have confidence in my own judgment because I am honest and dependable. I have a feeling of strength, power and courage. I am confident and poised. I have faith in myself. I respect myself. I appreciate myself. I can and do move forward from one magnificent achievement to another. That's the truth about me."

chapter 24

How To Use Your Mind

for Relaxation

MENTAL AND PHYSICAL RELAXATION IS ONE OF OUR GREATEST necessities in this modern age of speed, tension, noise and turmoil. Relaxation is not something which is done to us from the outside. It is an attitude of mind reflected in the body. Relaxation is a non-resistance to those things we fear or dislike. It is an acceptance of the inevitable, a mental willingness to let the universe be as it is; knowing it is good, however it may appear. Relaxation is a mental shrugging of the shoulders over those conditions or experiences which cannot be helped, knowing that in some way only good will result from them since the universe in which we live is good. Tension and stress are the enemies of health. They upset the smooth harmonious action of creative mind. When we are tense, we make hard work of the simplest tasks. When we are upset, we upset our family, our friends and our associates. Our human relations are painful rather than pleasant. Tension wastes our energy and shortens our lives. I know some people who seem to think it is a virtue to go at top speed. Hurrying, scurrying, driving, they gulp their food and neglect their bodies. They are always on the merry-go-round. Mental tenseness registers as tension in the muscular tissues and in upset digestion. Life acting through creative mind built your body in the first place; and if there were no interference, It would keep your body operating smoothly as long as you need a body.

Tenseness in the mind is usually the result of fear or resentment— fear of what may happen in the future or resentment over what has happened in the past. Fear is often expressed as anger. Striking out to protect itself, it takes the offensive.

Release your mental tensions by forgiving every person who has harmed you. Forgive every person, every condition, every situation which has caused you pain, anxiety or resentment. Let go of all past hurts and forgive yourself for all past mistakes. Everyone makes mistakes. Forgive yourself as you would forgive another. The mistake is not important. It is the continued repetition of the mistake that is harmful. Say to yourself:

"Yes, I made a mistake. I will watch carefully that I do not repeat it. I can't undo it so I will take some good from it. Right now I completely let go of the past. The past has no power over me, now. I realize the goodness of Life surrounds me. Life created me. It can and does sustain me. I trust It. Life loves me and I love Life. I have faith in Life. I now forgive. I release all sense of resentment and fear. I accept and maintain a mental state of love, understanding and faith. I let go of all strain or stress. I am relaxed. I do not try to manipulate the world. I do not try to hold the world together through the force of my will."

It might be well to ask yourself, "Now, do I intend, actually intend, to do something constructive about these things that worry me; or shall I continue to fret and stew?" If your business controls you, you are tense and worried. If you take control of your business, you are relaxed. If you allow your body to take control over you, if your body dominates you, you are continually in turmoil. If you take control, you are at peace. The wise person knows that circumstances do not control him. He knows that he controls his environment. He is not subject to circumstances.

Often we become tense, thinking about all we have to do and the short time in which we have to do it. A famous doctor once said, "The anxieties of tomorrow added to the frustrations of yesterday carried along with the problems of today are too much for any

man." We live but *one* moment at a time and anyone can meet the
present moment. Try not to anticipate trouble for the future. Try,
rather, to look forward with enthusiasm, expecting good, sincerely
believing that each day will bring more good to you.

To relax your body, talk to it lovingly, asking it to relax. Settle
yourself comfortably in your favorite chair and let go or stretch out
on your back. Close your eyes and say quietly to yourself:

"The muscles of my face are relaxed. My shoulders have let go. My
hands are relaxed. My fingers are relaxed. My feet and my toes are
relaxed. Every nerve, every muscle in my body is relaxed. I have
shed every one of my problems and all the problems of other
people. I am not anxious about anything."

Take a deep breath slowly and release it slowly, letting go of those
problems. Let go in mind and body.

Imagine yourself as relaxed, as limp as a wet bath towel hung
over the back of a chair. Recall how a dog turns around two or three
times and then lies down with his whole body.

Quietly consider a stream of water—a brook—as it winds its way
down the hillside and out across the prairie. The water in the brook
has its source in the great ocean of water. That water was carried
by the air currents up from the ocean into the sky where it formed
clouds which condensed into rain. The water fell on the hilltops
and collected in this stream of clear, sparkling water on its way to
the sea—its destination. The stream does not fight nor does it resist.
It flows steadily, persistently onward. The water in the stream moves
around the rocks, around the trees, around the hills. Nothing disturbs
it or frustrates it. It doesn't resist obstacles. It either passes around
or surmounts every obstacle. It persists. The persistent yet unresisting water finally wears away everything before it. Think of that
stream. You are like that stream. Your source, too, is in the great
ocean of Life.

Within you is the power to handle every situation as it appears.
You live but one day at a time, one moment at a time and you take
but one step at a time. You can always meet what this moment has
for you; and as you meet this moment, letting go of all past hurts,
recognizing your power to handle all problems as you come to them,

you find yourself relaxed, confident and better able to meet the next moment. You are a stream of infinite Life. Nothing disturbs you. The current of Life flowing through you, like the persistent yet unresisting water in the stream, carries away everything in the path of Its progress.

Affirm to yourself:

"I am relaxed in mind and body. Quietly and confidently I go forward to meet my good, knowing that each day brings me more and more of Life's abundant goodness. I have released every disturbing thought, every perplexing problem. I feel a deep peace stirring through every nerve, every muscle, and every organ of my body. Every part of me is relaxed. I am deeply quiet. My mind is calm and tranquil. I know all is well.

"A vision of perfect peace moves across my imagination. The day is warm and pleasant, calm and tranquil. I am walking through a quiet woods alone. A gentle breeze sways the trees above my head. The sun shimmers down through the stirring leaves, casting shadows on the cool, green moss at my feet. I smell the perfume of violets nestled in the grass. I feel the peace of summer. Slowly moving onward, I find myself on the shore of a tranquil lake in the heart of the woods. As I silently contemplate this beautiful scene, I feel serene and at peace. I feel soothed, healed, relaxed in mind and body.

"I feel the peace and serenity of all nature on this perfect summer day. Not a ripple stirs the surface of the water in the lake. All is calm—at peace and serene. I sense the deep soothing peace of nature as, in my imagination, I sit quietly beside the lake, a soft breeze caressing my cheek. The sun warms me. Every part of me is relaxed, soothed and healed. I feel the serenity of Life in this silent woods, by the tranquil lake, in the warmth of the sun. I am conscious of the beauty in the shadows around about me, in the gently stirring leaves above me. I am relaxed and at peace.

"Tomorrow morning I shall awake from a restful sleep, refreshed and confident. I shall know how to solve every problem as it comes, easily and confidently. I shall enjoy each moment of the day. Every day I expect good to come to me. Every moment is a moment in eternity and each moment is as good as any moment in all eternity. I am relaxed—serene—at peace. I move confidently into more abundant and glorious living."

chapter 25

How To Use Your Mind for

Success in Human Relations:

Social—Business—Marriage

EVERYONE GRAVITATES TO THAT PLACE WHICH IS MOST PLEAS-ant. Mrs. Post's problem for years had been one of human relation-ships. She was continually at odds with the neighbors and members of her family. Today she is one of the most popular women I know. Some time ago she said to me, "My whole life has changed and it came about through one statement I heard you make in a lecture a few years ago. Your words rang a bell for me. You said, 'Everyone gravitates to that place which is most pleasant.' I took that idea home to myself and proceeded to make the atmosphere surrounding me pleasant. It's wonderful how people now gravitate toward me."

People will respond to you when they like you; when they believe in you and have confidence in you; when they have confidence in your knowledge and when you are enthusiastic. If you expect them to believe in you, you first of all must believe in yourself. For them to have confidence in you, *you* must have confidence in yourself. For them to believe in your knowledge, *you* must believe that you know. You must have confidence in your knowledge. You can't give to others what *you* don't have to give.

Our secret belief about ourselves is reflected in our appearance and people are attracted or repelled by our appearance. The person who is timid and self-effacing gives outer evidence of it in his walk, in the way he dresses and in the way he talks. If one has a fighting attitude, an attitude of arrogance or superciliousness, it is immediately seen and felt by others who automatically react in defense.

When someone meets you, his first impression of what you are is through your appearance. He looks at you and unconsciously comes to a decision about you. How do you look? How do you act? How do you carry yourself? How do you dress? Unconsciously he may say, "I don't like his looks. He looks as though he doesn't care much about himself." If you look as though you don't care much about yourself, it isn't likely others will care much about you.

First impressions are made through the eye—your appearance; then through the ear—the way you talk. You are judged by the speed with which you talk, the pitch of your voice and whether it is pleasant or harsh; then through the ideas which you present—what you talk about.

You can drive people away from you by your appearance. (You, yourself, are repelled by the appearance of some people.) Through the way you express yourself, the way you dress, the way you carry yourself and through what you say, you attract or repel others. Your motives are revealed by the way you look and the way you talk. You are judged not only by what you say, but by the way you say it. Your attitudes reveal themselves in your appearance and in your speech, and largely determine how people will react to you. They like you or they don't like you! You cooperate best with people whom you like, don't you? Other people will cooperate with you if they like you.

To secure the cooperation of others, they must believe in *you* and have confidence in *you* as a person; also they must believe you know what you are talking about—that you have knowledge. You, yourself, must be convinced that the cooperation you want from the other person is right and good for him as well as for you. You must be clear in your own mind about what you want him to do and you must be ENTHUSIASTIC in your presentation of it. You should be persistent as well as enthusiastic. You must be artist enough to get him to see it as you see it. It sounds simple, doesn't it? Well, it is easy when you love the other person *as* yourself and when you first love yourself healthfully. To get the other person to cooperate with you, you must be able to paint the idea for him in his mind as you see it. You won't be able to do that unless you, yourself, see it clearly and are convinced of its absolute rightness.

Our very worst approach when we want someone to do something for us is to say, "*I want you to do it.*" If anyone were to say that to me, I would rebel. "I want you to do it! You owe it to me! If you loved me, you would do it!" Such demands draw out resistance in others.

Our desire is to live, to experience, to express; but we would be very foolish not to recognize that the other person desires exactly the same thing. We love him *as* ourselves. He doesn't want to be controlled any more than we do. He doesn't want to be owned any more than we want to be owned. He doesn't want to be possessed.

People are good to us and cooperate with us when they know it is to their interest to cooperate with us and to accede to our desires. When they know something is a good thing for them, they will automatically move in that direction. They, however, want to decide for themselves. They don't want their right of decision taken away from them. They want to make their own choices.

The only truth for anyone is that which is *self-seen*. Whatever truth we may have is of no value to someone else unless he can see it, accept it and use it. Whatever he should do for us or for our mutual good, whatever we wish him to do, will mean nothing to him unless he feels it is a good thing for him as well as for us. It should be good for both of us. We can't *force* the truth on anyone. It is his only when he sees it and when he uses it.

You may want me to do something for our mutual good; but when you say, "I want you to do it—I insist that you do it," it means you don't have confidence in yourself and somehow I automatically feel that lack of confidence. When you have confidence within yourself, you won't be arrogant, supercilious or overbearing because you won't be fearful.

When your mind is free of fear and resistance—all negative complexes—you can love and cooperate with the other person without fear and anxiety. When you know the laws of your own being, you can apply them to the other person. The trick is to put yourself in the other person's place. It takes a certain amount of imagination to do that but you can do it. Be sure your motive is right and know that the right motive will bring the desired response from the other person. If you are motivated by hate, fear and possessiveness, you will only get into trouble. You can and should be motivated by love, sympathy and a desire for mutual good.

Success in life, as we measure it, is largely dependent upon how well we get along with other people—the way we negotiate our way through the maze of human contacts. In getting along successfully with others we *don't* use other people; we *do* use ourselves. Naturally, we want other people to cooperate with us, but the way to secure that desired cooperation is through a proper attitude toward them. We desire mutual, healthy cooperation.

To get along in harmony with others we first must love and appreciate ourselves. The person who doesn't esteem himself, who is self-critical and self-depreciating, projects that depreciation and criticism onto others. As he does so, he automatically draws out their resistance and criticism. No one can love other people until he has come to terms with himself; until he appreciates himself and loves himself healthfully. He can't get along with others unless he can get along with himself, for his own problems are continually in the way of his healthy cooperation.

A better suggestion for successful personal relations never was made than that of Jesus when He said to love our neighbor as ourselves. He indicated that we should love ourselves in a healthy way and then we should love our neighbor *as* ourselves. The implication is that naturally we even love ourselves first but then we should move on to have the same emotional interest in our neighbor's welfare as we have in our own.

The selfish person cuts himself off from active cooperation. The selfish person loves himself only. When he learns to love other people as himself, he is no longer selfish. He cooperates—he is interested in others' welfare and, of course, gets along better with them.

A person cannot stop loving himself. But *healthy* self-love does not seek to possess others; it cooperates with them and so finds healthy self-expression.

The strong, healthy, vital, self-respecting personality gets along best with others. The strong person is the one who can best help, the one who can be the most sympathetic, the most loving and the most gentle toward others.

We must appreciate ourselves if we expect others to appreciate us. We must be sympathetic with ourselves. The person who feels himself to be inferior is weak and fearful in the face of the challenges Life puts before him.

It is so necessary that we think and live so that we have a high appreciation of the self. We must not resent ourselves nor be afraid of ourselves. We must have a feeling of confidence in the self, in others and in Life. If we believe we are sinners—weak and inferior, ineffective—we will not get along well with other people because we always will be trying to protect ourselves, thus building a barrier between ourselves and other people. Many of our troubles in human relations are due to a projection of our own sense of guilt, rejection, lack and inferiority.

To have comfortable and happy relations we must believe we are worthy of love and cooperation. Naturally, we can only have this feeling if we live in such a way that we feel we merit them. We will not believe that we can have, unless we believe we are deserving. Successful human relations are based upon the right motive. The only valid motive is the good of others as well as our own. This means a genuine, healthy love for the self and a similar love for all with whom we come in contact.

I PROMISE MYSELF:

To recognize my inner God-power so that nothing disturbs my peace of mind.

To talk health, happiness and prosperity.

To recognize the Divine and the beautiful in all others regardless of race and creed.

To look for a better day tomorrow and prepare for it.

To be as enthusiastic about the success of others as I am about my own.

To turn from the mistakes and hurts of the past and look joyfully
toward the future.

To be so busy in fully expressing my life in love and service that
I have no time to criticize others.

To be too healthy minded to worry, too sensible for anger, too intelligent to fear and too happy to recognize trouble.

To think well of myself and to proclaim this not in words but in
great deeds.

To think well of others and expect them to justify my belief in them.

To live in the faith that everything works together for good for me
since I love only the good.

To know that since God is for me nothing can be against me.

Today peace floods my soul. I know I am one with God and with
every child of God; therefore there are no enemies, no aliens, no
strange persons in my world. I have no resentment or resistance
to any part of God. I consciously draw the circle of love to include
everyone. As love and goodwill go out from me, only good can
return to me. I am free of all disquieting thoughts. The Perfect
Love of God expressed through me heals all enmity, struggle and
confusion. All situations, things and thoughts in my world are
reconciled. There is perfect adjustment. In this state of tranquility
and peace, I rest.

The Laws of Successful Marriage

Marriage is the greatest adventure in human relations. Surely a
successful marriage must be motivated by love and a desire for
mutual cooperation. No marriage can be successful unless each
partner loves the other *as* himself.

If you want to be married, you should desire *to be* a good wife
rather than desire *to get* a husband; or you should desire *to be* a
good husband rather than *to get* a wife. You will defeat yourself if
your desire is to possess someone. You don't want to be possessed,
do you? If you possess someone, you will be possessed. If you have
someone tied to you, you are tied to that person. If you build a wall
around yourself to keep others away, you are walled in, aren't you?
If you want to *get* me—possess me, control or own me—I am surely
going to run. But you can *attract* me.

What we attract depends upon our attitude. We always attract
the kind of people we, ourselves, are. Liars always find themselves

surrounded by other liars. Unhappy people automatically associate with other unhappy people and happy people naturally associate with other happy people.

Marriage is a *partnership*—a partnership in all departments of living. In Chapter XV we discussed the four major sides on which Life expresses Itself: *Work*—creativeness; *Play*—recreation; *Love*—emotionally expressing the self; Worship—intellectual and spiritual growth.

Two men may go into business together on the creative (work) side. They are partners in their creative activity. They go into partnership in order that both may be more, have more and do more as a result of their cooperation. One may do the office work and make the deliveries while the other goes out and gets the business. Merging their activities in this way, both are benefited.

In marriage two people enter into a lifetime partnership on all four fronts of expression. Their greatest success comes about when they most completely merge their activities; when they work, play, love and worship in closest harmony. Most people do not understand this; they often try to *get* but not to *give*.

I have counselled many people with marriage problems and have found very few who got married with the right motive. Most people marry for some compensation. They try consciously or unconsciously to profit individually rather than as a partnership. Frustrated, they say to me, "How in the world did John and I ever get together in the first place? We are so different. We just don't get along. We don't see eye to eye on anything." The answer is, both were unhealthy in their attitudes and motives or they wouldn't have gotten together in the first place. Each was seeking compensation for some inner lack. We could truthfully say both were neurotic.

A woman with a *superiority* complex is likely to be interested in a man with an *inferiority* complex. She wants to lord it over someone—her ego must be exalted—so she is interested in that kind of compensation. A man who feels inferior will be attracted to a woman who has a superiority complex—someone upon whose shoulder he can lay his head. What happens? In about six months time she gets tired bringing up a baby and he gets tired being led around by the nose. They wouldn't have been interested in each other in the first place if they hadn't been mentally ill and looking for compensation. Unhealthy minded people attract that which is unlike themselves.

Like attracts like, with the healthy minded. When you are healthy minded, you are attracted to a mate who thinks as you do and who likes about the same things you like. Partners who have the largest common areas of interest have the greatest likelihood of success and happiness. It is not possible for two people to have *exactly* the same areas of interest; but when healthy minded, the minor adjustments will be made easily. Healthy minded people are not looking for compensation; they are looking for cooperation. They are not trying to get something to satisfy their ego, as would the melancholy man who wants a wife to cheer him up.

It is unfortunate but true many people marry for money or because of sex drive or to get away from domineering parents or because of loneliness. They may be fearful of the future or tired of working. They try to escape something or seek to compensate for a sense of lack.

When two people get married with the right motive—to be partners through life in their work, play, love and worship—they get the good they hope for and they have the right to it. For example, they may accumulate money and lose it, but as healthy partners they continue to work together and rehabilitate their fortune. They don't fight about it—they are partners. If one gets sick, the other partner doesn't get angry. They work it out together.

If one or both marry with the wrong purpose, it is almost inevitable that at some time the one thing for which they got married will be withdrawn. If a woman married for money (which she wouldn't acknowledge) and later her husband through misfortune loses his money, unconsciously she will say, "Well, I didn't get what I expected." Of course, she won't acknowledge her real motive. She will go to a counsellor and say, "I can't stand him. Everything he does annoys me. Every morning he leaves his pajamas in the middle of the floor." If a man is dissatisfied emotionally with his wife, he may say, "I can't stand her. She is always on the go. She doesn't stay home where she belongs. I don't like her parents." These are not the reasons *why* they "can't stand" each other. These are but sparks which set off the fireworks. They are only excuses.

I knew a man who couldn't tolerate his wife because she always pinched the toothpaste tube in the middle instead of from the bottom. I knew a woman who couldn't stand her husband because he had the habit of snoring. Well, these weren't the reasons for their anger. These were only surface annoyances. The real reason lay much deeper. When a person is frustrated or feels he has been short-changed or humiliated, he usually becomes angry and this anger manifests in different and varied ways.

Nagging is one manifestation of anger. A man's ego has been deflated. He wants his wife to build up that ego. Unconsciously he thinks, "I will nag you until you do what I want; I will worry you until you do it." Nagging is continually worrying or "bedeviling" someone. If I were to ask my wife to do something and she didn't do it, if I kept at her continually, I would be nagging. I might know all along that she was aware of what I wanted but she didn't want to do it. I nag to make her miserable. I try to coerce her into doing what I want her to do even though I know she doesn't want to do it.

Another way people have of reacting to this feeling of being "let down" is in being grouchy. A grouch is a smouldering kind of anger. I once knew a psychologist who called it the "Wooden Indian Complex." The grouch is overly polite but uncommunicative. You know there is something wrong but he won't tell you what it is.

Unquestionably you want to make a success of your marriage. Whatever may have been the reason for your getting together in the first place, whether it was right or wrong, you are emotionally tied up with your partner and you may have children.

Is there a way of making your marriage a success? Yes, there is a way if you really *want* to make a success of it. You may not want to put forth the effort; but if you are not willing to make the effort, you certainly will not succeed. You *can* make marriage work.

In my years of counselling, many a wife has come to me with the same story. I always ask if she wants to make a success of the partnership. Invariably she answers, "Yes. It's most unsatisfactory as it is but I love my husband." Then I have the husband come to visit me. "Do *you* want to make a success of this marriage?" "Yes,

I do. Things will have to change but I want to make a success of it." That's good! Both want to make a success of their marriage. Then I get the two together. I have explained to each of them that marriage is a partnership and that each has his individual rights and his responsibilities. It is a matter of adjustment at those points where they don't agree. Recognizing that marriage is a lifetime partnership across the board in every department of living, they decide *how* they will build and operate this institution and together they decide to make a clear, comprehensive plan for their future.

They begin by taking four sheets of paper and writing out in detail how they are going to express their lives in *Work, Play, Love* and *Worship*.

They make their work plans—how will they build that side of their lives together? They plan what each will do. Each is important. A creative life is as necessary for a woman as it is for a man.

Then they plan their recreation. This doesn't necessarily mean he can't play golf nor does it mean she can't play cards with her friends. It is better if they play together; but if he is to have certain play activities which do not include her, she has an equal right.

What are they going to do together with regard to building their home? What are their plans for domestic life? What will they do in their life of growth and worship? Plans must be made which satisfy both and to which both agree. Only in this way can they have a program for a successful marriage. A plan is as necessary in a marriage partnership as it is in a business partnership. Then I usually suggest that they both sign the plan—call it a pledge. They are making a fresh start. I tell them they really are getting re-married. "You want him to be your husband. You want her to be your wife. You each want the other as a partner. Now you are going ahead with a definite plan." As a final suggestion I ask them to raise their right hands and promise they will never refer to the past, that they will do their best to carry out these plans in loving cooperation. I never have had a case which didn't work out satisfactorily when this method was followed.

I have had cases where one or the other didn't want to make the effort; where the man would say, "No! I am through!" or the woman would say, "I have no confidence in him. I don't want him as my partner." You can't force a partnership. You don't want any-one as your partner who doesn't assume that position voluntarily. You don't possess the other person. If the partnership isn't for mutual good, it is not good. If each is honest; if each wants to be a partner rather than *own* the other person or dictate and be the superior member of the partnership; if each will recognize that one partner is just as important as the other, the marriage will be a success.

This plan will work in all human relationships. You love your neighbor *as* yourself because your interests are mutual. It would be wonderful if the whole world could see and recognize this truth. Whether in business, marriage or world affairs, the interests of all partners must be mutual if the partnership is to be successful. The interests of wife and husband must be mutual. If I have a partner in business, certainly I must love and cooperate with him because when he makes a dollar, I get half of it! Our interests are mutual. I can't afford to love myself more than I love him. The interests of the merchant and the customer are identical. The interests of capital and labor are identical and perhaps sometime this will be recognized. People's interests are identical nation wide and world wide. Some day the leaders of all nations will know this is true. Living together is a cooperative enterprise. Selfishness has no place in successful human relationships.

In happy relationships there can be *no sense of bondage*. There must be complete freedom. You can't force anyone to be true to you. He will only be true when he believes it is to his interest to be true and when he wants to be a partner. Each person must choose where his greatest values lie. Of course, every thinking person recognizes that his greatest values lie in cooperative enterprise. He knows he doesn't get very far when he tries to go it alone.

When two people choose to be partners and build a plan of partnership; when they get married again, so to speak—with the right motive; when they agree never to mention the past, it is very likely they will get along in happiness and build a healthy enterprise.

When you get married, you expect freedom rather than bondage. In fact, you expect more freedom in the important areas of living than in so-called "single blessedness." In arriving at this greater freedom it is always necessary to give up a certain amount of liberty. When you drive your car down the street, you stop at a red light. You give up a certain amount of liberty, yes; but you have more freedom, actually, as a result of the stop light. If there were no traffic signals, there would be very little safety or freedom. If you didn't stop at the red light, very soon you wouldn't have any freedom at all. You give up something to get more. That is what you do in marriage.

We must *free* the other people from our opinions. This may be difficult to do—to let them have their own opinions and think for themselves. But I would say if we are to be happy in marriage, we never should interfere with the other's privacy—either physical or mental.

We *free* others of indulgences. If we indulge them, it is because we are trying to purchase something from them. If we indulge them, it is not because we love them; it is because we love ourselves. We should free them of any feeling of dependency. If we keep them dependent, we draw forth a resistance from them. Everybody knows that.

We must have confidence in and respect for our partner. Two men in a business partnership *must* have confidence in each other. When one partner is supposed to be out selling goods, the partner in the office must know the other fellow isn't spending his time in a card game or cocktail lounge. Partnership is not a duty, it is not a responsibility—except as you take the responsibility upon yourself. Partnership is a *privilege*.

If you desire a happy marriage, you must want to give as well as receive. Remember, you don't want to get a husband; you don't want to have a wife; you want to be a good partner. If that is your motive, you have the right to a happy marriage. So, carefully inspect and analyze your personality. Ask yourself, "Would I marry myself?" Look at yourself and see what you should build into your personality. Work with yourself until you can say, "I am a prize. I would be recognized as a prize by the ideal person—the ideal mate. That ideal mate would want to be a partner with me." You can't believe you will be admitted into the right of partnership unless you believe you have the right to it; otherwise it will be a struggle and whatever you get through struggle, you will have to struggle to keep.

One evening a few years ago I was lecturing on the subject of the laws of successful marriage. I suggested that a person should first *want* to be a partner, then work with himself until he knows he is a prize.

A woman who had been attending our lectures regularly brought a friend who had never before been in our lecture hall. In leaving, the friend said, "Now, I have some work to do." It seems that she and a certain man whom we will call Dave had been very much interested in each other but for some reason the relationship had been broken. She hadn't seen him for a year and a half and she hadn't heard from him for six months, but she still carried a torch for him. She went home after that lecture and thought deeply about it. She *did* want to be a partner. She wanted to be in partnership with the right person, and Dave seemed to be the right person. She started to think about what she should do to make of herself a perfect partner—so that he really would want to be her partner. She made plans without thought of time.

About three o'clock in the morning her telephone rang. It was a long distance call. Dave was on the line from Oregon. He said, "I haven't been able to sleep tonight. I have been thinking about you and I feel it was a mistake to break off our relationship. I think we belong together. If I send you an airplane ticket, will you come up here and discuss it with me? It is impossible for me to come to San Francisco right now; and, so that you won't be embarrassed, I will send you a round trip ticket." She told him yes, she would go. But, of course, she didn't use the return half of the ticket. Instead, she became Mrs. Dave, stayed in Oregon and according to the latest report she is a happily married woman.

This sounds like pretty fast work, doesn't it? But, that's what happened. It is easy to understand. After all, space is within mind and mind transcends space. While she was working with herself thinking about Dave, something happened within Dave's mind. How often have you and someone else started to think about and then to talk about the same thing at the same time?

We never should deny the other person the right of choice. The right to choose is what makes anyone an individual; and if that right to choose is taken away from anyone, he resents it.

If there is inharmony in your marriage, try to rediscover your mate. When you married your husband, you must have loved him, and he still must have some qualities you can admire. Make a list of those good qualities. Any adult can do that. Turn away from his shortcomings. Put your attention upon his good qualities. Your troubles start when you begin to make negative capital out of your differences; as a matter of fact it is the differences that make life interesting. Interest yourself in his welfare. Grow up! Become mature! Otherwise you will continue to love yourself, only.

Love is not possessiveness. No one wants to be possessed. It is a privilege to live with someone whom we love and who loves us but we *belong* to ourselves. Love relates us but it does not impose bondage. We want the other person to love us because that gives us privileges with that person but we get our happiness out of our own expression of love. Whatever we do must be good for both.

Every day I am more and more impressed with the amazing power of love. You love yourself but through growth you learn to love others! You continually expand your love. Your love is God's love expressed through your personality.

The love of the universe which we call God's love is poured out upon you in countless ways—through the air, sunlight and the good earth; and God doesn't ask for anything in return. Your love, to be a perfect expression of Divine Love, must be givingness without possessiveness. Send it forth! You have plenty to share and to spare. The well-spring of Love will never run dry.

The deep complex back of a feeling of *lack* of love and friends is one of rejection. What do you think people think about *you?* Whatever you believe they think, very likely they don't think it! But since that is what *you think* they think, it will be done unto you according to your faith. Heal yourself of what you think they think about you.

Banish the thought of age. Banish the thought that appearances are against you. Banish the idea of competition. Have confidence in yourself. Never say about anyone else what you don't want to come back to you. Read Matthew 12:36-37. You will have to account for "every idle word you speak." "By thy words thou shalt be condemned." By our words we condemn ourselves! Words spoken make pictures—motion pictures—and judgment is simply the consequence of the action of the natural law of cause and effect.

By no means try to reform or change others. People often project negative ideas or pictures onto others in an effort to turn away from their own sense of lack, guilt, and hurt. In their own thinking they project certain characteristics onto others in an attempt to cover up their own short-comings. They deceive themselves. Some people try to reform others, rather than reform their own opinion of themselves. The reformer is the fellow who needs reforming. He needs reforming because he, himself, has a sense of guilt, else he wouldn't strive to reform and make over other people.

Moral indignation—indignation over the immorality of other people (which is really none of our business) is an indication of something within ourselves which needs sanitizing. Our belief that it is the other fellow's fault—that he is bad and should be reformed—are but projections of *our* own sense of lack or of *our* inner sense of dissatisfaction. We try to relieve ourselves of our own short-comings, by projecting them onto others. This is a mistaken way of trying to relieve the self of burden.

Selfish motives are inevitably felt by the other person. They cannot be successfully covered up; there is no use trying. *Love is the answer.*

Let your smile be warm and friendly reflecting your good will. When you shake hands with someone, believe that your friendliness moves through your hand on through his and he feels it. Say to yourself, "I am conscious of my good feeling for you, my friend. I know you feel it through this handshake and you see it in my smile. Our interests are mutual. We understand each other. Good goes out from and returns to each of us."

A Mental Treatment for Companionship

My eyes are open to all that is lovely. I'm never alone. My love attracts love. My heart is responsive to love. I let His great love surge through me, healing, blessing all it touches, and through a thousand avenues it flows back to me. I am unified—mind, body and spirit—with all mankind. I see only that which is lovely. I hear only the music of love and I speak only words of love. I am the embodiment of love.

I do not listen to false prophecy. I am undisturbed by what others may think and do. I *know* there is the right companion for me—the right one who will complete my life and who will find completeness in me. I am the right person for him (her). Our love is the power of attraction which brings us together even from the furthermost parts of the earth.

The Law of Love can bring only right action. Love for the ideal brings my perfect companion to me—the one who needs me as I need him (her). I have faith in the infinite goodness of God. My love is steady, serene and true. I give the best I have and only the best comes back to me. I hold gently, lovingly and persistently to my ideal with sublime faith. I let Life bring my beloved to me. Even though he (she) tarry, I wait for him (her) with faith, knowing he (she) will come. That is the *Law*. "Love never faileth."

chapter 26

How To Build a
Powerful Personality

PERSONALITY IS THE BRIDGE BETWEEN INDIVIDUALS. IT IS THE means by which one individual communicates with another. The personality is not the real person, but it is all you can see, touch and hear of the person. It is the vehicle through which he expresses Life. You are infinite Life expressing through a personality.

Life with all its colorful qualities and dynamic faculties is *you,* for infinite Life is personalized as you. Through the use of your imagination you may express the qualities of Life as vitality in your body, attractiveness in your appearance, as personal power, and magnetism in your entire personality. Your personality is the instrument or channel through which your real self expresses. If your personality is drab and colorless, you are expressing the qualities of Life in a very limited way. If it is colorful, magnetic, and powerful, you are giving fuller and more complete expression to the infinite qualities of Life.

Everyone wants to build certain qualities into his personality; loyalty, sincerity, honesty, tact, poise, courtesy, politeness, beauty. Everyone wants to get rid of undesirable traits and substitute desirable ones.

You can have the personality you desire. You can make it according to plan. All the elements of a complete personality are already within you and you have the privilege of giving expression to any or all of these elements or qualities as you choose but *you* must choose. You must choose to express the positive qualities you want to experience. The power of choice is within you. The more actively you express Life and all that Life is, the more powerful, dynamic and magnetic your personality becomes.

Love for other people, love for Life, expresses through your eyes, through your voice and through your actions. Inner happiness expresses through your calm, friendly smile. Your goodwill is expressed through your firm handshake. Your self-appreciation is expressed through cleanliness of person and attractiveness of your personal self. Activating these inner qualities and letting them express automatically is a much better method of personality building than attempting to make objective changes in the personality, itself; such as trying to be cheerful when you don't actually feel happy or trying to walk with a spring in your step when you have an inner feeling of weakness.

Your inner power is directed by your imagination. So imagine yourself as the person you wish to be. Build the mental image clearly, distinctly and in detail. See yourself as vital, attractive, magnetic, powerful and making wise choices. See yourself relaxed, happy, confident, surrounded with people you love and those who love you. Hold this image persistently in your mind. The mental image will soon begin to take shape and form in your experience.

The healthy person lives, loves, laughs and is happy. Many people either fear Life or continually resist It, resent It and fight It. The worthwhile personality loves Life and gives himself to It with enthusiasm.

Think for a moment about this, consider a seed you are about to plant in the ground—a little black morning glory seed. That seed is a center from which Life expresses Itself. In that seed is the pattern of a plant. You plant the seed in the ground and all the productive elements of soil, water, minerals, air and sunlight flow together over the pattern in that seed. Everything the seed needs comes to its assistance and nature completes the project—a creation—a plant which blooms. The seed has fulfilled its destiny.

Here is man, also a point through which Life expresses Itself. Man, like the seed, is surrounded by all he needs to complete his project to become a healthy, effective, worthwhile personality. Why doesn't what he needs flow to him as it does to the seed? He, too, is surrounded by nature, by the good earth, and by people who may love him, cooperate with him, and give to him. Why doesn't Life serve him? The reason is, *man rejects* while the *seed accepts*. The seed doesn't argue. It doesn't fight its environment. It does not resist, resent or fight. Neither does it fear and try to escape. It gives itself to the soil. It does what it is designed to do and Life operates through it and for it. Man, however, often fears. He tries to get away. He refuses to cooperate, consequently Life cannot be good to him. He removes himself from the good which Life has for him. When Man resists, he builds a wall around himself, making it impossible for Life to deliver to him; and yet he is far better endowed than the seed, for he has the power of volitional motion. He can move about as he chooses. He can put himself into better and more agreeable surroundings while the little seed must accept its environment as it finds it and make the most of it. We should take a lesson from the seed.

The dynamic, powerful person loves Life, other people and himself healthfully. He sees the good in his environment. He sees the good in other people. He thinks expansively. He is true to his purpose in Life. He recognizes that he is surrounded by an infinitely good Life which gives to him as he accepts. He is a self-contained person sustained by a positive faith in good. He is relaxed and kind. He rejoices in the happiness of others. He is always glad to help others.

I remember a very lovely woman in her sixties, radiant, smiling, with very few wrinkles in her face and those the result of a ready smile. A "nice-to-be-near" kind of person who in her early life had experienced a great tragedy. Her fiance was killed in an accident, and she, herself, had been seriously injured about the face. After five years of lying in a darkened room wanting to see no one, she decided to dedicate herself to a life of service. She became a nurse, and a more radiant, glorious, dynamic, calm personality I never have met!

My friend, Johnny Hayes, told me the inspiring story of a little girl who was born a hunchback. Johnny represented a correspondence school for artists. He sold courses to people who wanted to study art at home and one day he answered a call from Mrs. Oliver who wanted the course for her seventeen-year-old daughter. She told him her daughter was artistically gifted but that she had a very serious problem. She hated everybody, including herself. She had become so sensitive, morbid and bitter she scarcely ever left her home. Feeling herself rejected by society because she was different from other girls—a hunchback—her disposition had so soured, her attitude toward Life had become so resistant that her family was desperate.

Now, Johnny was not only an artist, he was also an earnest student of mental science. He knew about the power of mind and he was able to help the girl in a most extraordinary way. When he first met her, she was surly, distrustful and belligerent; but he pretended not to notice. He started her off on her art course, promising to help her for this was the one thing in which she had a definite interest. The girl's name was Emma and she told him bitterly that not only was she ugly to look at but she hated her name as well.

"Well, then," said this wise man, "let's change your name. What name do you like? What name do you think is beautiful?" Surprised and intrigued at the suggestion, Emma admitted that she loved the name Patricia. "Very well, from now on your name will be Patricia. Patricia Oliver is a beautiful name. I shall speak to your mother about having it legally changed." The cooperative mother had Emma's name officially changed to Patricia.

This in itself, started an amazing transformation in the girl. As she began to identify herself with beauty, she felt and acted like a different person.

Johnny suggested some books—one of mine, in fact—and others. Casually, he left them for her to read. As the days passed, Patricia and Johnny had many discussions about the power of creative mind.

One day he said, "Patricia, now that you have such a lovely name, I want you to paint a portrait of the way you think the girl with that name *ought* to look. Make it a self portrait, of course, a portrait of yourself; but let your true, inner beauty shine through the physical likeness."

Patricia painted that portrait of herself and over a period of months she repainted it again and again. Each time she looked for the beauty in herself and each time she found more because she was searching for the beauty of her true self. Not only did Patricia's portrait take first prize at an art exhibit but Patricia became an entirely new person in the process of the painting. Her whole disposition changed in the months that followed. She became a shining, radiant personality who stepped confidently out into the world and took an enviable position as a fashion artist. Her success was soon assured and her salon was always full of friends. Johnny, who continued to be her friend, told me these new found friends often said of her, "When you stop to think of it, Patricia does have a physical handicap; but she is so bright, so gay and amusing, she makes you forget it entirely. Her inner beauty shines forth like the sun!"

Here you have a miracle in personality change and it shows what *any* person can do through guidance and inspiration even under the most adverse circumstances. You must *want* to change, however; you must desire good where the evil seems to be.

Remember, the individual is potentially perfect even though he may have covered himself over with a shell of unpleasant personality traits. As Robert Browning said, "Truth is within ourselves; it takes no rise from outward things, whate'er you may believe. There is an inmost center in us all, where truth abides in fullness; and around, wall upon wall, the gross flesh hems it in." And, "To know," says Browning, "rather consists in opening out a way whence the imprisoned splendor may escape than in effecting entry for a light supposed to be without."

The truth is, we are heirs to a perfection already existent within us. We may allow only a little or a great deal to manifest; but if we aren't expressing healthfully and expansively, it is because we have encased ourselves in a mesh of unfortunate personality habits, which keep the real perfection, the real person, in bondage. Our task in personality development is to replace our bad habits of thinking and acting with good, wholesome habits of thinking and acting.

Intuitively we know our wrong habits should be changed. This intuitive knowing is our own inner guidance trying to direct our actions into more perfect ways. Let's listen to it.

Try to see clearly that you are not bound by your habits of thought. Your true, inner self is intelligent and powerful. When you once recognize yourself as a God-being, you will know that you can direct your own life. Through your thoughts, your attitudes and your faith, automatically you will bring your good into experience.

Imagine yourself with a warm smile, expressing love and goodwill through your eyes. Imagine yourself greeting another person, saying to yourself,

"My eyes, my smile, my handshake, make him aware of my goodwill, my friendly feeling for him. My personality expresses my sincere good feeling and understanding. He knows I like him. He senses my goodwill. My appearance attracts him and causes him to have a good opinion of me.

"At all times I am nice to be near. I know that people automatically gravitate toward that place which is most pleasant. I am self-confident, courteous, tactful, and kind. I am cheerful and enthusiastic. I am nice to be near.

"I am a good listener. I rejoice in the success of others and I am sympathetic toward their problems. I give others freedom to think, to plan and to achieve as they choose. I do not try to dominate or control.

"I attract friends because I am friendly. I respect myself and I respect the opinions and rights of others. I expect good to come to me in every situation. I have a handclasp which is firm and confident. My voice is strong, magnetic and vibrant. I have a dignity that commands respect. My appearance reflects inner confidence and strength. Every part of my body is clean, immaculate, and pulsing with personal magnetism. I am perfectly groomed at all times. I choose my clothes carefully and wisely. They reflect my calm, unruffled but powerful personality. I am sincere and honest. My integrity is felt by all those I meet. In my imagination there exists a clear, distinct picture of what I believe is the ideal personality for me. I contemplate that ideal as myself."

chapter 27

How To Form

New Habits

WE LEARN TO SIT UP AND TALK. WE LEARN TO DRIVE A CAR. But suppose habit did not take over and in driving our car, we forgot to sit up? If it were not for our ability to form habits, we certainly would not be able to carry on a conversation, listen to the radio, and plan our activities all at the same time.

We learn to do a thing and then we transfer the doing of it over to the subconscious mind or the Father within. Automatic habit action is an amazing part of our mental machinery. It is little short of miraculous. We learn to operate a machine, to walk, to write. After we consciously learn the operation step by step, it is taken over by subconscious mind in us and thereafter acts through us as habit. The possibility of consciously forming habits of thinking and doing makes successful living possible.

Man is a volitional being so he can use his powers in whatever way he chooses. He can form either good or bad habits of thinking and doing. If he uses his powers destructively, he suffers the consequences. It is said that *every vice is a perverted virtue,* which means every evil is something good used in the wrong way or for the wrong purpose.

We can use our faith in the wrong way. When we use it as fear against ourselves, we sin against ourselves. We can direct our love or affections toward the wrong object and by so doing cause much trouble. We can use our imagination to give wrong direction to the powers of Life and bring us an experience of failure; but by taking conscious thought we can redirect our faith, our love and our imagination into healthful channels. We can use the power of our body, the strength of our arm, to harm someone else or to lift him up. We can form either constructive or destructive habits but habit forming is under our direction.

I have heard people say their habits control them and this is true so long as they do nothing about changing them. What mind has formed, mind can re-form. We cannot live and get along without habits but we do not want to be slaves to our habits and we do not need to be. Habits can and should be our servants. When we build constructive habits into our personalities, we experience Life as happiness. When our habits control us, it is because we have not taken the necessary steps to change them. We are refusing our God-given right to choose. We have within ourselves the power to redirect and consciously control the creative forces within us.

Sometimes people retreat from Life saying that "God made me as I am and so I must remain." But that is an expression of weakness. It denies the individual's power to choose and decide. No one ever was born a drunkard. In fact, no one *is* a drunkard. He is in reality a perfect person with the power to choose but unfortunately he has dropped into the bad habit of drinking to excess. He started it and *he* can change it. It is not really a part of him. He can decide whether he will stay on the old path or cut a new one. There is no selfish man. There is a man who has the habit of trying to get what he wants without regard for other people's rights. There is no proud man. There is the man who has the habit of reacting in pride. There is no failure but there is a man who has a habit of failing. There is no lazy man—only a man with the bad habit of laziness, one who hasn't found a constructive activity which interests him.

We have the power to choose, the power to redirect our lives. We all have habits—many of them good and some we would like to change. Let me suggest that you never should attempt to break a habit—rather you would substitute a new one. If you try to break a habit, it will break you! Just use your God-given power to choose what you want. You can get rid of any habit—not by *trying* to break it, but by substituting another.

As a youngster you may have coasted down hill on a sled. You took your sled to the top of the hill and pushed it down, making a track. You took it to the top of the hill a second time and this time the sled went down a little easier and faster. After a few trips the track was well cut. Then you needed only to take the sled to the top of the hill, put it into the track and it went down the hill without effort. However, it took conscious direction and effort the first time and it took some persistence. You can cut a new habit path or track whenever you choose. If the old track carries you into trouble or if you wish to go in a different direction, you can consciously cut a new path.

We now are told something like that happens in the brain and it may be interesting to know just what does take place physically in the brain and in the nerves. The nerves are telegraph lines. The sensory nerves bring information into the brain and the motor nerves carry messages out to the muscles to act. As the nerves bring information to a certain part of the brain, that information is passed on to another part where that information is analyzed and a decision is made as to what to do. This decision is carried to the mid-brain which in turn passes it on to the muscles with instructions to act in a certain way. This is a simplified diagram.

Someone says a certain thing to you. Information comes to you by way of the ear. You take the information, analyze it and decide what the reply is to be. This information goes to a certain brain center which in turn relays the instruction to the vocal apparatus telling it to say a certain thing in a certain way. An order may go to the muscles of the face directing them to frown or to smile. For every bit of information that comes into the brain there are thousands of ways of responding to it. You can smile or run or face it. You can fight or frown or make certain comments. The possibilities of choice are infinite. What you decide to do is determined by your reason, your emotions, your past experiences and many other factors. Something is said to you, you decide and then you act. A similar experience comes along another day but you have decided that question once so the information falls into a groove and the same order goes out that went out the first time. The second time it doesn't take so long to decide what to do and to act. That habit track is soon cut in the brain; and then when similar information comes to you, instinctively, immediately, automatically the order goes forth without your giving it conscious thought. Habit is automatic but it is acquired through conscious choice. Neurologists tell us that a fine electrical connection is actually established in the brain, a connection from the point of information coming in, to the point of orders going out, so no conscious thinking is necessary after the habit is formed. You see a certain person and you automatically call him by name. You smile or you frown depending upon the habit you have established.

There are many millions of such connections in the average brain. It is a very fine, complicated instrument of use. Suppose you have the habit of scowling when you see a certain person but you haven't had good results in the past by scowling so you decide to change your habit. The next time you see this person it will be easy to scowl but now you are careful. You do not allow that impulse to travel over the old road. You begin to form a new connection. You send out orders to smile. Then the next time, it is easier to smile and in a short time, an entirely new connection is made and you smile automatically; but for awhile you have to watch carefully that the "sled" gets into the proper groove. Soon the old track has fallen into disuse and the new one is used without conscious thought.

A man of my acquaintance had the habit of drinking whiskey to excess. He had pushed his "sled" down that path many times, several times a day, until the path had become very smooth. He often lost control of the "sled" and landed in a heap. So he started to form a new track, which he used for several weeks. Then, as he told me, "I went out and took just one little drink with the boys and away I went on a spree. I didn't seem to have any control. Why can't I take just one little drink and not go on a spree?" It is easy to see what happened. He went up to the top of the hill, shoved the "sled" just a little way down the old track thinking it would stay at the top. He didn't realize he couldn't do that so long as that old path was still smooth. The track he had established was very smooth. One little push and he couldn't control the "sled." I explained that when he had cut the new path deeply and the old one had grown into disuse, the danger wouldn't be so great and it might then be safe to take just one and let it remain there. Meanwhile, he would have to stay off that path. It was entirely too dangerous.

To form a new habit, *we must be convinced that it is desirable* and see why it is desirable. In the old type religion much is said about conviction, which simply means being convinced beyond a doubt. When a man is convinced, he has made a decision. Only then does he start a new plan of action. If no decision is made, he will stay on the old path. After he makes the decision, he must persist on the new path until it is deeply cut and well smoothed. Then it is as easy to follow as the old one. To illustrate, you meet a friend who is the picture of vitality and health. He tells you that he attributes his robust health to his habit of taking cold showers every morning. By his example, you may be convinced that a cold shower each morning is a good thing. You want the result that your friend seems to have. You become *convinced*. You decide to go through with it. You find that others of your friends have this habit so you make up your mind. You make a choice. In effect, you choose the result you want.

Forming the new habit will not be very difficult so long as you keep your attention on the result. You live in the feeling of having the good result you desire. When a decision is made, you unleash emotional energy. The decision is half the battle.

You decide, then you *prepare*. You may say, "Tomorrow morning I will start taking cold showers." You set the alarm clock fifteen minutes earlier. You promise yourself and perhaps you promise someone else whom you do not want to let down. That, by the way, is the advantage of signing a pledge. (Some people make their promise to God.) This is all by way of impressing yourself, for the promise actually is made to yourself. Then at the first opportunity you *initiate* the action. You have decided and before you or anyone else can talk you out of it, you start it. The longer you wait to begin, the easier it is not to do it. If you delay after you have made your decision, you are forming the habit of procrastination. You must give yourself no excuse. You would not say, "The weather is too cold," or "I got up too late." You say, "Today is the day."

You have taken the first cold shower—it was a task. You shivered and shook but tomorrow it will be easier and the next day still easier. Through *persistence* the new habit is formed. There may be a part of you which wants to continue in the old way and that part may argue, "Why do you wish to make life so hard for yourself?" About the third morning you may say, "I think I will take it easy this morning," and before you are aware of it, you are back in the old track.

Now this is important in habit forming: *everyone desires to be paid.* You have the right to a sense of *satisfaction* when you do right. When you are well started, give yourself a treat. We all like appreciation, so appreciate yourself. Prove to yourself that you do appreciate yourself. Buy a box of candy or treat yourself to a show as a mark of appreciation.

Here are the steps to take—whether it is taking cold showers, being an optimist, or living honestly, cheerfully, or living a good life:

> *Conviction* that the new habit is desirable and will bring the desired results.
> *Decide* to start.
> *Prepare* for it.
> *Initiate* the action and
> *Persist* until it becomes automatic.
> *Thank* yourself. Allow yourself to have a sense of joy in accomplishment.

Benjamin Franklin said it was possible for him to establish and make operative one new habit each week. One week he chose cleanliness, another temperance and another cheerfulness. No doubt, that is possible; but it would be wiser to establish one new habit each month or one each year than continue always to travel the old habit path if it leads to trouble and failure. Forming a new habit isn't difficult when one clearly sees in his imagination what takes place physically and then consciously goes about it scientifically.

Say to yourself:

"I am made to have dominion over my life. I am a creator because I am the infinite Life as a human being. I am a conscious point of Life expressing God—the God qualities—and using the God faculties. I do not fight the old habits. With honesty of purpose and clearness of sight, I choose new paths for greater good. I do not turn back or criticize the old.

"I am free. I know the truth about myself. I am free to act. The faculties of Life are mine to use. My body is mine to direct. My emotional power is mine to use. Whatsoever the Father hath is mine. I have the power to consciously choose how I will use the power of Life for my own good. I can direct my path to happiness, prosperity, and health. When I start a new plan of action, I persist until it becomes a habit.

"As I seek the Kingdom of Heaven, disease and lack automatically disappear. Resentment is eliminated for I have established self-control and poise as a part of my character. Envy and jealousy no longer plague me, for I express love and self-appreciation.

"I am the arbiter of my own fate and the captain of my own soul. I can do all things through Christ which strengthens me and Christ is the power of God within me. I have the power to choose and the power to act. I have the privilege of taking out of Life all those qualities which are within Life—vitality, understanding, wisdom, peace, power, beauty, joy. I no longer accept ideas of limitation. I have no thought of lack. I *am* and since I am, I *can* and with God as my power, I *will*."

chapter 28

How To Use Your Mind

To Stay Young

LIFE NEVER GROWS OLD. SINCE MIND AND SPIRIT ARE ETERNAL, they are not affected by time. Youth is a fundamental quality of Life and we are Life. We do not need to grow old and decrepit. We can use our power of mind to stay youthful, vibrant, and active so long as we remain on this earth. Whatever our years when we pass on, we still may feel young. We do not try to become young. We just come to the realization that we are eternally young.

As individualized points of Life using mind, we have built for ourselves bodies which *seem* to grow old. As a matter of fact, the body does not age, for it is continually being renewed. Today, scientists tell us that our body tissues are never more than a year old. At one time we were told that our bodies were renewed every seven years. Now we are reliably informed that mind acting subconsciously for us builds a new body every few months. Every nerve, gland, bone and muscle is rebuilt with new cells in a year's time. Actually, the tissues of the body are always young. Right now the tissues of the bodies we are using are as young as those of a year-old baby. Since our minds do not grow old—our minds being our individual use of the one infinite mind—and since our bodies are never more than a year old, we are always young.

Our new knowledge leads us to the conclusion that the experience of age is the result of mental attitudes. To a very large degree it undoubtedly is the result of accepting the dominant race pattern of age—the idea accepted by most people as they advance in years. When one retains a youthful attitude of mind, he has the experience, the spontaneity, the vitality and health of youth.

Even though we may have lost our youthful viewpoint and developed aged ways of thinking and old age habits, it still is possible for us to recapture the attitudes and the outlook of youth. This point of view may be held consciously and the pattern of youth maintained throughout one's whole life span. Many men and women do not let the years dull their perception nor block their creative activities, for they remain young in outlook. Gladstone was Prime Minister of England at eighty-five. Titian, the artist, did his best work in his nineties. Oliver Wendell Holmes was on the United States Supreme Court Bench in his eighties and in his nineties said, "It is faith in something that keeps you young in spirit."

One dominant trait of youth is ambition. However young one may be in years, if he is not ambitious, he is old. One may be old in years, but if he is ambitious, he still is young in spirit. When he no longer desires to build, create and grow; when he is satisfied to just drift along, he is experiencing age. When a man lets go of his desire to be, to do and to have, he is old. People with ambition live more years and each year means more, for they live more fully.

When people say they get tired of life, it means they are tired of the place they occupy, tired of doing the same thing year in and year out. Such people are in a rut. They are bored with life. They are fed up because they have no attractive and thrilling goal for the future.

If we would retain our enthusiasm for living at any age, *we always should have a goal* which draws us forward into the future.

Youth has a variety of experiences. Age narrows down its experiences. Our interests should be wide and varied. We should make new friends, read new books and venture out on new and interesting paths. Monotony ages the best of us. "Variety is the spice of life." Eternal change is the one thing that doesn't change. Everything is forever changing. Certainly in this amazingly interesting universe, it is foolhardy to let Life become monotonous.

Youth is plastic, adaptable, flexible. It has the quality of going along with Life rather than resisting Life. Like rubber it is resilient. Whatever happens, it does not go down and stay down. It always bounces back. Unless our minds and bodies are kept active, like the tire on your car they deteriorate through lack of use. *"Use or lose"* says nature. There is no substitute for use—for activity.

Youth is always open to new ideas and what's more it isn't afraid to act upon those new ideas. It isn't afraid to trust its hunches, its intuition, its inner-knowing. After we have had many experiences, we are inclined to get cynical. Just because we got hurt sometime in the past, doesn't mean we should be afraid of new ideas, or that we shouldn't grow, or that we should not be ambitious. We should develop the habit of anticipating a rich, full future by envisioning an alluring goal. *We should enjoy the present and look toward the future with joyful anticipation.*

People who have the attitude of age think about and talk about the "good old days." To stay young they should draw the curtain on past achievements as well as past failures. We stay young by being a success *now* and reaching out hopefully to greater success and satisfaction in the future. Personnel men in business, report that the greatest handicap of older people is their depressed states of mind. Older people are no less able to do productive work but young people have the advantage of a hopeful attitude.

Youth is always looking forward to something better. Someone has said, "When hope dies, old age runs to meet you."

Take this idea, put it on a card, hang it over your desk or over the kitchen sink and read it often:

I am always open to new ideas. My beliefs, my ideas, are not static. This is a universe of expansion, a universe of growth. That's my nature, too, and I will be true to my nature.

Youth is understanding and tolerant of others. Youth accepts people as they are. Youth doesn't pick flaws. Picking flaws is a bad habit—an aging habit. When we look for the good in others, we find them good.

If I knew you and you knew me,
If both of us could clearly see,
And with an inner sight divine
The meaning of your heart and mine,
I'm sure that we would differ less
And clasp our hands in friendliness;
Our thoughts would pleasantly agree
If I knew you and you knew me.

Nixon Waterman

Scratch the vilest sinner and you almost surely will find a warm, colorful personality underneath. We can't be magnetic and at the same time critical.

We like those best who see the best in us. Seeing the best in others brings out the best in them. We are always drawn to those people who think well of us rather than to those who think ill of us. We should recognize the good intention in others' actions if we wish them to see the good in ours. Let's be good-finders, not fault-finders. Either one is a habit. One makes for age; the other, for youth.

Youth is progressive, resourceful and not bound by precedent. Youth makes changes easily. As we draw the cords of habit tightly about us, we become aged. We should not allow ourselves to become slaves of habit. We should change our habits as the need arises. We should control our habits rather than permit them to control us.

Youth is enthusiastic. Enthusiasm has been called divine intoxication. Since "en" means "in" and "theos" means "God," "enthusiasm" means "in God"—a knowledge of God in you and you in God—indestructible, immortal and divine. Youth is intoxicated by that idea. Age is the era of depression, youth, the era of enthusiasm. Age is crushed, sensitive and disillusioned. Youth sees heaven here and now.

Youth is in love and love is the great rejuvenator. If you do not love, you are unhappy, and Life doesn't seem to be worth living. Always keep love alive, never let it die. Be in love whether the other person responds or not. The love emotion moving through you heals all disease and revives all hope. Love never fails. Certainly you want to be loved, for that gives you privileges with the one who loves you; but in any case—*love!* Love people, nature, your job, ideas, ideals and love God. To love is your greatest privilege.

If we go through Life giving wrong values to our experiences, we may get the habit of condemning ourselves and condemning others. People who condemn become hard and brittle. They are unforgiving, which means they break. They are resistant to Life. Consequently much physical and psychological trouble develops. *Criticism and anger poison the system.* That slow poison breaks down the tissues, clogs the body joints, causes heart trouble, nervousness, and indigestion. Those wrong habits must be eliminated if we are to stay young and pliable even in our bodies.

To retain a feeling of youth we should *develop a satisfactory philosophy of life* so that we can see some sense to living. We must have faith in the future. We must believe in immortality or likely we will say, "What's the use?!" We'll become discouraged, for we can see nothing ahead which stimulates and inspires us. If we can see this present existence as an experience in immortal Life, a phase of development, a part of the divine plan, then we will reach eagerly toward the future.

As we look about us, we see faces lined with anxiety and care, but it is an amazing fact of which we always should be conscious: the man of eighty is really no older than the year-old baby. His body is being renewed constantly, and the spirit is ageless. *We do not try to stay young.* We just try to realize that we are young. So long as we believe in age, counting our birthdays, we will be watching for signs of age and Life automatically responding to us will deliver old age appearances—dim eyes, wrinkled, faded skin, and creaky joints. We will be afraid to engage in new activities for fear we won't have the time or the energy to complete them.

Growing old is actually no more real than last night's dream. "Acting your age" means acting young. Why should we believe in age and decay? Why do we believe it is necessary to become feeble, that we must have poor organic functioning in our bodies? Is there any less God in us at sixty or seventy than at twenty? Has God gradually withdrawn from us or is God still incarnated in us? Is the healing power still within us or has it withdrawn itself? Is there any more God in one person than in another? As the years pass, does God withdraw Himself from us gradually? Let's heal ourselves of these ridiculous ideas.

Just about the worst thing we can do to ourselves is to use our imagination in wrong or destructive ways. Would it not be better to forget about age and think of Life? Some day we will step out of this body but *we never will stop living*. We, ourselves, determine *how* we live. We can live like old folks or young ones. In our imagination, let's give ourselves the stamp of youth and vitality, instead of the pattern of age.

Youth is not a time of life but a state of mind. It is not a matter of blushing cheeks and red lips and supple knees. It is a quality of imagination. It is vigor of emotions. It is courage over timidity. It is love of adventure over fear and boredom. Nobody grows old by merely living a number of years. People grow old by deserting their ideals. Years of experience may wrinkle your skin but giving up enthusiasm will wrinkle your soul.

Worry, doubt, self-distrust, fear, and despair bow the head and turn the spirit back to seek escape. You are as young as you feel, as old as your doubts. You are as young as your self-confidence and as old as your fear. You are as young as your hope and as old as your despair. But so long as your heart feels love, beauty, hope, cheerfulness, courage and joy, *you are young*.

Say to yourself:

"I incarnate the very spirit of youth which is the spirit of Life. My mortal experiences are but experiences in immortality. This 'I' is never obliterated. This 'I' is indestructible. It is immortal. I now decide how I will live, what I will do and what I will think. I now decide to act according to my true nature. Since I am immortal, I act like an immortal being. I anticipate never-ending Life. I am always active, alive, awake, and aware—doing the world's work, letting the power and energies of Life move through me as vitality, activity, peace, and perfect ideas.

"I have dropped the idea of age and I now accept for myself the idea of eternal youth, eternal vitality, energy, health, and full expression of Life. All the qualities of God are incarnated within me. I know that I never will come to the end of my path of attainment for it is a path of eternal unfoldment. I know that God holds nothing from me, that the fulfillment of all my desires is provided for me from the foundation of the earth and my desire and expectation is to live and to live forever."

chapter 29

How To Get Rid
of Fear

FEAR IS MAN'S GREATEST ENEMY. IT RETARDS HIS PROGRESS. Fear of what has happened in the past, fear of the future, fear of the unknown keeps him from going ahead.

A few years ago I was called to counsel with Mr. Cosgrove, who was a very sick man. It didn't take long to discover that his sickness was the result of a devastating fear. It developed that in his early life Mr. Cosgrove had made a mistake and for that mistake he had served a prison sentence. After his release he lived in continual fear. He feared his past would be discovered. He never allowed himself to accept any position in business where an investigation into his past was required. This necessitated a frequent change of employers, for Mr. Cosgrove was a brilliant and capable man—the type who from time to time would be up for advancement. He was married and had a fine family to which he was devoted.

For several months before his illness, Mr. Cosgrove had been associated with a large, successful company, and he had moved forward rapidly. He was making good. Now that a new position was opening up to him he was afraid he would be required to give bond. The fear of an investigation into his past had made him sick.

I went to the president of his firm and asked him if he knew Mr. Cosgrove was ill. "Yes," he told me, "I do and as a matter of fact I think I know why. He is afraid. You may tell him that for a long time we have known his history and it makes no difference to us. He has put his past behind him and has made good. He is now a valuable employee and we trust him. His past will not influence his promotion with us." For years Mr. Cosgrove had lived in miserable slavery, needlessly.

A child cries. He can't sleep. He fears. He believes there is a bear under his bed. When he is shown there is no bear under his bed, he is no longer afraid. He goes to sleep peacefully. Conditions haven't changed but the child's belief has changed. Yes, fear holds anyone—child or man—in mental slavery.

Mind is the greatest power you possess. Through your faith, you are always using the power of mind. Your power to believe is one of your greatest assets. Your right to choose how you will believe and what you will believe is the greatest gift Life has made to you. Through your use of mind, your habits of thought, you can and do direct your destiny. Believing in evil, sickness, failure, or unhappiness is using infinite mind power *against* yourself. Believing in, or having faith in health, success, and the goodness of Life is using mind power *for* your good. According to your faith Life responds to you whether that faith be positive or negative.

When the ancient character, Job, once cried, "That which I greatly feared has come upon me," he voiced the experiences of every man, for that which came upon him was the result of his use of mind—his negative thinking. To overcome fear and the results of fear, it is necessary to establish a positive faith.

You always have some kind of faith, for you are always using mind. You are always thinking—always believing—something. You cannot get away from your faith any more than you can run away from your legs, for your faith is your state of mind. You can, however, choose to redirect your faith. If you are having unhappy experiences, you can point your faith in a different direction and experience different results. You may be in a situation or having an experience you don't like. You can change that unpleasant experience by looking for the good in it, by knowing the good is there and persisting until you find it. You also can change it by turning completely away from it, by giving your attention to something else—something which will give you pleasure, something you desire—and then let that idea take shape and form in your imagination. As you do this, the law of creation will begin to operate over this new plan and bring a new experience to you. You might ask yourself, "Why do I have negative faith? Why do I *fear?* Is it just a habit of thinking? Have I really stopped to analyze my beliefs? Does my present faith rest on a rational foundation?"

Through a habit of morbidity, without consciously choosing, many people go through their entire lives with unreasoning fears because they have not made the effort or taken the time to decide what they should believe.

In Chapter IV, The Magic of Faith, we noted the four phases of Life in which we should have positive faith:

1. Faith in the great, infinite Life which surrounds us.
2. Faith in humanity which would include ourselves as well as other people.
3. Faith in the dependability of the laws of Life—the law of attraction, the law of cause and effect—which would eliminate all fear of luck, for things do not happen by chance.
4. Faith in immortality.

When we have faith in these four fundamentals, we have taken the foundation out from under all fear.

Ask yourself, "Do I believe in an infinite Life and do I trust It?" If you are honest with yourself, you will see that intelligent Life is the reality of everything—the vegetable, the animal, the mineral. Whatever form it takes, Life is all power and wisdom. It directs all growth. It is the universal creator. You see creative activity everywhere. You know there must be a creator, for something cannot emerge out of nothing. When you look at your watch, you know there must have been a watchmaker and that creator planned all the intricate operations of the watch. Take whatever time and effort is necessary to establish a positive faith in the Infinite Creator—in Life, Itself. Recognize since you exist and since you could not have come from nothing, Life must have become you. It gave you to yourself and furnished you with everything you need for your well-being—

air, sunlight, food, people to be your friends—all are yours to have, to use and to enjoy. Life loves you and It serves you when you co-operate with It. Since It does all this for you and more, have faith in It. Trust It.

Since you are Life, have faith and confidence in yourself. Since every person is Life just as you are, with the same desire for health, happiness and achievement as yourself, also have faith in them. When you have faith in people; when you love them and cooperate with them, they will love and cooperate with you. Take what seems to be some difficult person and find the good in him. Think of that good, be especially nice and kind to him and see what happens. You may be amazed!

We are all partners in this business of living, cooperating, working together—the buyer and the seller, the husband and the wife, the parents and the children, the employer and the employee. Mutual trust and respect call forth mutual cooperation. When we desire the same good for the other person that we desire for our-selves, he responds to our need, and we have fulfilled the law of successful human relations. We have used the Golden Rule. So many of us forget this.

Science shows us that Life is everywhere and acts according *to* and is governed *by* immutable law. *There is no such thing as luck.* Chemistry, mathematics, gravitation, electricity or mind—all are governed by law. You can learn to use the law. You are learning that as you read this book. "As a man thinketh in his heart, so is he." *You control your own destiny* whether you know it or not, for you think. You choose how you will use the laws of Life and you use those laws to bring happiness or unhappiness, success or failure. Meditate upon this until you have faith in the law of cause and effect and the law of attraction just as you have faith in the law of mathematics. That will rule out all fear of luck.

Since you are Life and Life is immortal—never-ending—then you know *you* are immortal. Sometime, of course, you will drop your present body, but that will be another experience in your immortal Life. Think about this until you believe in your never-ending, im-mortal Life.

Coming to a positive faith about those four phases of Life—Life

Itself, all mankind, which includes yourself, the laws of Life and immortality—will heal you of all fear. You will be free to move forward on a pathway of positive faith.

Say to yourself,

"Life is universal goodness and It pours Itself out to me. I am surrounded with good wherever I am. Life became me. It always sustains me. I accept my good now. I have nothing to fear. My thinking directs the greatest power in the world—Mind. My good thoughts attract to me only that which is good because I contemplate only that which is good for me and good for others. That which goes out from me inevitably must come back to me.

"I feel the goodness of Life in the very air I breathe. I see goodness and beauty reflected in the face of every person I meet. I know there is the seed of opportunity in every situation. I find my good everywhere, for I am always looking for it and always expecting it. I always find that for which I seek when I seek with faith.

"I am serene. I am confident. I do not fear. I know there is no such thing as luck. I know all is governed by law. I know that as I think, I shall experience.

"Since I know I am an immortal being, I do not fear the experience called death. I know that death is an experience in my eternal Life. Even though I may not fully understand it, I accept it as the beginning of a new era in Life just as I accept birth as the beginning of a new experience in Life. I trust Life. I have faith in myself—faith in the honesty and integrity of the laws of Life. I have faith in my fellow man. *I have faith that I will forever be, for I am Life.*"

chapter 30

How To Get Rid of
an Inferiority Complex

A DEEP-SEATED SENSE OF INFERIORITY, OR A SO-CALLED IN-feriority complex, crushes initiative. It is the exact opposite of courage. The person who suffers from a sense of inferiority cannot make decisions readily because he fears the results. If he cannot make decisions, he cannot be a success. He can't be a leader. Inferiority destroys achievement. It inhibits forward movement. The man who fears to move forward doesn't go and he hates himself for being so fearful.

A feeling of inferiority is reflected in a person's looks, in the clothes he wears, in the colors he affects and in the posture of his body. It speaks in his voice. It makes him old before his time. It causes conflict in both his mind and body. For him Life is a continuous struggle. He tries to force himself to go ahead but his fears hold him back. He is torn apart emotionally.

At least four out of every five human beings have some feeling of inferiority. It is found among college students and college professors; bank presidents and bank clerks; laborers and labor bosses. It is not confined to any special level of society, industry or intelligence. It is an emotional dis-ease.

Your emotions are the dynamic living power in you and you cannot dam up a living spring. It will break through sometime so there is not much use forcing yourself to act as though you are adequate if you feel inferior.

You cannot effectively handle these emotional states through will power, through forcing yourself, through making yourself act in a way you don't feel or forcing yourself to have faith in something you don't believe. This only adds to the confusion.

Every person has the desire to do, to be and to grow; he has the desire to perpetuate the race and preserve the self. Nature forces the young out into Life—to get married, raise a family, get a job and do the world's work. Nature continually forces the individual into new areas of living, into being superior to circumstances. This is evidenced in the baby who, after much effort, gets his toe in his mouth. It was evidenced in the builder of the Empire State Building and the Golden Gate Bridge.

Man, misunderstanding himself, his own powers, and the surrounding Life of nature, often through misinterpreting his experiences, comes to believe that he is inferior. To such a man, Life looks difficult, formidable, full of ugly pitfalls.

At an early age children should be taught to meet the problems of Life. If the child moves out with courage, he probably will be successful. When he is directed in the wrong way or allowed to drift, it is likely he will develop wrong habits of belief about himself and about his capabilities. He may form the habit of running away or of fighting.

A child may feel himself to be too short, too tall or too fat. Unless this uniqueness is explained to him, unless he is led out to have a good opinion of himself, he may believe he is inferior to others, a belief that will influence him throughout his lifetime, unless by some means he is set straight.

If a child gets the idea that he can run to his parents at any time knowing they will protect him and fight his battles for him, it is likely he will form the bad habit of believing he is weak. He may form the habit of always calling upon others, begging God, the government or his neighbor for help.

Parents unwittingly contribute to the child's sense of weakness when they say, "You are not very strong. You are not like other children." Some parents have an attitude of selfish love—the attitude of owning the child and not giving him his rightful independence. They dominate him, therefore, weaken him.

A boy may feel he is inferior to a smarter brother, or a girl may feel she is inferior to a more beautiful sister. There are those who are plagued by a feeling of humiliation. They feel they should apologize for some disgrace in the family or for being born on the wrong side of the tracks. Others feel they lack education, prestige or position. All these hurt feelings, if not healed, may crystallize into a complex of inferiority.

Some few people are healed of any feeling of inferiority. They live full, enthusiastic lives while many others go through Life as victims of their fear and their feeling of inadequacy.

The urge of Life pushes everyone out into activity and he desires to go. When he senses strength and courage, he moves out and wins. He moves on to better and better adjustments. If he forms the habit of hesitation, of withdrawal, he just muddles along in spite of his fears.

His fear and sense of inadequacy cause him to do many wrong things. He may try to *escape* from that which looks so big—so formidable. He may say, "I want to go off and live by myself," even though he knows to retreat means failure. The effort to go forward in the face of his fears is too much for him. He seeks solitude but through escape he never gets well. He may attempt escape through drugs, or he may drink to drown his sorrows—to get away from himself. He may develop the habit of fantasy or day-dreaming where he is the hero. In this way he gets a certain vicarious satisfaction. He may develop delusions of grandeur or he may try to escape through travel, always looking for new places, new sights. He may "talk big" until there is something to be done and then he is conspicuous by his absence. In order to escape his failures, he may seek excitement. He always may need boon companions because he fears to be alone with himself. He may try to compensate his sense of inadequacy by criticizing other people or he may just surrender—give up and become a hobo. Some withdraw from Life and become ascetics. Some become hermits and live alone, slaves to their fears. *The extreme escape is suicide.* It has been published that San Francisco has the highest suicide rate in the United States. It is interesting to note that it also has the highest alcoholic rate.

There are those who attempt to adjust by overcompensation. They become conceited. Life has forced them into activity, but since they fear, they build up a false front to protect themselves. They are arrogant and blustery, often pompous and sarcastic in their attempt to build themselves up.

Escape and *defense* are two wrong ways of handling a feeling of inferiority. The escapist becomes timid and shy while the person who feels he must defend himself against Life blusters and fights. He has a chip on his shoulder for he thinks that Life is opposed to him.

An objective adjustment never reaches the core of the problem. So long as one reacts to his problem through escape or defense, he is but protecting his inner feeling of weakness; he is not healed. *The fear itself must be healed.*

Objective training, even accomplishment and wealth helps very little. Getting rich or getting married, getting power or a high position in life—all outside accomplishments—will not heal the inner hurt. The adjustment must be made within. One must form a new opinion of himself. He must find his inner source of power and security.

It is most unfortunate when people believe their trouble is outside themselves—that they are imposed upon by their employer, their neighbors, their family, their parents, their government. It is a great mistake to believe the fault is in the environment.

When one's heart is broken or his feelings hurt, sensitiveness develops. That person becomes self-centered. He believes he is the butt of the ill jokes of Life so he drops into self-pity. He believes he is different from other people. He believes Life serves others better than It serves him. He gets some satisfaction out of saying he is different, that Life has been exceptionally cruel to him, that God singled him out for special trouble; but nevertheless, he is unhappy because he knows he hasn't measured up to his responsibilities. He hasn't accomplished and he isn't moving on healthfully toward his destiny. So long as he ascribes the trouble to something outside himself, he never will get well.

The trouble is not the defeat. It is in the fear of defeat. The problem never is in the thing we fear; it is always in the fear itself. It is in what happens within. The problem is never the thing; it is in what we think about the thing, and we can change our thoughts.

Here, then, is the center of the trouble: the urge to go out and meet Life comes in conflict with the fear of meeting Life. An inner conflict follows. The desire to go ahead collides with the fear of going. This conflict often causes mental and physical breakdown. When one makes an objective adjustment, he is but working with the symptom, and there is but a very temporary easing of the mental pain. He may push things around in his outer world, but if he does not make the adjustment within his own thinking, he will continue to be unhappy.

So long as he believes the trouble is *outside* himself, he will be unable to save himself. He may place the blame on conditions, on his family, or on the way Life has treated him; but he still has to meet Life or die. Escape or defense furnish no permanent relief. Any adjustment to be of value must bring out the inner strength of the individual. The trouble has been in his thinking, in his belief. His faith must be redirected.

If it is possible to think back and see how these wrong states of mind came about in the first place, then the offense can be understood; and *understanding is forgiving*. If a person can forgive what he says is the cause of his trouble, he will have drawn the foundation out from under his excuse for failure. Everyone has defects and shortcomings which have to be healed or transcended through understanding. Everyone has problems to be met. David was a shepherd lad but he became a great king. Moses was a foundling but he became the great law-giver of antiquity. Jesus was the son of a carpenter. Carver was the son of slaves. Milton was blind and Beethoven was deaf, while Lincoln was self-educated. These men did not let Life get them down. They became conscious of their inner power. They were not born with gold spoons in their mouths.

Riches or poverty—any condition—can be a curse or a blessing depending upon how one reacts to it. To the person who suffers

HOW TO GET RID OF AN INFERIORITY COMPLEX

217

from a sense of inferiority, I suggest that he picture someone else in the same circumstance and ask himself what advice he would give that person. He only has a problem to be handled, a challenge to his ingenuity. It is not actually a part of him. There is really no superior and no inferior. There is just a person who doesn't understand himself. Every person is a point of Life with the power to choose how he will direct the Life principle through himself so he should objectify his problems, put them outside of himself.

If you suffer from a feeling of inferiority, in your imagination see someone else in the position in which you find yourself. Ask yourself what that person should do and then relate the answer to yourself. Another suggestion I would make and which has been extremely helpful to many people: write out your history in the third person as though it were someone else. Write everything you can remember from your early childhood. *See yourself as someone else. Separate the belief from the believer. Separate the self from the problem.* Do this so you can see yourself as others would see you and then give yourself some good advice. You will heal yourself of your problem by getting a good look at yourself.

Here is something anyone can do, something I believe will heal every feeling of inferiority: everything you do, do it in such a way that you are satisfied with yourself! When you get up tomorrow morning, take your bath, shave, or put on your make-up, then look at yourself and say, "I did that all right." Dress, then look at yourself and say, "I did that all right." Eat your breakfast in such a way that you can turn back to yourself and say, "I did that all right." Handle every situation throughout the day in such a way that you can say to yourself, "I approve of you." Of course, you will make some mistakes but be able always to turn back to yourself and honestly say, "At any rate my motives were right and I am doing better."

I can promise that if you will do everything you do for three days in such a way that you can say to yourself, "I approve of you," by the end of the third day, you will throw your shoulders back and say, "I am getting over all sense of inferiority and weakness for I approve of myself."

Remember you are not running a race with Life. You are not

competing with other people. The only comparison you need to make is where you are today with where you were yesterday. Say to yourself, "I approve of myself regardless of what other people may think about me, and I know that when *I really approve of myself,* the world will approve of me for the world will take me at my own estimate of myself." This does not mean arrogance for one who is arrogant does not approve of himself. Arrogance is a defense mechanism.

You are not inferior. Mistakenly, you have believed yourself to be inferior. *You* are an incarnation of God and God is not inferior. Neither are you superior. Everyone is made of the same material and uses the same mind—the Divine Mind. The laws of Life are yours to use. Life responds to you as well as to any other person in the world. The Life in you is the same Life that was in Jesus or in Lincoln. The same creative mind is yours to use that is used by the greatest person in the world. Anyone can use it. It awaits *your* use.

Recognize yourself as a spiritual being. Know that at the point where *you* choose you may decide to use mind, your emotions, and your body as you wish. Know that your feelings and your body are your subjects and you direct them. Develop a sense of power by knowing that you are the commander of your own ship. Then live without apology and you never will need an alibi nor will you need to give excuses. The healthy minded person handles his problems. He has found the ability, the power and the intelligence within himself to handle himself; therefore, he handles his problems. He has dominion, for he has taken dominion over his mental processes. He has found inner strength.

The healing comes about through *repentance* and *conversion.* "Repentance" means "changing your mind," and "conversion" means "turning around." When you change your mind and turn around, you can face yourself without fear and embarrassment. You will approve of yourself for you have found your true self. You are self-sufficient without being arrogant. You look at Life without fear or timidity. You have faith in yourself for you are divine and immortal. You have faith in the integrity of Life. You believe the world is friendly and that your relationship to Life and to others is not temporal but eternal. You are an eternal being and you see every man and woman as an immortal being. You are interested in them as you are in yourself. You love other people as yourself and you love Life. "On these two commandments hang all the law and the prophets." "Do this and thou shalt live."

Say to yourself,

"I know I am an incarnation of the Divine Spirit of Life. Life has become me in a different way than it has become any other person. I am unique. I have special qualifications. The work that is before me can and should be done better by me than by anyone else. I am important to Life. It created me for Its purpose and I justify that purpose. I live in such a way that I approve of myself. I have no sense of inferiority. Within me are all the qualities and faculties of Life. With this understanding of myself, I rise above any sense of lack or limitation.

"I know that Life can deliver every good thing and It becomes all things in my experience. Through my imagination, through my creative thinking, I direct Life into wholesome, full and complete expression through me. I see myself expressing health, vitality, energy, love, beauty, and goodness. I remove every belief that Life cannot and will not respond to me in love, in happiness and in abundance. I accept the goodness of Life and I accept it *now. I believe I have that goodness right now.*"

chapter 31

How To Get

over Worry

Worry is the interest we pay on trouble before it is due. It never solved any problem. It is completely destructive and disintegrating. Still, many of us continue to indulge in it.

A man said to me, "I have worried so much about what may happen in my business that I can't digest my food. My mind is in a turmoil. I can't seem to stop this threshing around. This awful fear of what can happen is driving me mad. I can't think straight. I can't sit still. I can't sleep at night and I have butterflies in my stomach. I suppose you will tell me to pull myself together; and that if I stop it and get quiet, I will find the answer to my problem. I certainly would like to stop it, but how can I? I am sick all over."

"Well, what is this trouble with your business, Jim?" I asked.

"Oh, it hasn't happened yet and, of course, it may not happen; but I worry night and day. I know it doesn't help; it may even make matters worse but I can't stop."

By his own admission this man wasn't helping himself by worrying. He was actually doing himself harm. He was making himself weaker, less able to meet the problem if it did come upon him. And without doubt he *was* actually drawing the problem to him but he couldn't seem to help himself. He was moving rapidly in the direction he didn't want to go for that was what he was thinking about and expecting. His morbid state of mind had taken such complete control of him that he believed he was unable to handle it.

Jim's real difficulty was not the problem in the future. It was the worry which obsessed him, his *belief* that he could not control his mind. He was suffering from a wrong belief about himself. He had forgotten that he was made to have dominion over Life, over himself, that it was the Father's good pleasure to give him the Kingdom and that his Kingdom was his mind and his affairs. He had become a slave to a false belief about himself.

People succeed in tearing themselves down mentally and physically through this demon, worry. Doctors have told us that, excepting the diseases caused by microbes and those of old age, worry is responsible for a majority of our diseases. In addition to that, worry undoubtedly provides the condition for those microbes to do their deadly work, and it certainly fastens the effects of age upon us.

Worry is a malfunctioning of the mind. "Mal" means "wrong or bad." Malfunctioning means wrong functioning or bad functioning. A wrong use of mind results in dis-ease (not ease). It causes mental and physical pain and it tears down one's personality. The fact is *worry is against the law.* That may seem to be an unusual statement but worry does violate the law of health and happiness. It restricts our freedom and brings unhappiness to those about us.

The Buddhists say "The two devils of the emotional kingdom are anger and fear; anger, the burning passion and fear, the freezing passion." Anger, resentment, resistance are unhealthy reactions to what has happened in the past. Worry is a morbid unhealthy reaction to what you think will happen sometime in the future. It hasn't happened yet but you fear it will. When you worry, you reach out to the future for trouble. You seem to be hungry for it.

We all understand the vicious circle of worry. We get a little pain in the chest and we begin to worry about it. That morbid attention and worry causes the pain to increase. The increased pain causes us to worry more and soon we're on the merry-go-round; we are on a worry debauch. That circle must be broken. We sometimes even find ourselves worrying about our inability to quit worrying.

Jim, who was so worried about his possible failure in business, not only feared the future but he also worried because he seemed to be unable to stop worrying. This condition is well described by Freud as "the neurotic thought pattern repeating itself over and over with monotonous regularity." When we begin to let these negative states of mind control us, they do repeat themselves again and again. Our morbid thoughts go around and around with "monotonous regularity." After this goes on for a while, we get to where we doubt our minds. After we leave home, we may worry about whether we turned off the gas. We go back and find we had. We proceed again and then worry about whether we locked the door. We drop a letter in the letter-box and worry about whether we put a stamp on it or whether we put the right letter in the wrong envelope. We begin to doubt our mental processes, and when we begin to doubt our own minds, we haven't much left to sustain us.

Paul said, "God has not given us the spirit of fear but of power and of love and of a sound mind." *We are not born with fear.* Our fears accumulate. They result from our not having properly evaluated and understood our experiences. We have forgotten that we can quit making the mistake and do right any time we decide to do so and, as a result, have good come to us. We have the mistaken idea that we are weak, ineffective, inferior, that Life is opposed to us and that other people are our enemies when, as a matter of fact, our experience is a result of our thoughts and actions and only proves that Life is good to us. Life *immediately* responds to us. Life returns to us exactly in terms of what we send out.

A sound mind means an integrated mind. To be integrated means to be all in one piece; in other words, to think from the central core of ourselves, our spiritual nature; to know that at the point where we say "I" we can choose our thoughts and control our thinking. We can control our emotions and through our emotions control our bodies and our affairs.

Often in dealing with a "first-class" worrier, I say, "So you are worried? What were you worrying about a month ago today?" Usually he replies, "Well, I don't remember but I am sure I was worrying about something!" Most of us should ask ourselves, "What was I worrying about a month ago?" Very likely whatever we were worrying about, it didn't happen; and if it did happen, we lived through it and our worrying didn't help us in getting through it.

We should ask ourselves, "*Do I really want to get over this worry? Do I want this so much that I will actually do something about it?*" There are some people who get a morbid satisfaction out of worry; they want to hurt themselves, they believe they should be punished. But whatever the cause, the result is unhappiness. Then ask yourself, "What is it I am worrying about and why do I worry?" Write down your answers. Writing down what you are worrying about and why, also whether you wish to stop worrying, will enable you to look at the situation objectively. You have put the problem outside of you. Soon you will see the answer. Oftentimes when a person has written down what he is worrying about and why, with a sickly smile he says, "Now, isn't that silly!" When you face your problems, they don't seem to be so big. As a matter of fact, they cease to be problems, they are just situations to be handled.

The healthy minded person, as well as the mentally ill, has his problems. The difference is, the mentally ill person lets his problems handle him, while the healthy minded person handles his problems. The unwise person thinks of himself from the standpoint of his problems. He gets enmeshed in the problem. He lets the problem get inside of him. The wise person handles himself; and handling himself, he is able to handle his problems. He doesn't let them get inside him and control him. He thinks of himself from the point of adequacy, from the point of his ability to handle problems. He thinks of himself as a center of rational, choosing Life and he knows he can choose what he will think and what he will do about any situation.

As a worrier you have only accepted a feeling of inadequacy and inferiority but that is not the truth about you. You have been thinking of yourself from the wrong point of view.

When you write out what you are worrying about, some little devil of thought may rise up in you and say, "So you are going to be a sissy, are you? You can't take it. You can't stand the strain of a little worry. Don't you know you should worry? Don't you know there is much about which you should worry? Do you know if you lie down now, you will be a quitter? You will be a beaten thing all the rest of your life. You should be ashamed of yourself!" But having made up your mind to handle your problem, you will say to these negative states of mind, "Be still and know that I am God." or "Get thee behind me, Satan."

I have said that *worry is against the law.* Actually, worry is *suicidal.* When we worry, we concentrate our minds upon that which we don't want, and in doing so we create experiences we don't want.

In our study of the evolution and development of consciousness we find that only those points of mind which have the ability to reason can worry. To reason is to associate ideas. Man is the only animal which can associate ideas so man is the only animal which has the ability to worry. This means when we worry, we are simply using our wonderful power of reasoning in a destructive way. We are using this marvelous ability of associating ideas to get wrong ideas. The better we are able to associate ideas, the better job we can do of worrying. The strongest minded person can be the best worrier.

We use our powers of reasoning either for constructive or destructive purposes. Realizing that the strongest minded person can worry best, we who worry have something very wonderful with which to start. The fact is we can be very thankful we have such wonderful powers of concentration that we can actually worry ourselves sick. We have wonderful power. We can actually make a pitiable wreck of ourselves through our powers of concentration and reason and that's just what a worrier does. How wonderful it would be if we used this power of reason—this ability to associate ideas—to build ourselves and to make plans for glorious living instead of creating bonds of slavery for ourselves.

Some of the best educated people, those with the highest I.Q.s, worry most. They are not born to worry. It is not a part of their nature. They have given a false value to certain experiences. Their reasoning has been at fault.

A man once said to me, "I am worried sick. I lost my job today and I'd like to have you help me get another. I made a terrible mistake at the office. As soon as I discovered the mistake, I reported it and walked out before they had time to fire me so here I am, without a job." I asked him, "What did the manager say?" "I didn't see him. I left before he was told," he answered. "Then, how do you know you are fired?" He replied, "Oh, I am fired all right. There's no question about that!" I challenged him to go back and report directly to the manager. "Why, I wouldn't go back to that office; they would throw the furniture at me!" But I persisted; I persuaded him to go back. And what do you think the manager said to him? He said, "That was a costly mistake you made, my friend. I am sure you will be more careful next time. You'd better get back to your desk. Your work is piling up."

Emerson wrote, "Some of your hurts you have cured, and the sharpest you still have survived, but what torments of grief you endured from evils that never arrived!" Men have been sure they were fired or their wives had left them or their money was lost; but they weren't fired, their money wasn't lost and the wife forgave.

There is an answer to every problem. We may not be able to see the answer at the moment. It is not likely we will see it while we are blinded by worry, but the answer is there. We should look within ourselves and find that place of peace where we can say and mean:

"I am at peace and I will continue to be at peace. Whatever the problem, I will meet it when I get to it. None of these things move me. Under all circumstances I am profoundly undisturbed."

When we worry and fear, we have forgotten who we really are. We have neglected to recognize this surrounding Life of love. We have forgotten that "All things work together for good for those who love God, for those who are called according to his purpose."

Remember Life brought you here, and since It brought you here, It must be interested in you. Life evidently was interested in expressing Itself in a unique, special way and so became you. There never has been another nor will there ever be another person in this world exactly like you. Since you are special, you must be here for some special purpose. Common sense certainly would deny that your purpose for being here is to be unhappy. It could not be that in bringing you here Life wanted to be unhappy through you, continually hurting you, thwarting your ambitions, frustrating your desires, and bedeviling you.

If an intelligent Life became you for a purpose, It *can be* and *is* your sustainer. The master teacher, Jesus, pointed out that even the sparrows are fed and sustained by the Father of Life. The lilies are dressed in beautiful clothes and have everything they need. How much more does an intelligent Life care for you? Man is the highest point in the evolution of Life on this planet. Life has devoted Itself to you. Certainly Life is intelligent enough to preserve and sustain Its highest values. Can you not trust your sustainer?

Since you are where you are, do what is before you to be done in the very best way you can. Let the intelligent Life principle, which desires to work out Its purpose through you, tell you what you should do and then start doing it. Let It answer your problems for you. Seek the Kingdom of God as Jesus suggested and let the things you need come to you and you to them.

In the 37th Psalm, David suggested that you "fret not." This is fundamental in healthy living. Don't be disturbed! Fret not! "Trust in the law and do good; so shalt thou dwell in the land, and verily thou shalt be fed." Can you believe that? You can feel assured that only good will come to you if you do your best with faith in the integrity of the law of cause and effect. Others may get hurt but it will not come near you.

David also said, "Oh, how I love thy law." We should remember that the law of cause and effect is infinite, immutable, honest, and dependable. The mistakes we may have made in the past have no further effect when we cease from evil and do good. The law of cause and effect still operates. We choose a new course and immediately we begin to experience a new result.

Again and again we have heard the statements "Love they neighbor as thyself" and "Love fulfills the law." When we use the law with love, we remove our attention from what seems to be our problem and we become interested in the drama of other people's unfoldment. Many times we say of some person who always seems to be in trouble, "If only he would get his mind off himself for a little while; if only he would think of what he could do to help someone else, he would be all right."

Let's quit morbidly making the self our complete center of

attention. Let's turn our thoughts and efforts to helping others out and making this world a better place in which to live.

No one can deny that "All things work together for good to them that love God" and God is all Life. This is not a promise. It is a statement of law and Life operates through law. If you love Life, if you love the expressions of Life—all people, all things (which would, of course, include yourself)—then all things will work together for good for you. Through this mathematical law of cause and effect, your employer, your employees, your spouse, your children, your neighbor, your friends—*all things will work together for good for you.* Only *you* can decide how you will use the law. No one is above the law but everyone must use the law of love, of faith, of the Golden Rule for the right purpose if he is to be happy and fully expressed.

You cannot believe that you are of a different Life than other people or that the law does not operate for you. You cannot believe that you came into this world through some error, some mistake, or that you are lost. You are important to Life as you make yourself important. You are the instrument through which God expresses. You are the hands and fingers of God. Do not let those hands and fingers become atrophied and weak through lack of use.

We get into trouble when we don't fully express the Life which made us for Itself alone and our hearts are hungry unless we unify with our purpose. We are important to Life or we would not be here. We are important to God. We are made to express God. Do we justify that importance?

Many people through fear, anxiety, resentment and resistance become almost valueless.

We are important as we make ourselves important, as we do what we are designed to do, as we fulfill our purpose. When we live the best we know, we can trust. We should accept a valid purpose for living, one to which we can give ourselves unreservedly, a purpose which draws out all the powers of mind, spirit and body. When we are true to an ideal, we can trust Life to deliver to us because we are doing what we should do. This cures every sense of fear and worry. Why shouldn't we be well, happy and free when we fulfill our purpose, when we do what we are designed to do? When we live up to our highest ideals and trust, we will be free from worry.

Say to yourself:

"I am healthy, happy and free. I do what I am designed to do in the best way I know. I love my family, my friends, my neighbors, my associates. I love Life. I express Life in a wholesome and thoroughly creative way. As the best goes out from me, only the best can come back to me. Love and goodwill continually flow out through me, blessing everyone I contact and every situation in which I find myself."

chapter *32*

How To Make Every Situation

Pay Dividends

Do THINGS JUST HAPPEN HIT OR MISS, OR IS THERE SOME REAL cause back of every experience? Is there a sound reason for every human contact? Is Life governed by law or luck?

If we can understand that *all* of Life's happenings are governed by law, then we may take the good out of every experience and find a way to make what seems to be a bad situation deliver good to us. We often find ourselves in a place which is not comfortable. In fact, we often are disappointed in situations which looked promising but which didn't turn out as we had hoped or expected. We are where we are, however we got there. It is up to us to decide how we will make the best of it, how we will take the good out of it, for in every situation, there is the seed of opportunity.

On the whole most people lead very inefficient lives. They spend much time and energy without getting worthwhile results. We spend our time with people who bring no good to us and devote hours and days to matters from which we receive very little value. Nature is constantly putting good in our path but often we are blind to our opportunities. We attend meetings and get little good from them. We fail to take the good from our human associations when there is tremendous good all around us if we will but recognize and use it. A multitude of opportunities surrounds us each day and we should select and claim for ourselves those opportunities which will deliver the greatest good. Every contact with friends, neighbors and business associates should bring us good. Every person we meet has some good for us if we will accept it; and we, too, have something in the way of good which we can deliver to every person and every situation we meet.

History tells us that the Island of Crete was inhabited by people noted for their low standard of living. They had a bad reputation for lying and avarice. Perhaps you have heard the old saying, "He lied like a Cretan." As a matter of fact, an old Greek Philosopher, Epimenides, who lived in Crete seven hundred years before the time of Jesus, said, "Cretans were always liars, evil beasts, and gluttons."

Paul, organizer of the Christian church, journeyed to the island of Crete and placed there a man by the name of Titus to establish a Christian community. It was evident young Titus didn't like his assignment. In the New Testament you can find a letter Paul wrote to Titus in which he said, "For this cause, left I thee in Crete, that thou shouldst set in order the things that are wanting." This must have been an answer to Titus' call for help and relief. Without doubt Titus had said, "For pity's sake, don't make me stay here. It isn't a decent place for beast or man." Titus was in a tough spot. He wanted to get out and go somewhere else, fast; but Paul's answer was, "Even a prophet of their own said the Cretans are liars, evil beasts, and gluttons . . . for this cause, left I thee in Crete, that thou shouldst set in order the things that are wanting." To make a long story short, Titus remained in Crete. He didn't run away. His challenge became his great opportunity.

Today the old ruins of Crete are being excavated and foundations of stately churches and beautiful shrines are being uncovered; and whose name do you think is on those churches and shrines? In whose honor were they built? Titus—St. Titus!

Our lives would be wonderfully improved if we could recognize the opportunities surrounding us and accept the good they have to offer. Good exists in every situation in which we find ourselves.

I heard the story of a man who lived in the far North, beyond the Arctic Circle. He went into that country as an adventurer, married a native woman, and had a family. As time went on, he became very unhappy. He wrote to a friend that he wanted to get away, that he couldn't take it any longer; he was planning to run away from his responsibilities, come back to the United States and become a writer.

The friend wrote back, "Stay right where you are. Write stories about the far North, the field you know intimately and well."

Following his friend's advice he became a very successful author of stories of the Far North. Magazines were eager for his stories and he was paid well for them.

Every person and every situation is an opportunity. Every person who crosses our path does so for a reason. That person probably doesn't consciously realize or understand the purpose and we usually do not understand why the opportunity is presented. Not once in a hundred times do we inquire of ourselves, "How can I take the greatest good out of this situation?"

My very good friend, George Herman, who has been unusually successful, certainly in accumulating this world's goods, told me not long ago, "I have learned that *every situation, however bad it may seem to be, is a good thing for me if I believe it is good.* When something seems to be entirely wrong, when it seems that I have made a horrible mistake, I have learned to look at the situation and say, 'Yes, I may not see the good in this now but it is there. I know if I give this my honest and loving attention, good will come out of it.'" He tells me that with this attitude, no situation ever fails to bless him.

Would it not be wonderful if we could evaluate every contact and discover the good which it holds for us? This universe is not operated by luck and chance, but by law. Law is as precise in our individual affairs as in the solar system. We may see but little of the plan back of the whole operation—but there is a plan! It is universally admitted that a thinking consciousness is back of all that is and we each are in that thinking consciousness. Certainly we are cared for. Everything is given to us to use. All contacts come to us for our growth, for our understanding and experience.

Lacking understanding, we often fail to see the good but every-thing that crosses our path contains good for us. We fail to recognize the opportunity and the possibilities in it and yet it is all as surely law-governed as the movement of the stars in the Milky Way.

Each of us has a destiny to fulfill. There is something within each of us which demands satisfaction. I am sure that many times without our conscious knowledge we are led by an inner intelligent wisdom into situations and conditions for the purpose of learning a lesson. We all have had the experience that when we refuse to meet a situation, when we run from it, try to escape, we are put up against this or a similar situation again and again until we meet it. When we meet it, when we have learned our lesson, we always go on to something new and better.

A few years ago, a young man was convinced that no opportunity existed for him at the radio station where I had a program. He was unhappy and disgusted. He said advancement depended entirely upon "pull" and he had none. I asked him if there wasn't something about the place that needed to be done, something that wasn't being done. With quiet disgust he said, "Plenty!" "Then, why don't you do it?" I asked him. To which he replied, "What! Do you think they will pay me for it? Not much!" "That's entirely beside the point," I said. "If there is something that should be done, why don't you do it and do it with a sense of gratitude that you have the opportunity to do it. It isn't going to cost you anything except effort. Try it. More than that, try this, too. Make everyone you meet happy. Every time you have any contact with anyone around this place, don't leave him until you have made him happy. Say something to make him smile. Make his day seem a little brighter. Try this for a week." I could almost see the thoughts moving around in his mind as I made these suggestions. He seemed a bit dubious at first but he agreed to try it for a week. In less than two weeks he had a much better job at the same station. One day some weeks later I heard him say to another employee, "Jack, you are angry and discouraged but listen here! Your opportunity is right at the desk where you are right now. You don't need to think you can get out of here and get along better somewhere else." And he continued to lay before Jack the plan I had given him.

Man, being a self-conscious point in mind, has the power of choice. He chooses how he will accept the various circumstances in Life which are presented to him. He decides what his reactions are to be, whether he will accept his opportunities and how.

If we fail to take advantage of these opportunities, we are the ones who lose. Nature, however, is good to us. If we fail to recognize one opportunity, another is presented and then another. We may miss a thousand opportunities while we are taking advantage of one. But nature never tires. Life continues to present us with what is good for us until finally we learn to accept it.

How are we to obtain the greatest value from these various contacts? When we go to a meeting, how can we be sure that we will come away with some good? Two things we should always remember: expect to give and expect to get. Every person you meet has some good for you and you have some good for him. *Seek to give and expect to receive.* The other person may not accept what you have for him. He may not understand the possibilities of an exchange, but that need not keep you from getting your good and you will get it by expecting it and by having the attitude of giving out good.

We often see people come to a public lecture, settle themselves, smile at their neighbor, beam forth their goodwill, make others happy, join in the consciousness of good, and enter into the spirit of the occasion. These people always go away with some good. They are open for good to flow out from them and for good to flow to them.

May I tell you about an old friend, Colonel Dan Morgan Smith? He was an attorney and a fine speaker. In the days when the Anti-Saloon League was campaigning for funds, they hired Dan to travel, lecture and raise funds for that cause. He told me he was scheduled to speak in a small town in New England one winter Sunday evening. A severe storm came up. The wind, snow and sleet were so heavy no one was out on the streets and he didn't expect anyone to come to the church where he was scheduled to lecture. However he decided to brave the storm and leaving his hotel, he went over to the church.

Only the janitor was there when he arrived but he waited.

234

THE MIRACLE OF MIND POWER

Finally, two little old ladies came in and sat down quietly without saying a word. No one else came even though they waited for some time. Colonel Smith thought to himself, "I think I will go back over to the hotel. Perhaps I can scare up a bridge game." Then he remembered that in every challenge there is an opportunity. He said to himself, "I came here to speak and speak I will!"

He told me he gave the best lecture he could to those two little ladies and when he had finished, one of them said, "Well, if it's that important, I will put in fifteen thousand dollars." The other lady spoke up and said, "Well, if you can, I can, too."

The Colonel got more money from that congregation of two ladies than from any meeting of any size at any time on his lecture tour.

A woman once said to me, "No one ever invites me to come for a visit. I invite others to my house but they never return the invitation. People don't appreciate me." It was easy to see that when she invited people into her home, she really invited them in to get something for herself. She invited them because she was lonely, not because she wanted to alleviate the loneliness of others as well as herself. If we want cooperation from others, we must be willing to cooperate. I like to think of each of us as some sort of substation in universal life. *Good flows to us as good flows from us.* It cannot be dammed up within us. When we pass it out, a vacuum is created and more flows in for we know that nature abhors a vacuum.

It is important that we do not try to force our good onto others. It is provided for us and we can accept it or reject it as we see fit. When we have the attitude of passing our good on, leaving others free to take it or reject it as they wish, we shall find other people are channels through which good flows to us. They give to us willingly and spontaneously if we give out willingly and spontaneously. As a matter of fact, good does not belong to any of us. It is simply ours to use temporarily. We keep it circulating. We pass it on and more flows in.

Happy is the man who sees an opportunity in every challenge, who sees in every person a potential friend and who makes of every moment an adventure.

chapter *33*

A Morning

Meditation

EVERY MORNING IS A FRESH BEGINNING. EVERY DAY IS THE world made new.

Today is a new day. Today is my world made new. I have lived all my life up to this moment, to come to this day. This moment— this day—is as good as any moment in all eternity. I shall make of this day—each moment of this day—a heaven on earth. This is my day of opportunity.

This morning the power of Life (which is the only power there is) pours through me in an unlimited way. My mind and my body are thoroughly cleansed and I thrill to the possible good experiences which lie before me today. I am thankful for all my experiences of the past which have taught me how to successfully meet each situation as it comes.

I am thankful for all my God-given equipment which helps me to meet today, and I shall use it well.

I am blessed with a perfect body. It is dependable. Every organ, every cell of this body has its function and is directed by an inner intelligence into perfect action. This body is a fine piece of equip·ment and its energy and skill will do whatever is required of it, this

235

day. It responds to all my needs. I have absolute confidence in this body. It is made of the eternal energy of Life.

My mind is a fine piece of equipment. Since my mind is *my* use of the *one* mind (the mind that knows all, sees all, and creates all), my mind knows the answer to every problem and *knows* that it knows. Since there is one mind common to all individual men, my mind is never weak. It is the mind that was in Jesus, Socrates, Plato, Shakespeare, Lincoln, Emerson and Edison. I have all the equipment necessary for me to successfully meet this day.

This morning I have greater real assets than ever before in my life so I can move forward today into greater activity than ever before. I can be and do what I should be and do.

This morning I have more experience to draw upon than ever before in my life. I also have more mental strength for I have a better understanding of myself. For this I am thankful!

Every day I go forward. Life has great expanses to be explored. There is a most interesting road before me to travel. There is much to be done; and I do all that lies before me to be done with efficiency and strength, with courage and enthusiasm.

I know I am in this world to be a wholesome, glorious expression of Life. So I ask myself, "What can I do today to make this a better world? How can I help someone? How can I relieve some pain, suffering or heartache? How can I best serve Life?" I, too, want to say with that great master, "I am come that they might have Life." That is also my motive—to serve. I know when I serve unselfishly, I am best served.

How can I do the task before me in a better way than I ever *have* done? How can I make someone happy? I know when I make someone else happy, my own happiness is intensified.

I now resolve that every person I meet today will be a better person because I will inspire him to greater hope, faith, freedom and happiness. A new life begins for me today whether I am twenty, forty, sixty, or eighty.

I will go through this day with courage, with faith, with enthusiasm. I will carefully examine my thoughts. I will guard my mental house so that no negative thoughts find entrance.

My motives are beyond reproach. My acts are governed by an

inner intelligence and wisdom which knows more about me and my needs than I consciously know about myself. "The Lord is my shepherd; I shall not want. He leadeth me beside the still waters. He restoreth my soul. He leadeth me in the paths of righteousness. I will fear no evil. Thy rod and thy staff, they comfort me." My inner subconscious mind—the Lord or Law of my Life—leads me into right situations. It built my body. It sustains my physical equipment and directs my affairs. It thinks through me. It directs and guides me. It created me and sustains me.

I have right ideas. I have strength. I fear not; for the Father of Life—Nature—Infinite Mind—in me doeth the work.

I never fail. I cannot fail. I abide under the shadow of the Almighty so no harm can come to me. Every moment I am sustained —maintained—directed—led. "I can do all things through Christ which strengtheneth me." Christ is the power of God or Nature or Life within me. I depend on this power within me. I no more can be separated from It than the wave can be separated from the ocean or the shaft of sunlight from the sun.

I listen closely to that inner voice of wisdom and I do not make mistakes.

The Divine Mind within me, called by some "subconscious mind," by others "God" or "Creative Mind," is my great servant, counselor and protector. It is not limited by time or space. It keeps me from doing anything which might harm me or harm another person. It leads me—guides me—into right action at all times. It is the source of all my ideas. It leads me into paths of peace. I let no thoughts of fear, anxiety or worry control me, for all problems in my world are adjusted by this infinite inner mind. I depend upon it to digest my food, to keep my heart beating, to keep my blood circulating and all my body processes functioning. I choose to let it direct me to be at the right place at the right time, to do the right thing and to say the right word.

My inner subconscious mind—the one infinite mind—leads me safely through this day. As I go forward into this day, I have no resistance—no resentment—toward any person, any situation. My mentality is clear. I have no hatred, no unforgiveness in my heart.

I am relaxed and fearless. I feel no strain. I feel only perfect confidence.

This is the day! The day in which great good can come to me. I expect it. I accept it. I give thanks for it. I know that all of my loved ones also are led, cared for, and sustained by the same infinite, creative mind. They are guided, sustained and protected by the power and the wisdom of the infinite Life which surrounds them. They are sustained and protected because the love of infinite Life is devoted to them. Today no one or no thing can hurt them or me. As I go forth to meet my day, I am protected from all harm because I know neither fear, hatred nor resentment.

Faith in Life and love for Life and men is my watchword for today. Since I am master of myself today, I am master of every situation. There is that within me which is stronger than anything outside of me. Every step I take this day is in the direction of more good—greater happiness. Each step I take affords me a glorious vision of magnificent achievement.

Hail to this day!

I look to this day for it is Life—the very Life of Life. In its course lie all the realities of existence. The bliss of growth—the glory of action—the splendor of beauty. Yesterday is now a dream and tomorrow is a vision. Today well-lived makes of every yesterday a dream of happiness and of each tomorrow a vision of hope.

This day is Life's magnificent gift to me.

PART THREE

chapter 34

An Evening

Meditation

THIS DAY IS NOW DONE. IT HAS PASSED INTO MEMORY. WHAT-
ever was in it of good or of ill cannot be relived. Today I did my
best as I saw it at the time. My very best having gone out from me
only the best *can* come back to me. I am confident that my efforts
of the day were good, serious efforts. Tomorrow I will have had the
experience of *today* to build upon. I will have greater understanding;
therefore I will be able to do much better tomorrow than today.

I have grown in stature because of meeting the challenges before
me today. Having done my best this day, this night I am at peace.
I am tranquil in mind. I have served Life with my best. I have not
tried to *get* only; I have desired also to *give*. I expect as a result of
serving Life, Life will serve me. Since I have tried to use the
infinite, creative law to create more good rather than struggle to get
someone else's good, I am at peace, knowing that I have fulfilled
my mission of the day.

As the sun sinks below the horizon and the shadows of night fall
across the world, I am relaxed and quiet in mind and body. I am
grateful for each experience of this day. Even though some things
may have happened which I do not understand; which may seem to

have been opposed to my good, I know that since my *motive* was good, since I sought only to do right, out of every circumstance only good can eventually come to me. I know that in every adversity there exists an opportunity. I know that new life arises out of the ashes of what has looked like failure. I am thankful for the many opportunities afforded me today to make others happy—the opportunities to alleviate some pain and unhappiness.

I am thankful for my health of body of this day—for the vitality which carried me through every moment. I am thankful for the good ideas which came up to my conscious mind from the deeper levels of the subconscious mind within me—those flashes of inspiration when I knew what to do and where to be—those hunches which enabled me to do the right thing in the right way. I am thankful for the opportunity afforded me to say a kind word of helpfulness to someone confused and in trouble. I am glad I could cause a smile to move across the face of one who had felt sorrow. I am thankful that I had the opportunity to do a good turn for my neighbor. I am thankful for the happiness that came to me as a result of my giving out of myself and of what I had. I am thankful for the love and goodwill of my fellow men who, as I, are walking down the pathway of Life. We are all trying to make of this path a road of achievement and happiness rather than a road of sadness and sorrow.

I am glad that every act of mine today moves on forever, that it has eternal significance. *My* smile cheered someone today; and since that person was cheered, he in turn cheered someone else and *that* one passed it on. It goes on eternally. Thousands of people in this world will eventually feel the result of that smile. My warm handshake moves on throughout the ceaseless years. My every act is eternal. My life counts. *Everything* I do never ceases to influence the world. Coming generations *unconsciously* feel the influence of my good acts of today.

The dollar I spent today was a blessing to the merchant, who in turn was enabled to bless the wholesaler, who in turn blessed the manufacturer. This dollar which *was* mine moves on back to the farmer, the miner, the worker, and to their children, providing an education or a healing, thus making the whole world a better place in which to live. I realize that the money I spent was the substance of Life—a divine messenger I sent forth on its way to serve. It has served me; and now it will serve countless others, down through the ages.

Today I met my obligation to Life. Now I release the day and let it become a beautiful memory. I have forgiven myself and I have forgiven all others. The memory of today holds no bitterness. I recall only the good, the true, and the beautiful. I have gone back over my day and eased every uneasiness. I have let go everything that seemed to be a hurt. I understand and I forgive. If someone seemed to be selfish, I know that at worst he but acted selfishly for the man himself is an incarnation of divine Life. His selfishness was but a habit which is far outweighed by his virtues. In time, he, too, will see that less than love and goodwill doesn't pay. He is fundamentally good. His action was only a mistake and I forgive every mistake of my neighbor as I hope my neighbor will forgive my mistakes.

I now draw a curtain across the day and prepare for rest. In my imagination I now make preparations for tomorrow. I see myself rising tomorrow morning completely rested with plenty of energy—vital and alive. In my imagination, I see myself going about my various activities, doing whatever I should do, with good results coming out of every act. Every person I meet receives some good from me and I from him.

I see myself meeting each situation as it comes with courage, faith, and enthusiasm. I anticipate for tomorrow a day of magnificent achievement. Today is done. I have made a plan for Life to flow over tomorrow. I have drawn the curtain on today. Tonight I shall rest and store up energy for tomorrow.

I believe that good experiences are my divine right. I trust God and the immutable laws of God. I have no resistance against the past nor do I fear the future. I shall meet tomorrow's challenges tomorrow. I shall carry no strain into my sleep—no sorrow—no grief—no sense of loss. I have forgiven all mistakes. Now, I relax into peaceful sleep. Relaxation is pleasant and sleep is sweet. The darkness of the night with its peace and tranquility provokes for me a deep and peaceful slumber. I trust Life completely.

I now drop every wearisome thought and place all my affairs and the affairs of my loved ones in the care of the great, infinite, loving

Life, Itself. I know that my loved ones and I are protected and sustained. I know that directed by Divine Mind, I am always at the right place at the right time and doing the right thing.

I now abandon myself completely and wholly to that infinite, intelligent power which keeps the sun and the stars in their places and which also directs the bird in its flight and tells the lost dog the way home. Infinite Life surrounds me with Its love and cradles me in Its everlasting arms. I am grateful for sleep. I trust the infinite intelligence within me to keep me alive and to keep my affairs healthy. Since all my affairs are the affairs of infinite Life, Itself, they are directed by infinite intelligence.

I live continuously in the consciousness of the presence of good. Good surrounds me and enfolds me. The Kingdom of Heaven is within me.

I have released every problem to infinite intelligence for I know, "He that keepeth thee shall not slumber." I now sleep in complete confidence and trust and I say with the old prophet:

In peace I lay me down to sleep for thou, Jehovah, alone maketh me to dwell in safety. When thou liest down, thou shalt not be afraid. Yea, thou shalt lie down and thy sleep shall be sweet.

chapter 35

I Am, I Can,

I Will

THE FINAL ANSWER TO ALL OUR PROBLEMS, GREAT OR SMALL, is definitely to be found within ourselves. Is there something you would like to do and be, which so far you have failed to accomplish? Are you frustrated in your desire to express Life or do you feel that you actually are in control of your world? The answer to these problems and the power to solve them are within yourself. The solution is in the realization of who and what you are.

In a previous chapter we compared the creative level of mind— that is, mind acting on the subconscious or subjective level—to the soil in our garden. Subconscious mind is personalized as our subconscious self. *As conscious beings we each are conscious points of mind and have the power to choose what we will have and be.*

Emerson, in his essay on Self-Reliance, says, "Though the wide universe is full of good, no kernel of nourishing corn can come to him but through his toil bestowed on that plot of ground which is given to him to till. The power which resides in him is new in nature, and none but he knows what that is which he can do, nor does he know until he has tried."

We always are believing something about ourselves and, therefore, are planting thought seeds in our subconscious soil. Those thought seeds grow into form according to the pattern within the seed. Weed seeds grow into weeds and vegetable seeds become vegetables. Negative thoughts of sickness, poverty and unhappiness, if allowed to take root in the great subjective creative medium, grow into experiences.

We wish to select the right thought seeds and we should learn to till and cultivate the plants so that they will grow into the fruits of right experience. Our ideas, our beliefs, our mental images are the seeds; and everything reproduces according to its kind.

We always are identifying ourselves mentally with something. We always are believing something to be true about ourselves. We constantly say we are something—sick, well, rich or poor. Much of the time many of us identify ourselves with the negative and therefore experience that which we do not want. When we say, "I feel bad," the idea is caught up in our imagination. The subconscious mind or creative soil being impersonal accepts what our conscious thought suggests, takes us at our word, at our belief, and immediately starts bringing it forth into our experience.

It has been said that the ancients knew certain words of power which have been lost to modern man. These words have not been lost but their importance is not understood by one man in a hundred. They are words we use many times every day and they are the most important words in our vocabulary. The words of power are "*I am.*" Day after day and time after time we believe and say, "I am this. I am that." Our declaration, planted in the creative soil of mind, like the soil of the garden, sprouts and grows and the thing or condition we have decreed becomes manifest.

When we say, "I am unlucky" or "I am sick," we are giving to creative mind a definite pattern of action, not realizing the damage we are doing to ourselves. If we say and believe, "I am a failure," unconsciously we make a mental picture of failure, and the creative power within us proceeds to objectify that picture. No successful man ever thought or said he was a failure.

Instead of identifying ourselves with negative ideas, let's learn to identify ourselves with positive ideas for we become in experience that with which we identify ourselves. We should learn to identify ourselves with the highest ideal we can know and understand. Actually, The life of ourselves is perfect life.

We can say:

"I am Life. I have within me all the qualities of perfect Life. I incarnate the infinite God-Life. The very power of my body and the power in all my affairs is the same power that holds the sun, the moon and the stars in their places. It is the power which makes the rose bloom. It is the power back of the wind and the power with which I breathe. That infinite, invisible power is personalized in me and through my conscious thought I can direct it to right action in my body and my affairs. Nothing denies me my right to choose."

All the power anyone needs is available to him as soon as he recognizes it and everyone may learn how to use it.

We can say:

"The intelligence within me is the intelligence of infinite mind. There is no limit to that intelligence. It is endless, bottomless and infinite at the point where I exist. The universal mind is the mind which I use and any information which I need can be revealed to me as I need it. The power of God is my power. The presence of God is manifest as my presence."

By thinking in this way we identify ourselves with infinite being. When we accept this as the truth about ourselves, we automatically give to Life a more perfect pattern for our experiences. When we know this larger truth about ourselves and when with conviction we declare it to ourselves, the creative, subconscious mind says in effect, "He knows he is a god. He knows there is no limit to his possibilities." Then our experiences will begin to unfold according to the new pattern.

Instead of saying, "I am a failure," let's say, "I *am* a success," or "I *am* healthy. I *am* intelligence." When we do this, a different seed is planted; we have declared the truth about ourselves.

Jesus said to Peter, "Thou art Peter (a rock) and upon this I will build my church; and the gates of hell shall not prevail against it." Peter had been one of the most vascillating and uncertain of men, unpredictable and unsubstantial. When Peter became imbued with a new belief about himself; when he identified himself with stability, he became a rock of faith and strength.

When we acquire the great realization about ourselves, we can truthfully say:

> "Since *I am* an incarnation of the eternal Life, I can have, I can be, and I can do all that is normal and right for me to have, be and do. I can experience that which I should experience. My real self is none other than the eternal being. *I am; therefore I can.*"

This is a wonderful idea to plant in the feeling, creative part of mind. It is an all inclusive concept and the only correct concept. God incarnated in me, as me, is the truth about myself and that understanding gives me the right to believe and say:

> "I can do that which is right for me to do. I can have that which is right for me to have. I can be that which is right for me to be. It is possible for me to accomplish. *I can.*"

Everyone knows that he must have confidence in himself if he is to accomplish anything worthwhile.

Knowing I have the intelligence and the power I can say, "I WILL. *I am!* Therefore, *I can!* and, therefore, *I will!*" Whenever we are confronted with a problem, big or little, we can take these three mental steps. *I am; I can; I will.* When we accept this concept without reservation, we find the situation which faces us is not an obstacle. It is rather a challenge to our power and to our recognition of who and what we are.

One of the greatest evils in human experience is a feeling of weakness and inadequacy—the fear to go ahead because of a belief that we do not have the proper equipment to meet the challenges before us. When we finally recognize ourselves as incarnations of infinite Life using the infinite, creative mind; when we open the channels of our consciousness to infinite intelligence, power and guidance, we literally may become "supermen." To some extent every person can experience this.

I have seen people's lives completely changed through an understanding and continued use of this one simple statement—*I am, I can and I will.*

Knowing the truth about yourself, applying the truth you know to yourself and beginning to express that truth in your every action, you can change your whole outlook and experience. When you do this, you will be using the intelligence and power of universal, creative mind which is all the intelligence and power there is. There is no power to oppose it. *I am; I can; I will!*

chapter 36

The Key to Health,

Happiness and Prosperity

WE HAVE DISCOVERED OUR RELATION TO THE *great universal mind and life.* We have found this "I" of ourselves is *individualized Life* knowing *Itself* as a person and we know we use the mind of Life in every decision we make. We have learned we are not only connected with cosmic mind, we are unified with It. We use It because It is in us as the human mind. Each one of us is a conscious, thinking, directing point in the one life and each one of us may choose how he will use mind, how he will think and how he will act.

The entire philosophy of the Christian religion, which is really the philosophy of most great religions, is built upon two fundamental premises—the incarnation of God in man and the continuity, eternality and immortality of life. This was basic in Jesus' teaching—the identity of God and man—and therefore the immortality and divinity of man. This idea is reflected in the world's greatest art. This conviction has inspired the greatest poems ever written. Since the true nature of man is God, his Life never comes to an end.

It is not that man is now master of the universe around him because he split the atom but rather he split the atom because he believed himself to be master of his universe. Basically, perhaps unconsciously, man has believed in his own divinity. Faith led the search. Faith led to the achievement, not the achievement to the faith.

It is most important that man believe in these two premises we have mentioned: that he is an *incarnation of God Power* and that he is *immortal.* Certainly a man believing himself to be an accidental by-product in nature's creation would be justified in feeling that it was hardly worth the effort to attempt great achievement in the limited life span allotted him here on earth.

When the scientists split the atom, something tremendous was discovered. It was announced with awe that within the atom, of which all substance is composed, was the Life force Itself; the intelligent energy out of which the world of form around us has come into being. Man, through this discovery, is able to see more clearly the divinity of his nature, his oneness with infinite Life, Itself.

To any thinking person these two fundamentals are self-evident. They are no longer a matter of opinion. The absolute union of God and man is as evident as the fact that we exist. This invisible oneness has existed from the beginning of time, before we knew anything about it or anything about ourselves. This is true whether we realize it or not and whether we understand it or not. It will be no truer after we discover it; but when we do discover it, we will be able to use it with purpose. Insofar as that unity is concerned, nothing ever has happened to it; and nothing can happen to it. No one can dissolve it. Only ignorance can keep us from enjoying it.

Within Life is a great craving which impels us toward the discovery of the self. Today this isn't just a religious theory. It is practical mental science. The concept which the modern scientist holds regarding the physical world is very different from the concepts held a hundred years ago. Scientists now see that substance is energy and "Energy and substance are equal, identical and interchangeable." The physical universe is a projection of, or the surface appearance of, the world of reality. Substance is one with mind, with universal energy.

Modern psychology has rediscovered the truth of the statement in the Bible that "in Him we live and move and have our being."

Look within yourself and discover the reality of yourself, your own awareness. That is as far back as you can be aware of anything. At that point you are one with the infinite Life, Itself.

People sometimes say, "I can accept that but how do I take these facts and make them come alive? How can I improve my circumstances in life, raise my salary, pay my income tax, buy a new home, or bring love and friendship into my life? What does knowing that I am one with infinite Life or that I shall go on forever, do for me *now?*"

Obviously, being one with all power, all energy, all intelligence and all the Life there is, there can be no real limit to what we as individual points of Life can do. As we know more about ourselves and about how to use the laws of Life, we push back the horizon of our experience.

Raise your salary? Improve your environment? Find love and friendship? Of course! You merely use the natural laws of the universe—the Law of Cause and Effect, the Law of Compensation, the Law of Attraction, the Law of Increase; and these laws work with the same exactness as the laws of physics, chemistry, electricity, mathematics; as precisely as the law of gravitation.

The saving of civilization as a whole, as well as the safety of us as individuals, I believe, lies in our realization of the unity of all Life, all people, everything; the recognition that *we live in a universe.*

We never will progress satisfactorily so long as we insist upon believing that we as individuals are separate from or lower or higher than others. The world will be torn with dissension so long as people believe in race superiority or race inferiority. Human beings *differ* as to race, color, language and geographical location; but the superiority or inferiority of one race over another—never! *Only that individual is superior whose thoughts and motives are superior.*

In our desire for the good things of Life, we do not rob someone else for there is plenty to go around. Neither does it do the rest of the world any good for us to be unhappy. Already there are too many tears. We are helping the world only when we are happy, when we are vitally alive.

Imagination is fundamentally creative but we choose what images we create and give to creative mind. Our faith may be either positive or negative. It may be strong or wavering. The picture we make may be either clear or cloudy; but in any event through our faith, actual plans are made in our imagination through which Life flows for us; and it is done unto us according to our faith.

A child may grow up in an environment of poverty and limitation. He may come to think that limitation is the normal experience for him. He pictures a future of limitation. Limitation becomes his subconscious thought pattern. Poverty will continue to be his experience until by some means or other he changes that thought pattern. *He did not consciously make the plan* in the first place, but *he can consciously change it.*

A child may have been surrounded by much sickness and complaining in his early years; but if he never makes the effort; if he never argues the matter through until he sees the truth about health being normal, he probably will come to the conclusion that sickness is normal. A belief in sickness and disease will dominate his imagination as long as he lives.

Unconsciously we may *believe in luck*—good or bad. If so, we will seem to be governed by luck. If we believe that the average experience of the human race must be our experience, we will be governed by the law of averages and remain in bondage to our dominant subconscious state.

All trouble is the result of maladjustment—spiritual, physical and mental—and in most cases it is unconscious. *The dominant state of the subconscious mind is reflected in our bodies and in our affairs. We each have the power through our conscious thinking to create new, subconscious states of mind. Our bonds of limitation and trouble will drop away when we no longer hold patterns of limitation in our imagination.*

We may redirect our faith. We may make and re-make our lives. We do not need to be bound by old beliefs. When we substitute new, positive states of mind, we create a new set of experiences. We have been in prisons of our own making. Now as we learn to identify ourselves with freedom, abundant riches, health, success, peace and happiness, those prison walls automatically crumble.

Our outer world is a reflection of our inner world. Outer experiences are but surface appearances. There is something back of that surface which gives reality to it. Life is the great reality. The law of Life is mind. Form is Life brought into the field of our observation. The objective world can be explained only by the subjective world back of it. The mental scientist works in this field of causes.

For many hours, through many pages, you, the Reader, and I, the Author, have thought together. Undoubtedly we have worked out many problems through thinking together. You have embarked upon the greatest, most thrilling experience in your life. *By consciously using the power of mind, you can be and do what you want to be and do. You can use your mind power to help others. There is no limit to your possibilities.* The power you use is within yourself. It is not necessary to search elsewhere for *you have the key.*

Index

Best Seller!
THE LEARNING BLOCK

By Dean E. Grass

This book introduces a new technique of teaching through mind conditioning that works. It shows the teacher how to make his efforts with his students more successful; it teaches the student how to think and study more effectively; it brings to the parent the much-needed understanding of what makes a slow learner (the learning block) and what can be done to overcome this handicap.

The author has tested his methods in the classroom for over thirty years and has come to the conclusion that the mind acts as a computer that responds to both negative and positive conditioning. He brings out the fact that classroom instruction is a form of hypnosis and good or bad results may be obtained, depending on the teacher. Thus the teacher will learn in this book how to apply the new technique of positive conditioning which makes the student happier and more willing to learn, by the kind of positive mind conditioning that unlocks "the learning block."

What educators say about *The Learning Block:*

Richard E. Hammerle, *Past Principal – Christopher Columbus Junior High School, Canoga Park, California*

"As educators, we are constantly looking for new ways to work with children. Mr. Grass has been interested in mind conditioning for many years . . . his research has been very interesting and positive, and it opens the doors for others to continue research in the same areas."

Robert P. Malcolm, *Principal – Christopher Columbus Junior High School, Canoga Park, California*

"The philosophy that is developed in regard to programming the mind is something that all of us in education should become aware of . . . I feel that this should be a handbook for all new teachers and a guide for those of us who have been in the profession a long time."

Dr. Ewing A. Konold, *Professor of Education – San Fernando Valley State College, Northridge, California*

"*The Learning Block* should open the doors to many phases of research. Techniques and details should be explored in many areas of mind conditioning . . . . Educators have overlooked this phase of mental development long enough."

Softbound – $6.95

Best Seller!

SELECTIVE AWARENESS

By Peter Mutke, M.D.

Dr. Mutke gained an international reputation for his original research into breast development with hypnosis. Complete instructions for controlling headaches, muscle spasms, influencing circulatory system, weight reduction, self-image and breast development, improving sports performance and learning, and healing after surgery.

GIL BOYNE — Peter Mutke's brilliant structuring of a new view of self-therapy through self-hypnosis and self-programming gives specific instructions for:

1. Learning to deal with headaches, muscle spasms and other pains
2. Influencing your circulatory system
3. Directing weight reduction
4. Overcoming smoking
5. Self-image and breast development
6. Learning how to learn — how to take tests
7. Overcoming insomnia
8. Improving sports performance
9. Healing after surgery

Formerly a professor at John F. Kennedy University in California, Peter Mutke, M.D. now teaches "Selective Awareness Therapy" at the University of Berlin in West Berlin. This book has been translated into German and is the textbook for his course.

Softbound — 195 pages — $7.50

SUCCESS THROUGH SELF-HYPNOSIS

By John Roger Martin, Ph.D.

Many will recognize Dr. John Martin as the author of "Psychologist's Casebook," which apppeared in Redbook Magazine as a regular feature for five years.

This is an usually effective teaching book for both laymen and professionals.

Soft Bound — $6.95

HYPNOSIS:
New Tool in Nursing Practice

Edited by Gil Boyne

GIL BOYNE

In this first-of-its-kind textbook, I have collected the writings of a number of registered nurses who have used hypnotism in a great variety of special situations in medical settings. Among more than four thousand persons I have trained in hypnotherapy, there has been an increasing number of nurses who seem to intuitively grasp the central realization that hypnotism is the original and most effective "placebo effect."

The registered nurse is a "natural" hypnotist with a special capacity to use hypnotism creatively with hospital patients. It is the nurse who provides comfort and reassurance, administers pain-deadening medications and allays the patient's anxieties. There are at least three major reasons why the nurse is ideally suited to use hypnosis in patient care.

1. The patient's on-going, primary contact is with the nurse. Physician-patient contact is usually brief in duration and content.

2. Hospitalized patients often develop powerful feelings of helplessness and dependency which can trigger regression to a childlike ego-state. When this happens, the authority of the nurse is greatly magnified and the patient becomes highly responsive to suggestion, direction and instruction.

3. Because most nurses are female, they are often perceived by the patient as a mother surrogate, since it was mother who tended their needs and cared for them when they were sick as children.

The writers in this anthology have bypassed the technical writings of theoretic and experimental investigations, and have devoted themselves to addressing patients' problems with pragmatic methods based on therapeutic response.

The rapid changes in medical practice, the tremendous escalation of hospital costs, and the heavy demand on the physician's time have brought us to the realization that nurses must be given greater responsibility in the therapeutic treatment process rather than being restricted to the role of dispensers of comfort and medicine. It is my conviction that nurses are about to assume a new dimension in health care, gaining recognition as vital forces in the healing process.

Hardbound — 197 pages — $20.00